WAR *changes* CLIMATE

How Two World War Changed Climate

-The Naval War Effect -

By
Arnd Bernaerts

Order this book online at www.trafford.com/06-0815
or email orders@trafford.com

Most Trafford titles are also available at major online book retailers.

Note for Librarians: A cataloguing record for this book is available from Library and Archives Canada at www.collectionscanada.ca/amicus/index-e.html

ISBN: 978-1-4120-9059-9

We at Trafford believe that it is the responsibility of us all, as both individuals and corporations, to make choices that are environmentally and socially sound. You, in turn, are supporting this responsible conduct each time you purchase a Trafford book, or make use of our publishing services. To find out how you are helping, please visit www.trafford.com/responsiblepublishing.html

Our mission is to efficiently provide the world's finest, most comprehensive book publishing service, enabling every author to experience success. To find out how to publish your book, your way, and have it available worldwide, visit us online at www.trafford.com/10510

www.trafford.com

North America & international
toll-free: 1 888 232 4444 (USA & Canada)
phone: 250 383 6864 ♦ fax: 250 383 6804
email: info@trafford.com

The United Kingdom & Europe
phone: +44 (0)1865 722 113 ♦ local rate: 0845 230 9601
facsimile: +44 (0)1865 722 868 ♦ email: info.uk@trafford.com

10 9 8 7 6 5 4 3 2

WHAT ASTA AND TONY MAY HAVE THOUGHT IN SUMMER 1939

Asta Lindskog had only ten minutes for her lunch break at mobile phone giant Ericsson's canteen in Stockholm. And now the soup was too hot. She turned the spoon through the soup bowl. Her thoughts drifted to the looming war hoping that the British Prime Minister Neville Chamberlain could persuade Adolph Hitler not to make war. If not, what would be the future for little Eric and sweet Signe, her children of four and two, and the spoon moved quickly. "Calm down", she ordered herself, "it will not come to the worst". When realizing the soup was suddenly too cold her mind jump: "Sweden will hardly see a mild winter if navies at war churn and turn the Baltic Sea about as I just did with the soup." The war started within few weeks time and all countries around the Baltic Sea experienced the coldest winter for more than 100 years.

Tony Blair was sure, Neville Chamberlain's persuasion policy was bound to fail, when naval vessels of the Deutsche Kriegsmarine took positions in the North Atlantic in August 1939. He felt it was time to present his yet strongest belief, "that there is no bigger long-term question facing the global community than the threat of climate change". He hitch-hiked to Munich but none of the leading Nazi gave him a chance to express his concern on global climate. No one wanted to listen to an unknown young man. Hitler wanted a war and started war on 1st September 1939, which caused climate to shift the course immediately. Our earth cooled down for four decades.

In late summer 1939 Asta and Tony are fiction, the climate changes by war at sea not, as the book will explain in great detail.

Everything comes from water!!
Everything is maintained through water!
Ocean, give us your eternal power.

From the drama Faust II, Thales, by Johann-Wolfgang v. Goethe, (1749-1832)

TABLE OF CONTENTS

A. CLIMATE CHANGE ISSUES

INTRODUCTION

In the summer of 1939, a major world war was looming. British Prime Minister Neville Chamberlain desperately tried to persuade German Chancellor Adolph Hitler not to push the world into another major war. But the threat of climate change was not among the arguments Chamberlain used to convince his opponent and his efforts were in vain. Hitler wanted a war and started it in September 1939. The war lasted six years and initiated a big climate change.

The book is about oceans, wars at sea and climate changes. It focuses on two major climate changes, which happened because man abused oceans through naval warfare twice during the last century. Last and most dramatic climate change occurred during World War II, sixty-five years ago.

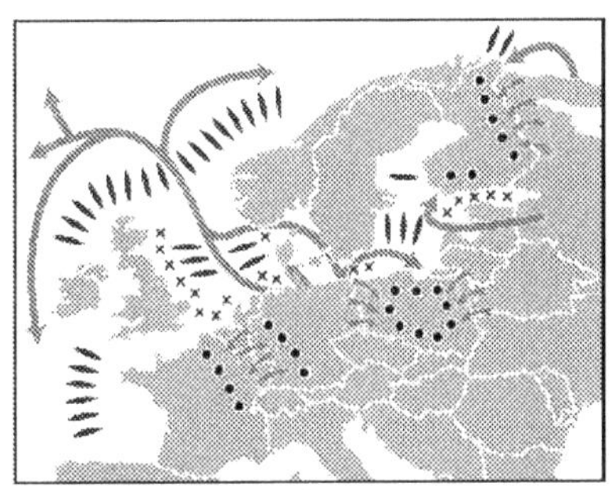

Fifty million people were killed and the infrastructure and the economy of many countries ruined. But there are even more tragic consequences, which have not been tackled very seriously yet. With the commencement of the World War II, warm climate changed to a cold phase, which lasted four decades. Nowadays, more than half a century after the above mentioned events, leading politicians and scientists warn that climate changes are the greatest threat to mankind. They claim that the threat is caused by industrial release of carbon dioxide into the atmosphere. This works like a greenhouse effect that makes the earth's temperature rise.

The British Prime Minister Tony Blair recently said that there is "no bigger long-term question facing the global community" than the threat of a climate change[1]. Unfortunately, the focus is misplaced. It is not the atmosphere, which determines the fate of the climate. It is the ocean that does it. J.W. von Goethe would have agreed:

Until one has experienced the sea around one,
One has no idea of world and its relation to the world[2].

The war at sea caused a major climate change starting with 1918 and then another one after the end of 1939. If the oceans, as the driving force of the climate, had influenced scientific research since the early days of meteorology, 150 years ago, it would then have been possible to clearly stress that, at the advent of the two World Wars during the last century, extensive fighting at sea endangered the normal course of the climate.

How would the course of international conflicts have been managed if the world's leading statesmen of the 20th century had been concerned with climatic changes due to the impact a war at sea could have had on the ocean and consequently on the climate? Could World War II have been prevented if global climate change had been as much a concern as today? Or would the leaders have tried to persuade warring navies to leave oceans and seas out of the conflict?

But no one had alerted the warring nations at any time over the last 150 years that going out on sea to fight a war would have an inevitable impact on the status of the oceans and, consequently, on the climate. In August 1939, no one demanded to Adolf Hitler, in strong diplomatic notes, to abstain from any military activities out in the oceans.

The inevitable happened. Within six months, the Second World War (WWII) commenced and Northern Europe was plunged into the coldest winter in more than 100 years. By mid-February 1940, Europe was in the grip of arctic conditions that had not been experienced since the Little Ice Age, in the 18th/19th

---

1 www.bbc.co.uk/climate/policies/uk_policy.shtml Topic: Climate Change from the BBC Weather Centre/ Policies/ UK Policy; "PM Tony Blair described climate change as 'the most important environmental issue facing the world today'";

2 Johann - Wolfgang v. Goethe , 1749-1832, "Italian Voyage", 1787;

century. And neither the scientific community nor the political leaders had any idea about the link between war and arctic temperature conditions.

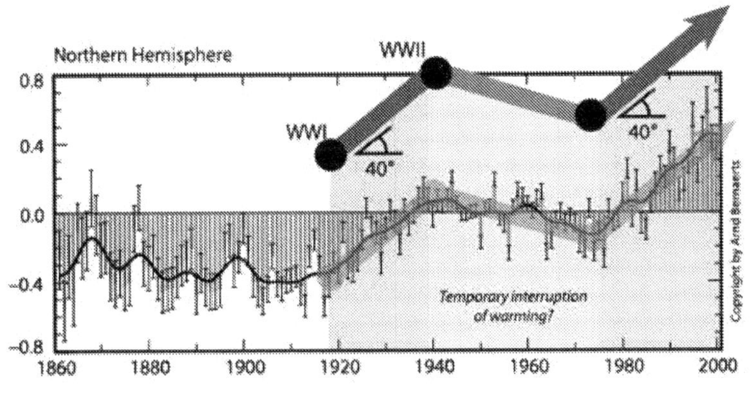

Deviation of temperature from long term average.

It is an irony that Adolf Hitler's deputy, Field Marshal Herman Goering[3], in a speech designed to boost the morale of the German population which was striving to overcome the unbelievable hardship of a cold and snowy winter, could get away with the statement he made on the 15th of February 1940:

Nature is still more powerful than man.
I can fight man but I cannot fight nature
when I lack the means to carry out such battle.
We did not ask for ice, snow and cold –
A higher power sent it to us.[4]

How wrong was Herman Goering! He, Adolf Hitler and the German Reich were alone responsible for the sudden

3 Hermann Goering a celebrated WWI air fighter pilot joined the Nazi movement as early as 1923 and became head of Germany's armed forces in 1938. The following year he officially became Hitler's deputy and legal heir. After WWII commenced Goering was placed in charge of the Luftwaffe. In 1946 he was found guilty at the Nuremberg War Crimes Trail;

4 Herman Goering in a speech in Berlin on the 15th of February 1940; reported by The New York Times, on the 16th of February 1940;

transformation of both regional and global climate. While the war continued for five more years and the war at sea turned global after Japan's attack on Pearl Harbour, in December 1941, it did not only generate three extreme cold winters in Europe but also generated four decades of cold that lasted from 1940 to the early 1980s. This happened after an extensive series of devastating naval activities in the Atlantic and Pacific regions.

A major climatic implication in oceanic affairs already started with the development and use of screw-driven steam and motor vessels in the mid 19th century. For almost a century, 10,000 vessels criss-crossed the seas, travelling more than 10,000,000 nautical miles every day. It can be logically assumed that, over the years, each ship cruising through the seas will force more heat into the sea than out of it. The more heat the oceans hold, the warmer the atmosphere gets.

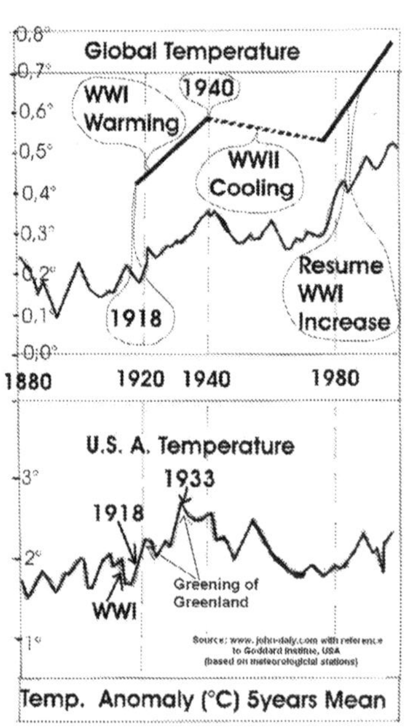

But this simple fact had not been given any serious attention by the scientific community until recently. This book aims to raising the issue while concentrating on the two wars at sea, from 1914 to 1918 and from 1939 to 1945, when seas and oceans were turned into battlegrounds and huge water areas were turned upside-down by naval vessels and by activities such as shooting, aerial bombing, torpedoing merchant vessels, sea mining, and depth charging of submarines.

"Everything is maintained through water!" says Goethe in his drama, Faust II. Understanding global nature in this way needs to be also reflected in the field of climate research and in any definition on climate. Goethe would certainly have agreed with the definition on climate as the continuation of the ocean by other means[5]. In this book you will find facts, circumstances

5 See: Arnd Bernaerts, Letter to Editor, NATURE, Volume 360, 26 November 1992, page 292;

and evidence about the impact of naval warfare on modern climate.

The facts presented aim to leading the way to a new thinking on climate, based on the conviction that only the one who is able to feel the eternal power the oceans have on our global nature affairs will be capable to uphold the principal driving force on earth, namely, the oceans which ultimately control the weather and climate.

Want to change climate?

Is man responsible for global warming? This has been debated for more than 20 years. And most of the claims say that modern civilization is responsible for higher atmospheric temperatures caused by man-made greenhouse gases. The mouthpiece for this claim is the Inter-Governmental Panel on Climate Change (IPCC), founded in 1988.

The main argument of the IPCC is based on carbon dioxide (CO2). Proud to convey the "consensus" of hundreds of leading scientists from around the world, this organisation hardly ever hesitated to confirm its belief in the Assessments Reports[6] as being correct.

The IPCC Report from 1990 states:

> *"Emission resulting from human activities is substantially increasing the atmospheric concentration of the greenhouse gases: carbon dioxide, methane, chlorofluorocarbons (CFCs) and nitrous oxide. These increases will enhance the greenhouse effect, resulting on average in additional warming of the earth's surface. The main greenhouse gas, water vapour, will increase in response to global warming and further enhance it".*[7]

Arnd Bernaerts, "Legal Means for Understanding the Marine and Climatic Change Issue", in: Thomas A. Mensah (ed.), Ocean Governance: Strategies and Approaches for the 21st Century, Honolulu 1994, pp. 157f;

6 For example 1990, 1995; and the Report 2001 on http://www.grida.no/climate/ipcc_tar/wg1/index.htm

7 IPCC First Scientific Assessment Report, Climate Change, J.T. Houghton, et al (ed), Executive Summary, page XI, Cambridge July 1990;

After the end of the 19th century, the world's global surface air temperature has increased from 0.3 to 0.6°C, the 1999 Report further states[8].

IPCC's CO2 claim proved highly successful. The science on climate change received many billions of US dollars every year for research, in addition to meeting the costs of infrastructure, meteorological services, satellites, ships, etc., all paid from the public funds. The CO2 claim was the basis on which politics has been made since the Rio de Janeiro Summit, in 1992, which agreed on the United Nations Framework Convention on Climate Change of the same year. Only five years later, a treaty on curbing greenhouse gases was negotiated in Kyoto, Japan. The negotiation resulted in the agreement that is world-wide known: The 'Kyoto Agreement'[9].

The Russian Federation, an opponent of the treaty for many years, approved it in late 2004, due to the promises and persuasion of the European Union. Twenty years of hard lobbying proved to be a great success story for climate science. The last big industrial country still holding back its approval of the treaty is the USA. But with Russia on board[10], the Kyoto Treaty went into force on the 16th of February 2005. The strong belief and conviction of the man-made planetary climatic catastrophe due to greenhouse gases have created a mighty political tool within the community of climatologists.

Seeking funding, having visions, lobbying for one's own belief is all fair deal. But what will happen if the greenhouse strategy is found to be grossly exaggerated or even proves wrong in due

---

8 IPCC First Scientific Assessment Report, Climate Change, J.T. Houghton, et al (ed), Executive Summary, page XII, Cambridge July 1990;

9 The Kyoto global warming pact, negotiated in Japan's ancient capital of Kyoto in 1997 and ratified by 140 nations, went into force on the 16th of February 2005, seven years after it was negotiated, imposing limits on the emissions of carbon dioxide and other gases scientists blame for rising world temperatures, melting glaciers and rising oceans;

10 With the United States staying out, Russia was the last hope for the treaty's supporters to get the necessary 55 countries accounting for at least 55 percent of global emissions in 1990. Russia accounted for 17 percent of emissions, second to the United States;

course? Could it all result with global community having lost dozens of years to understand the mechanism of natural climate system?

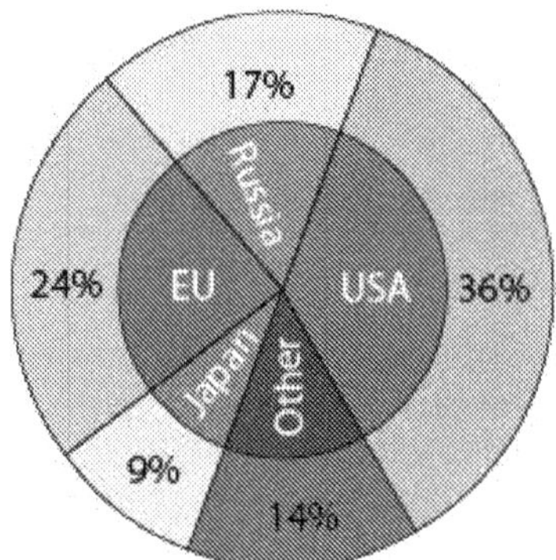

Country share
CO_2 Emissions in 1990

Not everybody is with the IPCC and its findings by "consensus". While the mainstream of science and climatologists support it, there are also voices opposing the IPCC's conclusions. The most prominent document in this regard is the "Oregon Petition" from 1998 signed by 17,000 scientists protesting against the Kyoto Agreement. The petition requested acceptance through the following statement:

> *"We urge the United States government to reject the global warming agreement that was written in Kyoto, Japan, in December 1997, and any other similar proposals. The proposed limits on greenhouse gases would harm the environment, hinder the advance of science and technology, and damage the health and welfare of mankind.*
>
> *There is no convincing scientific evidence that human release of carbon dioxide, methane, or other greenhouse gasses is causing or will, in the foreseeable future, cause catastrophic heating of the Earth's atmosphere and disruption of the Earth's climate. Moreover, there is substantial scientific evidence that increases in atmospheric carbon dioxide produce many beneficial effects upon the natural plant and animal environments of the Earth".*[11]

Neither the IPCC claim nor the Oregon Petition are satisfactory and reflect a fairly correct assessment and analysis of the

11 See: Anti Global Warming Petition Project; http://www.oism.org/pproject

Earth's climate during the last 150 years. A thorough analysis of climate events and human activities will show that it is possible to establish considerable links between the two. After all, the global weather system is based on the law of physics. That will be explained, demonstrated and discussed in details throughout this book.

Want to have a freezing winter? Start a war!

The following section will provide an initial example. It is one of the climate change experiments made by man that should have been subject to a detailed assessment when the experiment started, on the 1st of September 1939. If the meteorologists of the 1930s failed to recognise that a climate change is inevitable in case of war at sea, the post-war climatologists had 60 years to rectify the failure of their pre-war colleagues.

On the 14th of February 1940, virtually only hours before the German Vice-Chancellor and Air Field Marshal Herman Goering denied any responsibility for the weather with the words: *"We did not ask for ice, snow and cold – A higher power sent them to us"*, The New York Times reported that a record cold gripped the European Nations and that at least 56 people died from Scandinavia to the Danube, while the Baltic Sea was frozen. The newspaper informed its readers about the situation as it follows:

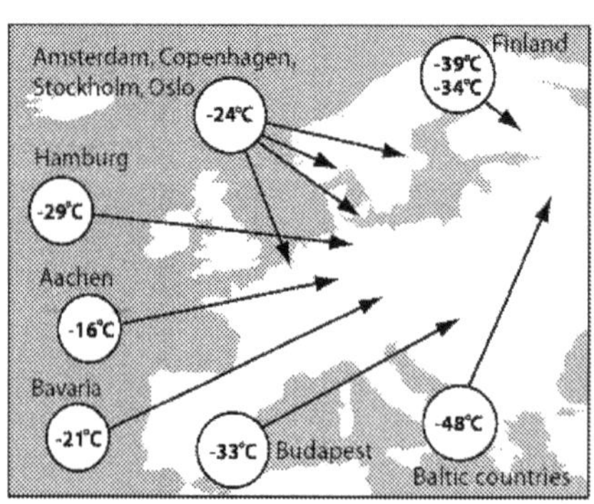

Reported temperature, February 14th - 17th 1940

"Europe suffered tonight in the paralysing grip of the bitterest cold in more than 100 years".

"The cold wave extended from the Arctic fringes of Norway and Finland to the Netherlands and Hungary".

"The Netherlands Weather Bureau recorded the lowest temperature ever recorded in this country, 11.2 degrees below zero Fahrenheit." (-11.2 F corresponds to -24°C).

> "Water transportation in the Netherlands is completely paralysed. The canals have been covered with thick ice for more than six weeks. Hundreds of persons abandoned their homes in the face of crushing ice packs boiling up from ice-blocked canals, rivers and seas."
>
> "In Copenhagen the temperature has dropped to 13 degrees below zero Fahrenheit (-25°C)".
>
> "The Baltic Sea was frozen over for the first time in many years. Islands along the coast of the Netherlands and the Baltic were isolated. All day they sent out SOS calls for coal and foodstuff".
>
> "In Estonia, Latvia and Lithuania, more than 10,000 persons suffered severe cases of frost-bite. At least five persons froze to death in the three Baltic countries where temperatures reached 54 degrees below zero Fahrenheit (-47°C) for the first time in 150 years".

Only five and-a-half months earlier, Hitler had started a war in Northern Europe. Then there was bitter cold, lack of coal, shortages of food, frozen water pipe lines. Keeping transportation going had become a nightmare since the cold wave had started during the second week of January. To boost the morale of the population under these difficult circumstances, Herman Goering appealed to them in a speech, in Berlin, on the 15th of February 1940 (NYT, the 16th of February 1940):

> *"These troubles, naturally, take precedence over yours. They are not a German patent – look at the nations around you having the same difficulties."*

The arctic winter in Northern Europe continued for another week. In Sweden, all cold records were beaten during the days of 19th/20th of February, with 32 degrees below zero F. (-35.5°C), the coldest since 1805 (NYT, the 23rd of Feb.'40).

Only a few lines from the outstanding war time reporting of The New York Times are enough to illustrate the astonishing result of one of the most captivating climate change experiments.

Since the 1st of September 1939, thousands of naval vessels were permanently engaged in war, guarding merchant ships, patrolling sea areas, and exchanging fire with shore batteries or with other naval vessels. Thousands of planes flew on bombing, fighting or patrolling missions every day. Up to 100,000 sea mines were dropped in the sea of which several thousands exploded. Many thousands depth charges were thrown over board to destroy enemy submarines. U-boats torpedoed vessels. Hundreds of ships were sunk in the sea. Some exploded with extreme force due to their loaded cargo consisting of ammunition or gasoline.

Baltic and North Sea waters were churned, mixed and turned upside down as never before. It was as if someone violently stirred a bowl of soup with a spoon to cool it quickly. Waters of Northern Europe went to a similar process which paved the way to the arrival of polar air which established there for many weeks. The impact on regional winter conditions should have hardly come as a surprise. The arctic cold during January and February 1940 was an inevitable result of the war at sea. It will be discussed in more details at a later stage of this presentation.

Not one cold winter alone

If the war in Europe had ended with the winter 1939/40, a few weeks after Herman Goering's speech in mid-February 1940, a description of the winter 1939/40 as "weather modification" would presumably be correct. The climate, the same as the statistics of weather data over a longer period, would hardly have left a trace. Consequently, the extreme icy January and February 1940 would have 'gone under' in the weather statistics.

But the war continued and the war winter of 1940/41 in North Europe came up with the same conditions as the year before. Same phenomenon occurred again during the winter of 1941/42 when Germany was at war with Russia since July 1941. This extreme winter is the most stunning regional weather modification event. As a result of the war at sea for over six months, the Baltic became arctic and temperature became colder than that of the North Pole.

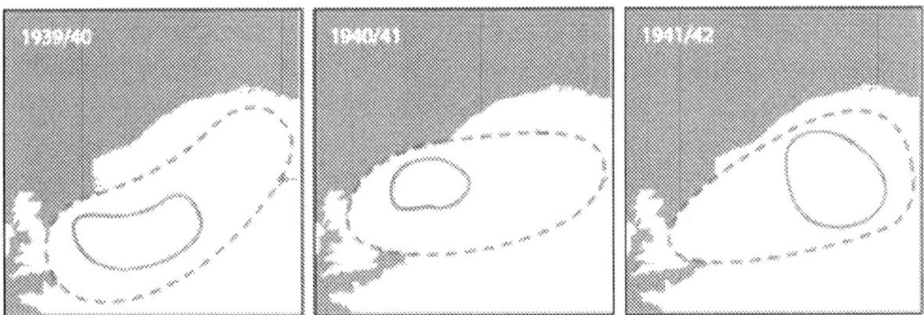

Record cold areas during the war winters 1939 to 1942.

But WWII is not the only example of weather modification as a result of fighting at sea. Even the war at sea during World War I (1914-18) left a similar trail in the weather data records of the British Isles (the winters of 1916/17 and 1917/18). Fighting in the waters of Great Britain became very fierce and deadly with newly developed military weapons, sea mines, submarines, and depth charges. Each of the mentioned five war winters proved how the war at sea left its clear fingerprint on the regional winter conditions. One can only wonder why meteorologists at that time were not capable of seeing a link between altered seawater conditions due to naval warfare towards the end of a year and arrival of icy air from the north or the east during the following winter months.

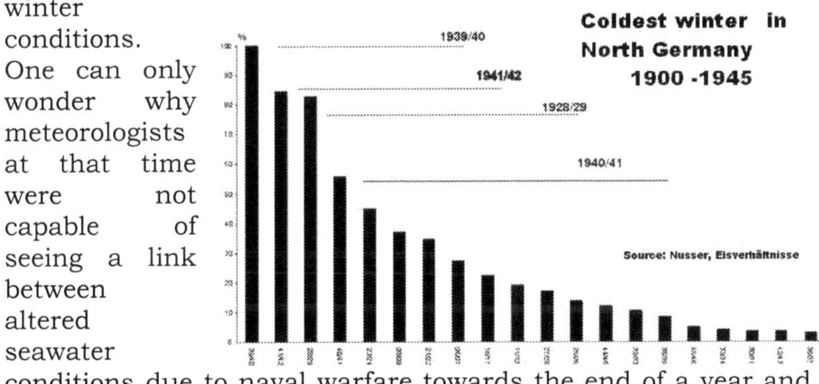

Act together to change global weather

But the story on how war at sea determined a climatic change will not end with some cold regional winters in North Europe. Act globally and you can globally change the climate for the better or the worst. With Japan's attack on Pearl Harbour, on the 7th of December 1941, naval warfare went global, resulting in a colder temperature phase which lasted over four decades at a global level. Therefore, the winter 1939/40 was part of an already huge global climatic change event.

After having mentioned that all cases of war at sea can be directly linked to climate-relevant events, two further highly interesting climate changes during the 20th century may have been man-made with a somewhat "extended link" to the war at sea. There is, in the first place, the sudden warming at Spitsbergen, in 1918, as a result of the naval warfare around Britain, and in the North Sea, this having an impact on the Norwegian Sea and current. The other aspect, the warming of air temperatures since the mid-1980s, is certainly a remote possibility but altogether not impossible.

Issues raised so far need further evidence and explanations, which will come step by step. But to start with, it will be necessary to give an assessment on how the world climate would presumably have looked like if man had failed to industrialize and had remained a small population.

Starting point will be around 1850 when the so-called Little Ice Age ended. Climate would presumably have been totally unspectacular without two World Wars generating two climate changes during the last century, namely 1918 and 1940. The temperature increase after the 1980s is perhaps not a change but only a continuation of the rising trend from 1918 to 1939. Indeed, it is one of many interesting questions. But as man-made changes to climate are a major concern, it could only have happened with the advent of industrialization one and a half century ago.

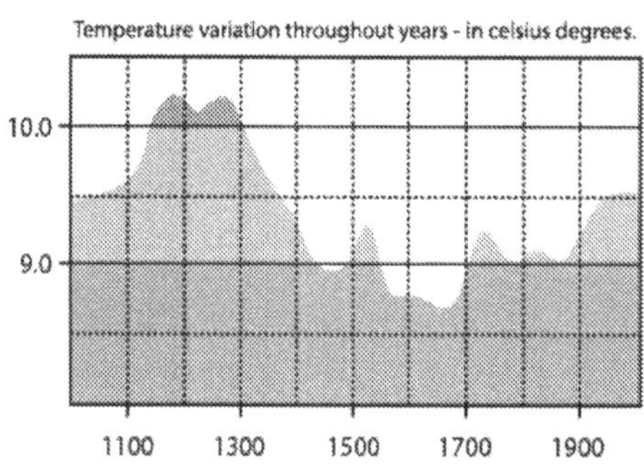

How modern climate evolved 150 years ago

Global warming is not a new thing, and the matter did not started just 25 years ago. Since 1850, global air temperatures have started to get warmer. Warming in this sense can only be measured and evaluated against previous temperature records in an endless chain of repeatable cycle of Earth's climate changes going from warm periods to glacial conditions and vice versa during the past one million years. With the end of the Ice

Age, the globe became about 4-5°C warmer. More recently, a medieval warm period (between 900 and 1450 AD) was at the upper most level, followed by the so-called Little Ice Age (between about 1450 and 1850 AD). This period shall be briefly discussed as it may hold some clues to how the world climate evolved until it reached the current status, at least with regard to the general trend.

The Little Ice Age

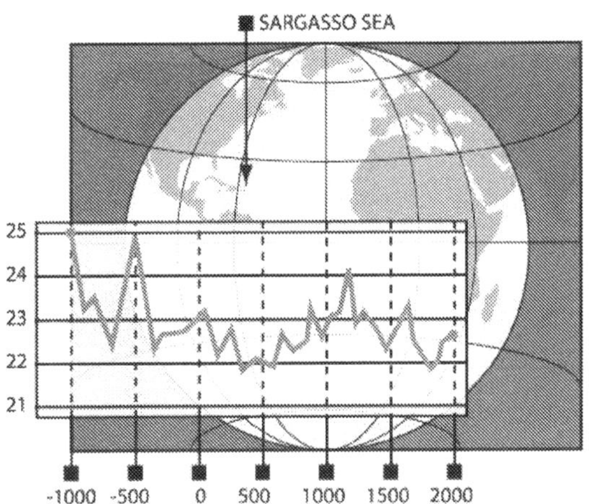

The world was cooler through out the Middle Ages. Even though during the Little Ice Age the temperature fluctuation was in the average just 1-2°C colder than during the previous warm period (from 900 to 1450 AD), the social implications of this phenomenon were immense. Life in the Northern Hemisphere became rather uncomfortable. Low temperatures and higher cloud coverage affected farming severely. Several great famines occurred, which led to a number of wars in Europe.

Possible causes for this cold phase that prevailed for almost 400 years are still being debated[12]. The number of contributing causes is numerous and includes, among others, notions like: intensity of the sun's rays, earth's rotation around the sun, surface albedo by ice and snow, volcanic activities, ocean-

12 Richard D. Tkachuck (//www.grisda.org/origins/10051.htm) states: The causes for this cooling may have derived from a combination of changes in the energy output of the sun and changes in the atmosphere of the earth which resulted from volcanic activity that reduced the amount of energy absorbed.

atmosphere conveyor system, etc. Current climatic conditions and processes could be better analysed if the natural processes of the Little Ice Age were understood properly. In the absence of either an earth science or even of a reliable data collection during the above mentioned cold phase, a complete picture of the causes which triggered and sustained the cold phase would probably never be established.

Despite this incertitude, it can be said with a certain amount of certainty that a high volcanic activity had considerably contributed to this scenario. For example: the eruption of the Huaynaputina (Peru), in 1600 AD, caused the most severe short-term cooling effect in the Northern Hemisphere, in the past 600 years. The huge fissure eruption of the volcano Laki, in Iceland, between 1783 and '84, was the greatest historical volcanic eruption hitherto recorded anywhere in the world. The explosion of Mount Tambora (Indonesia), in 1815, catapulted 150 cubic kilometres of rock dust into the air, this resulting in the coldest single year on record in many places in Europe and North America and producing, in 1816, a "year without a summer". The last big one, Krakatoa, in the Sunda Strait (Indonesia), erupted with tremendous force in 1883.

The Krakatoa volcano and science

(a) An event leading to climate change?[13]

After a long row of severe volcanic eruptions during the Little Ice Age, the Krakatoa was the last major volcanic eruption in the world. As a result, the world got warmer. When Krakatoa erupted, on the 27th of August 1883, about 50 cubic kilometres of lava, mud and ashes reached heights of more than 10,000 metres. It took about three months for the volcano 'dust' to have circled the whole global atmosphere from the South Pole to the North Pole.

---

13 From: Bernaerts, Arnd, 'Conditions necessary for the protection of world climate', Geesthacht 1992; (available on www. seaclimate.com, Previous Essays (8_13); published in German by Verein der Freunde und Foederer des GKSS-Forschungszentrum Geesthacht e.V. : ISSN 0934-9804

During the following years, air circulation in the atmosphere was above normal and then sank to a bare minimum in 1888[14]. For more than three years, the solar radiation intensity was about 10 to 15 % lower than the normal level. The minimum value of 76% was reached in the late summer of 1885[15]. The high drop of the radiation values during such a long period should have left significant marks in the weather records. But nothing serious happened. Neither did the Little Ice Age return, nor did 'a summer without sun' happen again as it did in 1816. Does it really not matter if warming coming from the sun is partly blocked out? Did the laws of physics refuse to work in this case, or were the emerging community of meteorologists not able to grasp what was going on in those days?

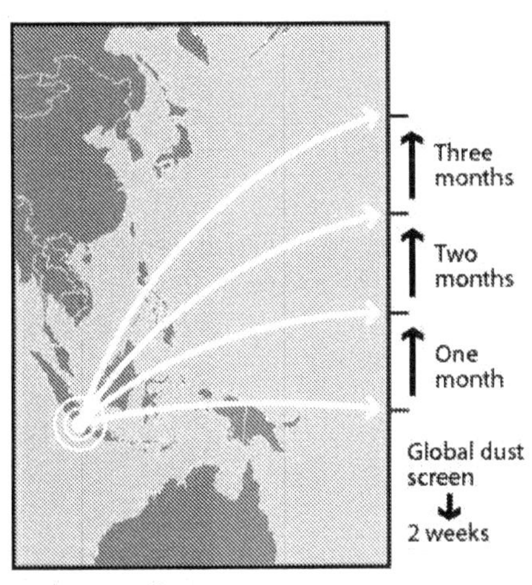

Krakatoa, 27th August 1883

(b) Krakatoa raise the interest in meteorology as a science

Eruption of Krakatoa was widely acknowledged with interest. The Deutsche Kaiser was so impressed that he ordered the establishment of a scientific institution, the German Sea Observatory, within weeks from the Indonesian event. The institute started publishing the venerable magazine *Meteorologische Zeitschrift* in January 1884. Its first article was a report on the volcanic eruptions from 1883, particularly that of Krakatoa. The first sentence says: "The year 1883 will occupy a remarkable place in the history of earth with respect

14 Wagner, Artur; Climatic Changes and Climate Fluctuations, Brunswich 1940, p.42.

15 Wexler, H., On the effects of volcanic dust on insulation and weather', in: Bulletin American Meteorological Society, Vol. 32, No. 1 & 2, January 1951, pp. 10-15, and pp. 48-52

to the effects of the earth's interior on its crust and everything found upon it." That sounded very promising. The British journal NATURE also published frequent scientific findings for a couple of years. But nothing exciting happed in climatic terms. The weather continued just as it had before. Only in some continental regions, average temperature decreased during the next five years. Because the Krakatoa eruption did not cause major changes to the weather statistics, science lost interest after a few years. Was Krakatoa so unspectacular indeed? No! The stability of the weather was extremely interesting, because only the oceans saved the world from a new dramatic cold period for a couple of years.

(c) Ocean as a stabilizer

After the eruption of Krakatoa, on the 21st of August 1883, unusual observations were reported. For example:

On the 3rd of September: During the past few days, there has been a fairly even, gray Cloud mass, normally covering the entire sky, above the cumulus and Stratus clouds;
On the 3rd of September: At midday hazy gray air. Hazy, gray air condensing into Dew towards evening;
On the 5th of September: Air appears yellow and watery;
On the 7th of September: The atmosphere appears to be filled with very small, evenly distributed clouds of vapor;
On the 13th of September: The yellowish "haze" continues in the upper atmosphere;
On the 11th of October: Fiery atmosphere, cloudless sky;
On the 5th of November: Pale atmosphere;
On the 10th of December: The air was very clear and looked like the air in the Southern Indian Ocean during the typhoon season;
On the 13th of December: Lead-colored sky.

These early observations could possibly have been dismissed as coincidence if the period until 1886 had not been accompanied by a permanent phenomenon, a "hazy fog", a strange, smoky cloudiness in the atmosphere, which was observed everywhere around the globe, in the tropical as well as in sub-polar areas. One of the descriptions given was: "The hazy fog appears as a constant companion of the extraordinary optical phenomena in the atmosphere during the entire period of the atmospheric-optical disturbance". How the young science viz. meteorology could not be concerned with what was going on? Had the oceans been recognized as stabilizers, the greenhouse effect would be understood much better today. The explanation is easy.

The “hazy fog” was a compound of volcanic dust and oceanic water vapor. This “extra stuff” from the atmosphere wrapped the earth like in a blanket. This blanket protected the earth from losing heat too quickly and thus compensated for the deficiency of blocked-out sunrays (10-15%) for a few years. The interdependence is evident:

- Air circulation, initially above normal, decreased to a ‘bare minimum’ in 1888. The above mentioned blanket determined a more maritime climate during the early period, while the continuing lack of ‘usual’ energy supply for the oceans over a longer time period pushed the water body temperature so much down that high air pressure systems got the ‘upper hand’.

- The “hazy fog” was stronger at the tropics. The warm tropical oceans released more vapor than colder pole water areas.

- During the Krakatoa-relevant five years, the average temperature in inner continental areas dropped more than in coastal zones; a clear indication that the heat capacity of the oceans had weakened over the period in discussion.

Oceans as a climate factor were inexistent in those days as far as science was concerned. One can only wonder how the matter had been discussed then. One serious opinion was whether the eruption had thrown a huge amount of water vapor into the air; while an opposing opinion was that the “hazy fog” was predominantly dry dust fog. There was no mention about the highly dominant role of the oceans.

(d) Relevance of Krakatoa in modern climatic study

It does not seem reasonable to discuss carbon dioxide (CO2) and Greenhouse effect on climate seriously as long as the impacts of more climatically relevant Krakatoa eruption on global weather conditions are not debated. The eruption of Krakatoa was the first scientific phenomenon of its kind which was carefully observed. But the unique and early opportunity to understand the principal mechanism of climate was not used properly because the mechanism of the weather and its reliance on the oceans were so poorly understood. Any convincing assessment on the former is still not available today. It would be particularly a matter for the Intergovernmental Panel on Climate Change (IPCC) to explain the historical conditions of the climate change issue to further and broader understanding. The perpetuation of the moderate climatic conditions from the explosion of the Krakatoa (1883) until the end of the decade was a physic-dynamical sensation, with many interesting clues on how to handle the CO2 issue.

However, the Krakatoa was the last major worldwide volcanic eruption after a long row of severe volcanic eruptions during the Little Ice Age. As a result, the world got warmer. Without industrialization, global air temperature would have been rising. A strong increasing trend is therefore defiantly natural and man is not to blame. This is widely undisputed. The next section will give an overview of other possible reasons which could have contributed to global temperature status during the last 150 years.

Factors affecting climate change since the 19th century

Since mid-19th century, when rapid industrialization went on at a much larger scale, man became an active user of nature in many respects. That brings up the big question whether temperatures had risen due to the end of the Little Ice Age only or human activities had contributed to this rise. Although it is assumed that both factors were involved, our main concern is the anthropogenic aspect. How did mankind contribute to temperature rise during the modern time period?

Carbon dioxide is certainly a possible contributor to making today's world warmer, but let's not overlook the fact that it represents only one of the contributing factors. Industrializing the world during the last 150 years practically meant accelerating the use of fossil resources such as coal, oil, gas, etc. for transport and energy production. Burning and combustion of organic substances produce gases, particularly carbon dioxide, which together with methane, water vapour and nitrous oxide are called greenhouse gases. Any discussion on climate is principally focussed on this phenomenon.

There are a number of man-made contributory factors that may have had specific impacts on the atmospheric seasonal heat budget, e.g. local warming in cities *(due to housing, roads, and other resultant factors)*, smoke and dust over long distances or deforestation of huge areas. Each may have had temporary or long lasting implications, but none of these is a major source for the strong warming trend during the last 150 years.

Shipping, which is one of the presumably decisive warming factors, has been given little attention until now in contrast to the greenhouse effect caused by atmospheric gases. The contribution of shipping, fishing, naval vessels, oil platforms, leisure boats, etc. is not comparable to that of cars, power plant and air planes in feeding the atmosphere with carbon dioxide (CO2), except for a small fraction. Each and every moving boat and vessel ploughed the sea to a depth of one to 20 metres, day and night. Since moving force of ships changed from sails to coal steamers and motor vessels propulsion, they churned the sea surface layer as a kitchen blender works on a milkshake.

The main aim of this investigation is to demonstrate the absolute dominance of the ocean in climatic affairs. Insofar as we can talk about the role shipping played in the warming of earth's climate since changing over from sailing to screw driven ships, the aspect of navigation is closely related to climatic changes like the sea war issue. If it is established that two short wars can dramatically change the course of climate for decades, it can also be proved beyond any doubt that shipping had been a major contributing factor to atmospheric warming during the last 150 years as well.

Greenhouse warming gases

The discussion about greenhouse gases had started in the early 19th century but the thesis acquired an extraordinary success only during the last 20 years. Forceful efforts of the global community of climatologists were recently crowned with success when the Kyoto Protocol[16] was enforced, in February

16 The Kyoto Protocol is an amendment proposed to an international treaty on global warming -- the United Nations Framework Convention on Climate Change (UNFCCC). Countries which ratify this protocol will

2005. The Protocol requires an overall reduction of emissions on market economy basis of offer and demand[17].

For the climate science, the group of greenhouse gases include carbon dioxide[18], methane, water vapour and nitrous oxide. They appear naturally, but are also produced through industrial processes. Inclusion of water vapour among these gases is an unfortunate if not a misleading action. Atmospheric water vapour needs to be considered on its own merits when the matter concerning air temperature warming is discussed.

Humidity and gases

Atmospheric dynamics principally happen because of the variation of heat concentrations. The term humidity refers to the water-vapor content from the atmosphere. While water vapor has the characteristic of appearing in various concentrations throughout the atmosphere, CO2 is distributed evenly. To this extent, it is a substance that is neutral for the climate and gains relevance only indirectly, in association with water vapor. The following explanations refer to this:

a) Figuratively speaking, distribution of greenhouse gases can be compared to a gridiron whose meshes are the same distance

---

be committed to reduce their emissions of carbon dioxide and other greenhouse gases which are linked to global warming. It also reaffirms sections of the UNFCCC.

17 It is said that such a market mechanism will help find cost-effective ways to reduce greenhouse emissions. There is no carbon audit regime yet. A carbon audit regime is an effective means of accounting for greenhouse gas control efforts. It establishes that the claimed reductions in emissions, or carbon sequestration, have actually occurred and are stable.

18 Carbon dioxide (CO2) results from the combustion of organic matter if sufficient amounts of oxygen are present. Plants use CO2 during photosynthesis. Both carbon and oxygen are used to construct carbohydrates. CO2 is present in the atmosphere at a low concentration and acts as a greenhouse gas. CO2 is a heavy odourless and colourless gas formed during respiration and through the decomposition of organic substances; absorbed from the air by plants in photosynthesis.

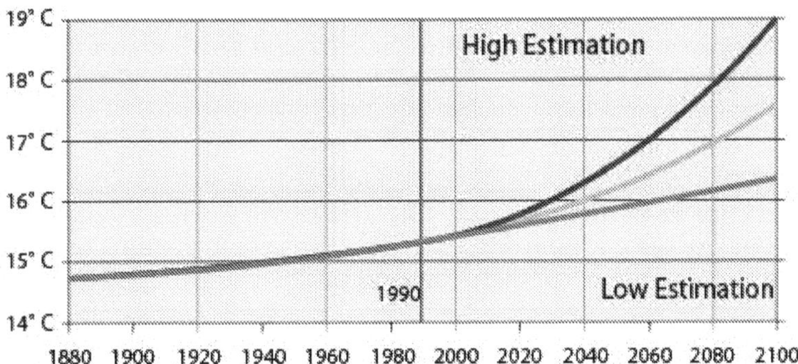

Temperature developments according IPCC

apart. The only variable is that the mesh network can be drawn tighter (e.g. by more CO2) or loosened. This net, by the way, changes only in accordance with the seasons and never with more than 1-2%. CO2 concentration has increased with about 25 % since 1850[19].

b) Water vapor, on the other hand, appears in varying concentrations. A saturated cloud stores within a certain volume which is many, many more times bigger than the amount of energy of the same volume of the CO2 gridiron. A hurricane, which derives its energy from the ocean, produces about 300-400 billion kw-hours of energy daily and releases 10-20 billion tons of water.

While there is an active exchange of water and energy between the ocean and the atmosphere, the greenhouse gridiron does not change. It would be interesting to hear from IPCC with how many kilowatt-hours of energy and with how many tons of water the greenhouse CO2 gridiron contributes to a hurricane as it develops and moves through a region. As the development, strength and maintenance of a whirlwind depends on the condition of the ocean, it seems unlikely for the greenhouse CO2 gridiron to make a significant contribution to this process - except perhaps in computer simulations.

c) To this extent, it is difficult to understand how any significant amount of heat energy could be transferred from

19 From 280 ppmv to 360 ppmv in year 2000

this gridiron to the ocean, thus leading to a rise of the sea level. Practical experiences show that, when the air is dry, the land heat does not come from the air, and that, when warm air encounters cold water, the ocean immediately protects itself with a defensive shield which takes the form of daze, mist or fog. Admittedly, the interaction between the ocean and the atmosphere is very complex. It requires considerable time and efforts to be explained plausibly. However, it is a mystery how anyone can explain with conviction that the seas can be heated by a cloudless sky at night, for example. The oceans are earth's central heating system. After the sun, the ocean is the second heating factor of the atmosphere. No one has plausibly explained yet how warm air coming from the bedrooms and living room is influencing the central heating system.

Dimension matter

If the sun were "turned off," the temperature of the atmosphere would be only 28°C above absolute zero, viz. -245°C. With the sun and "greenhouse gases" but without water, the average temperature on earth would be of -11°C, resulting from a daytime mean temperature of approximately +135°C and a nighttime temperature of approximately -175°C. The moon provides such conditions at night. CO2 would delay the cooling towards the absolute minimum only for a short time. Its functioning on earth is not so much different.

What matters is the amount and concentration of water in the atmosphere. If the atmosphere is divided into two warm or energy bearing zones, viz. water and greenhouse gases (CO_2, methane, etc.), then the atmospheric humidity has as much warming capacity as a two-meter layer of ocean/sea surface and the greenhouse gases as much as a one-meter layer. Practically, this means that a rise in the atmospheric temperature by 1°C must cause a drop of an equivalent amount in the upper three meters of the ocean. But because water vapor is usually in a much higher concentration at lower altitudes, its weather impact is much more effective then that of CO2. CO2 is permanently distributed equally throughout the atmosphere. Weather and temperature functioning are extremely different. Water vapor is about 96 to 99 % responsible for the greenhouse effect; and on a foggy day even 100%.

Since so much has been written about the greenhouse effect, whatever written here will be insignificant. Basic understanding about carbon dioxide issue is relevant only as far as it is needed to provide a comparison between possible contributors to the warming trend, including human input. While atmospheric water is a highly remote subject in IPCC reports related to climate, the shipping issue is completely inexistent.

Oceans and shipping

Oceans and shipping should have been the hottest topic in the climate change debate since meteorology was established as a science, in the late 19th century. Instead of that, oceans were ignored up to late 20th century and even today they do not enjoy the top position they deserve as a decisive climatic force, second after the sun.

a) The starting point is that the oceans are huge and deep. If all continents were leveled, the globe would then be covered by one ocean all around the sphere, at a uniform depth of 3,000 meters. It is not only quite a lot of mass, but water is also an excellent thermal store. Heat capacity ratio between ocean and atmosphere is of 1:1000. The sea can store heat for hours, days, decades or even centuries. Atmospheric heat capacity is almost completely limited to the amount of water vapor available. If not sustained by sunray or ocean heat, atmospheric heat is gone within 2 to 3 days. Humidity is particularly important for the winter seasons at higher latitudes when the sunshine is short, modest or not existent at all. Merchant and naval vessels, fishing and leisure boats plough warmer surface water to lower sea levels in the summer time. During winter, the process is reversed. The more the ships turn the surface water layer around during cold winter days, the warmer the water from lower levels will be and contribute to the rise of the air temperature.

b) Oceans and seas were subject to extensive 'stirring and mixing' since the start of the global warming, 150 years ago. There are over 30,000 registered trading ships. If half of them travel about 275 nautical miles (about 500 km) every day, then the waters of the oceans are "churned up" to a width of about 5 to 30 meters and a depth between few and 20 meters over a path which is equal to eight times the distance from the earth to the moon or 1,500 times the distance from the English Channel to the east coast of North America (all these figures are rough estimates). In a year, this would mean that the Atlantic Ocean from Iceland to the Ross latitudes is "ploughed up" to depths which have as much heat capacity as the entire atmosphere.

c) But there are not only merchantmen out in the sea. If all ships are to be taken into account, viz. fishing vessels, coast guard ships, tugs and millions of leisure boats during the summer season, we can easily double or triple the churning effect in the coastal waters and seas as compared to the figures calculated above in respect of merchant shipping. And shipping is presumably not the only contributor: dragging, sea bed drilling, off shore wind energy farms, etc. may also contribute. Actually every contribution, as little as it may be, adds to statistics, possibly resulting in a change of climatic data.

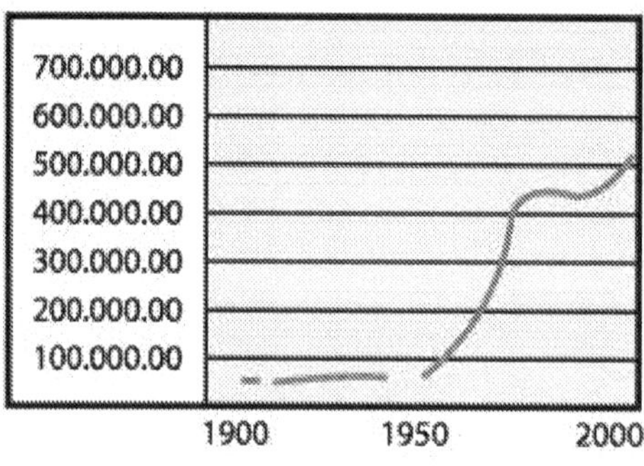

d) There are virtually no continuous series of measurements, which would lead to some acceptable conclusions about the isotherm structure and its influence on the upper layer of the ocean to a depth of at least 50 meters, over a long period of time. But the temperature difference can be of several degrees within a few meters, in summer as well as in winter.

e) The turning and churning of the sea by ships and boats is an ideal means to increase the warmth of the oceans. Any temperature increase expends simultaneously the volume of the water body. IPCC comes to the following conclusion concerning oceans[20]:

20 IPCC, Climate Change 2001: WG I: The Scientific Basis, Summary for Policymakers.

- *Tide gauge data show that global average sea level rose between 0.1 and 0.2 metres during the 20th century.*
- *Global ocean heat content has increased since the late 1950s, the period for which adequate observations of sub-surface Ocean temperatures have been available.*

Causing Sea Level changes is an important consequence of climate change, IPCC claims[21] and says: The pattern of sea level in ocean basins is maintained by atmospheric pressure and air-sea fluxes of momentum (surface wind stress), heat and fresh water (precipitation, evaporation, and fresh-water runoff from the land)[22]. That a significant proportion of ocean warming and expansion could have been caused by various uses of oceans and seas has not yet attracted IPCC's attention. This investigation will demonstrate that two World Wars were responsible for the only two major climatic changes since meteorology became a scientific discipline about 125 years ago.

Who contributed?

CO2 thesis supporters vs. sceptics

The earth's temperature has been rising for several decades now. That is a fact generally acknowledged. But the question concerning the causes of this phenomenon has received a lot of different explanations from the scientists. While the vast majority is blaming CO2 as the primary cause for this rise in air temperatures, claiming that its increase is unprecedented in the last 1,200 years, a minority suggests that atmospheric carbon dioxide -- often thought of as a key component of "greenhouse gases" -- is not the cause for global warming. They claim, for example, that rising global temperatures are a natural cause for increasing the level of carbon dioxide, and not the other way round. Environmentalists warn that adverse effects of man-made causes on environment, if left unchecked, may be irreversible. Reduction of rainforests, continued growth of hydrocarbon industries, increases in livestock and depletion

---

21 IPCC, Climate Change 2001: WG I: Changes in Sea Level, Introduction (Sec.11.1).

22 IPCC, Climate Change 2001: WG I: Changes in Sea Level, Ocean Processes (Sec. 11.2.1)

of ozone, etc. are all considered crucial factors in the debate. Sceptics maintain that the climate change is a natural phenomenon and that human influence on nature is highly overrated. It is interesting that neither camp has much to say about the strong interrelation between the thermal status of oceans and atmospheric warming.

For a better understanding of the rationale of this investigation, the principal causes for global warming will be provisionally rated on the basis of their contribution, to give each possible cause a 'dimension'. If this investigation succeeds in proving that two major wars changed the course of climate twice in the last century, it will also prove that shipping and other ocean uses also contributed to global warming. Although WWI and WWII saw an aggressive churning of the seas, it was hardly more than a fraction of the turning of the seawater surface layer by vessels year after year since engine propulsion revolutionized shipping, 150 years ago.

Meanwhile, it is obvious that this investigation would identify four main causes for the warming trend which started after the end of the Little Ice Age, in 1850. These causes are: natural phenomena, carbon dioxide, shipping and naval warfare. Other interesting causes, e.g. huge deforestation, urbanisation and building of large networks of roads since industrialization started, etc., play only a distant secondary role. Although these issues deserve greater attention, they are of little interest for this investigation because they represent second or third rank contributors.

What matters?

Global warming or climate change? This question should not be taken lightly as it means quite a lot for the understanding of our matter. Before suggesting a rating for major contributors, as mentioned above, it seems necessary to make clear what we are talking about.

Actually, the relevant United Nation's Convention on Climate Change (1992) should give an answer to this question. While the term "global warming" is frequently used, it is not mentioned in UNCCC. Instead, the Convention defines:

> "Climate change" means a change of climate which is attributed directly or indirectly to human activity that

> alters the composition of the global atmosphere and which is in addition to natural climate variability observed over comparable time periods".

One can only wonder how a text "Climate change means a change of climate" could be presented as an international law. It is simply absurd. Instead of defining what 'Climate' means in the first place, it introduces the term "Climate System" as follows:

> "Climate system" means the totality of the atmosphere, hydrosphere, biosphere and geosphere and their interactions."

This definition also does not make any sense either. According to common scientific understanding, 'Climate' refers to the weather situation over a long period of time, usually 30 years or more, or to meteorological conditions, including temperature, precipitation, and wind that characteristically prevail in a particular region. In a strict sense, 'Climate' is a mere accumulation of weather data expressed in statistics. If one wishes to give Climate a useful meaning, one should define it as the 'continuation of the oceans by other means' or as a 'copy of the oceans'.

The common term 'Climate' is often accompanied with uncertainty. 'Climate System' is even worse. Therefore, the definition 'Climate Change' is an insult to common sense. All these definitions always need further explanation depending on what subject one is talking about: sunshine, rain, wind, temperature, etc.

This investigation explains the reasons for the ranking of contributors to 'climate system changes', then selects the temperature issue, thus concentrating on 'global warming'.

Rate of Contribution

As a starting point, attention focuses on IPCC's warming assessment from 2001[23] according to which global average surface temperature (the average of air temperature over land

---

23 IPCC, Climate Change 2001: Working Group I: The Scientific Basis, Summary for Policymakers

and sea surface temperature) has increased since 1861. During the 20th century, the increase has been of 0.6 ± 0.2°C. The record shows a great deal of variability; for example, the warming occurred with more intensively during two periods: from 1918 to 1939, and from 1980 to 2000.

Discussion on possible causes for global warming leads to heat regulators. The global heat status is largely determined by a balance between the energy that Earth receives from the Sun and the heat that Earth releases back into space. This is called global energy balance. There are many causes for the alteration of the global energy balance, e.g. aerosols and cities. Indeed, heat balance is what occurs on Earth. In this exercise, the oceans are second in place after the sun but much more relevant than any subsequent source. On distant third place comes the atmospheric water vapour. Less than 0.05% of the ocean is in the atmosphere at any time. In tandem, the water masses of lakes, seas and oceans, and evaporated water co-ordinate and control the global atmospheric heat balance. Weather would not exist without these two factors.

We should always be aware that the sun is the principal player as far as climate is considered. However, for this investigation, its contribution is regarded as constant and stable throughout all seasons and years.

The following rating that we suggest represents an individual guess but may be of significant importance in categorising the scope of the theme.

Natural variability

Any 'natural variation' of the atmospheric conditions will have something to do with earthly water conditions, as they exist in the oceans and in the atmosphere. These conditions can suffer diverse influences. The Little Ice Age is certainly such a case. Volcanic dust may not only alter radiation but also influence the amount of water vapour and its height above sea level. A recent NASA study observed that the eruption of Mount Pinatubo (in 1991), a very small volcano compared to Medieval Age eruptions, increased Arctic Oscillation. During the two years following the volcanic eruption, the Arctic Oscillation caused winter warming over land areas, at high and middle latitudes in the Northern Hemisphere, despite a cooling effect due to volcanic particles blocking the sunlight. This winter warming is a strong demonstration that the oceans and water vapour compensated for the loss of sun radiation. A similar situation after Krakatoa had been explained in a previous chapter. But if the amount of volcanic particles is severe and sunrays are blocked out for a longer period, oceanic heat capacity will weaken after some time and a cooling is inevitable. That was presumably one of the principal reasons for severe winter conditions during the Middle Ages. The latest Intergovernmental Panel on Climate Change (IPCC) report (2001) reaffirms in much stronger language that the climate is changing in ways which cannot be accounted for as being natural variability. How did they know?

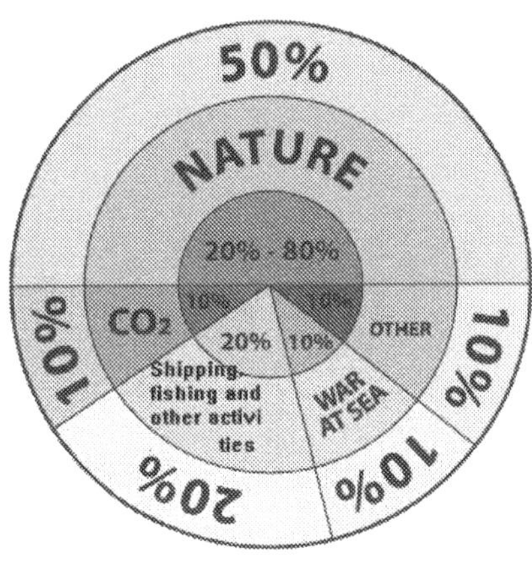

One can, with high certainty, assign a considerable amount of responsibility for warming to natural variations due to absence of serious volcanic activities during the last 120 years. However, the margin will be somewhere between 20% and 80%. In so far, it seems reasonable to work with an assumed figure of 50%.

The role of Carbon Dioxide

The higher the concentration of carbon dioxide, the greater the warming: this is the conclusion of the IPCC on this matter. According to them, the rising levels of CO2 anthropogenic emissions (primarily through use of fossil fuels) are responsible for the sustained temperature increase.

Since the beginning of the industrial revolution, atmospheric concentrations of carbon dioxide have increased with nearly 30%, methane concentrations have more than doubled, and nitrous oxide concentrations have risen with about 15%. IPCC experts believe that the increasing concentrations of greenhouse gases are likely to accelerate the rate of climate change. Scientists expect that the average global surface temperature could rise with 0.6°C-2.5°C during the next fifty years, and with 1.4°C-5.8°C during the next century. Of course, there will be significant regional variations, claiming that there is a "high" level of understanding among experts concerning the mechanism of greenhouses gases.

There is little one can do against the established 'beliefs' in certain circles. This investigation gives CO2 only a marginal rank as a contributor, viz. 5 to 15 % of 10%. This low rating derives particularly from the fact that the atmosphere is not the driving force for the warming mechanism but a mere appendix of the oceans. Furthermore, since its first report, in 1988, IPCC has never offered as an explanation more than the conclusion, by consensus, that there is a link between the rising of CO2 and the rising of the temperature level. This is hardly a convincing argument.

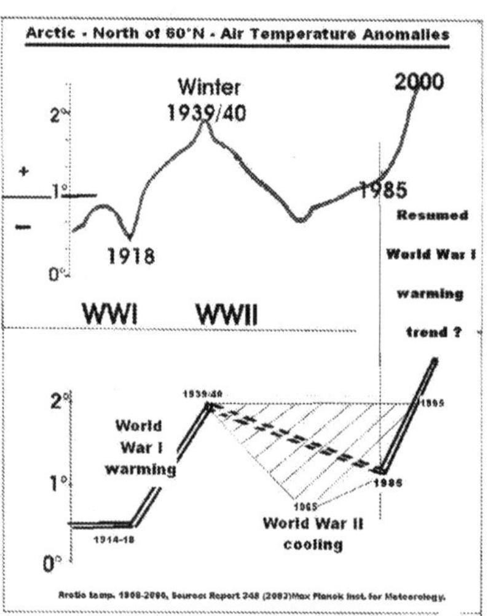

Shipping and ocean uses

Why shipping, as a major user of oceans, has not crossed the mind of the scientific community as a potential contributor to global warming since motorization of vessels took place, in the 19th century? We are of the opinion that shipping is considerably more relevant to global warming than various greenhouse gases, at the same time not hesitating to place it at a rank twice or thrice higher than CO2, or at least of a percentage of 20%. As this argument is currently difficult to prove, the turning and churning of oceans and seas by naval warfare shall be presented instead as causes for major climatic changes and global warming with a rating of 20% contribution to global warming.

War at sea issue

Central point of this investigation is how naval warfare during two world wars, in the 20th century, contributed to global warming. An in-depth analysis will show that the overall picture provides clear clues. World War I initiated a two-decade warming, from 1918 to 1939. World War II initiated a four-decade cooling period, from 1940 to about 1980. What makes things even more interesting are the three consecutive arctic war winters between 1939/40, 1940/41 and 1941/42, caused by military activities in the North and Baltic Sea. The emergence of these three winters will be presented as a powerful demonstration of how naval warfare drove temperatures to Ice Age level, changed regional weather conditions and left a significant imprint on climatic statistics,. This phenomenon is commonly called climate change.

Rating the impact of war at sea on global warming during the last century is somehow not easy as the warming period during WWI was largely neutralized by a much longer cooling period after the beginning of WWII. Furthermore, it cannot be completely excluded that the warming period initiated during WWI re-emerged after the end of the cold period, around 1980. It cannot be completely excluded as well that the forceful warming process which took place during the last 10-20 years has some connections with WWII naval activities.

As the prevailing opinion in this investigation allocates to various kind of ocean uses more relevance for warming than to the war at sea activities, the rating for the war at sea contribution is set at 10%.

Other contributors and summary

One could possibly name many dozen aspects and sources, alone or in combination with others that might contribute to warmer or colder regional and global air temperature. To the best of today's knowledge, none of them belongs in the premier league as a major player. Not to be ignored, they are given a rating of 10 %.

An overall allocation of the causes of the warming process could be divided evenly between natural and anthropogenic forces, at 50% each. More interesting are the assumed positions concerning anthropogenic contribution: direct ocean-related contribution represents 60% of the total while contribution related to other causes is only 40%, including 20% due to CO2 and other related gases.

The war at sea as significant factor will be elaborated in detail in order to demonstrate that modern naval forces were strong enough to force serious weather modification, including two major climate changes during the last century. The main aim of this investigation is to raise the awareness that anthropogenic atmospheric changes derive primarily (50% and more) from making use of the seas and oceans.

- B - Four-month war – One arctic winter 1939/40

Autumn 1939 scenario

On the 1st of September 1939, Germany attacked Poland by land, air and water. Soon, the Nazis deployed 5,000 planes in Poland (NYT* the 25th of September 1939). On the 25th of September 1939, 240 German planes bombed Warsaw, dropping 560 tons of bombs, including the first 1,000 kg bomb. 30 transport aircrafts dropped 70 tons of firebombs. Meanwhile, 1,000 batteries shelled the city day and night. Warsaw burnt for many days. Poland surrendered before the end of the month. Total casualties were estimated at 1 million, including 200,000 dead men and 700,000 war prisoners.

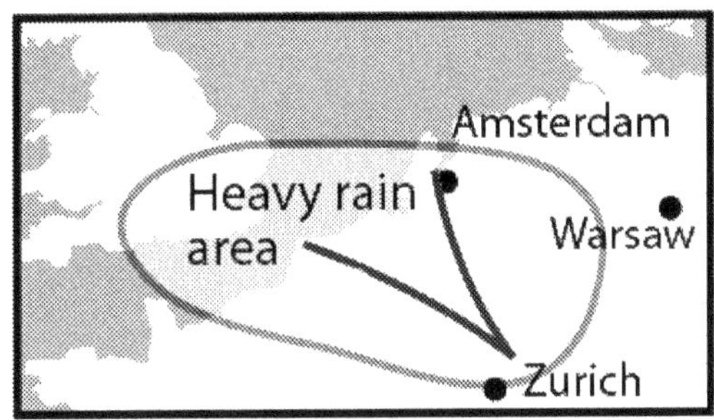

200% to 300% rain above average during October & November 1939

On the 3rd of September, Great Britain and France declared war to Germany. A several hundred-kilometre long military defence zone between France and Germany (viz. the Maginot Line and the Westwall) became operative immediately. Two million soldiers faced each other in September 1939. Since October, the number increased to over three million. Attacks and encounters occurred on a frequent basis. During one of the first attacks, 700 French tanks and planes moved seven miles over the Saarland border, while 300 air planes attacked German positions in the Aachen industrial region and munitions area, some 125 miles further north (NYT, the 7th of September 1939). Similar encounters, of smaller or larger proportions, occurred frequently. But the biggest clash was postponed due to extremely wet conditions, although Hitler had planned to invade France in late autumn.

---

*) NYT, The New York Times

On the 30th of November 1939, Russian troops invaded Finland with an army of 500,000 men (ca. 30 divisions), 2,000 tanks and 1,000 airplanes, while Finnish strength was much weaker. Fighting took place along a 1,000 kilometre front line, from the Barents Sea to the Gulf of Finland, with few access roads and very low temperatures (-46°C around Christmas 1939), in the permanent darkness of the northern Polar Circle and with only a few hours of daylight in southern Finland.

On the night of 26 to 27 December, Anatolia was hit by a major earthquake which caused the death of 30,000 persons and generated a tsunami in the Eastern Black Sea.

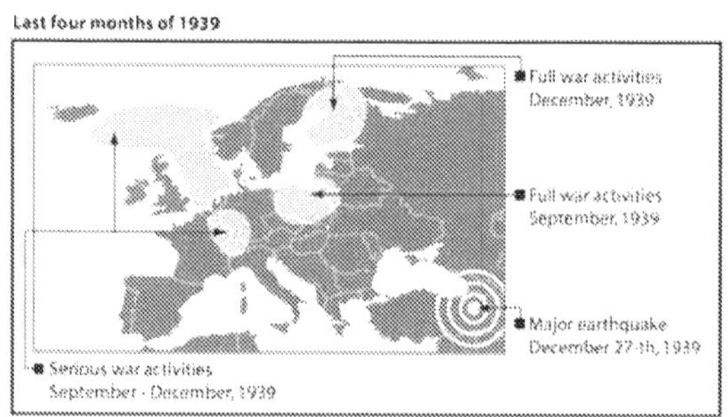

In August 1939, many naval vessels had already been sent to distant positions. When war commenced, warring nations had an armada of 1,000 naval vessels in service. The Baltic and North Sea and Eastern North Atlantic were the preliminary areas of activity. From hour zero, many hundreds of naval vessels were permanently engaged in patrolling, escorting, mine laying, mine sweeping, depth charging submarines, shelling coastal batteries, enemy vessels or enemy air planes.

The importance of autumn 1939 for climate research

The autumn of 1939 has a unique importance for the climate research. Even though naval activities were modest compared to what the world saw a few months later and which lasted the next five years, on the 1st of September 1939 climate statistics were free from any “external” influence. Northern European waters had never experienced such a devastating force powered by newly developed military means used firstly in WWII. WWI circumstances differed from those of WWII because during the former naval warfare the destruction progressed rather slowly before becoming serious, in late 1916, with the deployment of new weapons such as U-boats, sea mines, depth charges, etc.

The winter 1938/39 has been the warmest in the past few hundred years. Since the end of the WWI, Europe has been warming year after year. In the 1930s, no abnormal phenomenon has been recorded either in Europe or in a wider region that could have had an impact on the 'natural course' of the climate. In fact, the months between January and August 1939 had been slightly wetter than the average but, otherwise, thoroughly normal. Things changed only when WWII started. The impact of naval warfare on natural environment occurred very suddenly. Ocean and atmospheric matters run according to physical laws, for which the principles of conservation apply, except when something of huge proportions change the situation suddenly; an excellent example was the autumn of 1939.

Thanks to accurate climate data recorded in the autumn of 1939, conditions and circumstances that produced the arctic winter all over the Northern Hemisphere, in January 1940, and which maintained in Northern Europe until March 1940 will be discussed in details. To provide a complete picture, the war from China (1936) and an El Niño event 1938/39 which broke out in July/August 1939 will also be included in our presentation.

Methodology of presentation

While investigating what happened to European weather during winter 1939/40, one should logically start with naval activities in the concerned area as they were preconditions for the climate change. Instead, the result, viz. extraordinary winter conditions in January and February 1940, is presented first, whereupon certain relevant aspects are explored subsequently. The agenda will be as it follows:

- Extraordinary winter conditions making it the coldest winter in Northern Germany in more than 110 years and very extreme winter all over Northern Europe.
- Northern European waters and sea under stress. What does it mean to see naval forces in action?
- Warming and cooling process in North and Baltic Sea. Physical conditions and seasonal processes are explained in order to demonstrate that changes were inevitable and that the arrival of arctic cold was not really such a surprise.

- Shut down of west-wind-drift. Europe's mild climate depends on the flow of moister Atlantic air through its continental realm. War prevented it.
- Forcing rain in Europe – Drying out USA. Seasonal weather stability depends on the amount of water in the atmosphere. War in Europe and China dried the winter sky through excessive rain in autumn.
- Other contributors? War in Finland – Turkish earthquake – El Nino? Other major events in late 1939 are presented for the completion of the picture. None of them did seriously contribute to creating record arctic winter conditions during Europe's first war winter.
- Which aspects prove any relationship between conducting a war at sea and the resultant change in weather and climate conditions?

Four-month war brewed arctic winter
War and Naval warfare

This investigation is not concerned with history but only with climate change. Describing military events which happened in Europe after September 1939 would require from any historical writer to distinguish between activities on land, in the air and on sea. In our presentation, these military aspects are of interest only as far as they relate to climate. As climate should be defined as 'continuation of oceans by other means', a distinction can be made straight and to the point. It is of interest what happened above and under the sea surface: activities such as ship propulsion, shelling, mining, bombing, torpedoing, depth charging, ship scuttling and sinking, ship fire and explosion, loss of cargo, oil, chemicals, bulk general cargo, etc. Each and every activity that resulted in 'churning and turning' of seawater could be of interest and importance in this study. If the ocean undergoes a change, a subsequent change of atmospheric conditions is inevitable.

However, the suddenness of changes during the initial war period is nevertheless surprising. After only 100 days at war, North Europe tumbled straight into severe Little Ice Age conditions that are comparable to those of more than 100 years ago. On the other hand, 65 years have passed and science has not yet taken up the issue of analysing these phenomena. It is a fact that many trained meteorologists were called to military service, that weather data was considered top secret because of its military impact and that Met Offices had little time at hand to do scientific work. But these can hardly serve as an excuse for not doing anything after the end of WWII. Not even a reasonable assessment of general weather conditions during the extraordinary winter of 1939/40 has been made. But this is a preliminary requirement before elaborating causation and effect. The first to be done is to draw a picture of what it meant for Europe to go back in the Little Ice Age.

General winter weather scenario

Even Northern Spain recorded a temperature of -18°C at the beginning of WW2. Severe winter period lasted from mid-December 1939 to March 1940. Cold centre was The Netherlands and North Germany, generated by arctic air from Siberian interior. Extreme conditions were felt in Finland, Sweden, South of Norway, Denmark, Southwest of England, North of France, Hungary, Yugoslavia, Romania, Poland, Baltic countries and Western Russia. In the south of the line London-Budapest-Bucharest, weather was extremely cold and erratic for some days but mean value was not exceptional. In Switzerland, for example, winter was short and weather in February 1940 was close to normal. By mid-January, newspapers reported extraordinary temperatures as it follows: Finland and Baltic countries –48°C, South of Sweden -35°C, Denmark -26°C, Poland –40°C, Budapest -32°C, Paris –20°C.

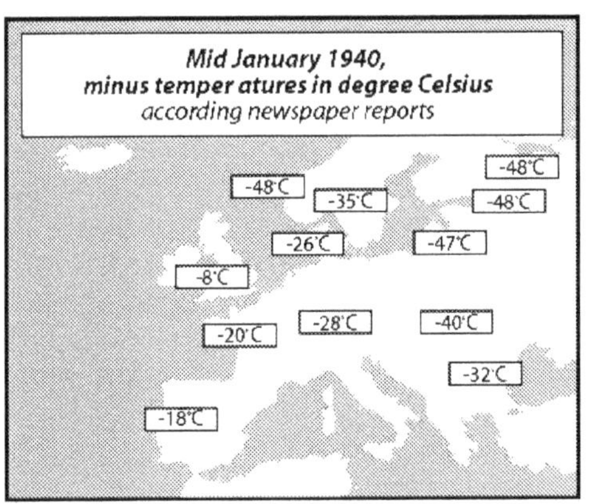

Although weather remained cold until mid-February, a second cold wave gripped Northern Europe with temperatures of -25°C in Sweden, Denmark and Holland, -33°C in Budapest, and -47°C in the Baltic countries. Subzero temperatures lasted at Potsdam/Berlin until the 15th of April, with only about 20 days without freezing temperatures in-between.

Winter conditions in Northern European Countries

A brief assessment in respect of the most affected countries in Northern Europe will be listed and remarks given if deemed helpful in further discussion. The list will start with Great Britain that is always of particularly climatic interest due to its location between maritime and continental weather conditions. Germany, which reported a record winter in its northern and eastern areas, will be dealt with at the end of the next section.

Great Britain

In January 1940, England was plunged into cold: it was the coldest month since 1895. The South was particularly affected, probably the coldest month for 100 years, as the chronologist of the Royal Met Society (H.C. Gunton)1 wrote a few months later. According to Kew Observatory, January 1940 was the coldest since 1791 and had the highest percentage of frost days. Also Greenwich figure was the lowest recorded during the past one hundred years, which was 0.5°C lower than the means for the long-remembered January 1881.

January 1940 is also remarkable for its high snow figures throughout many parts of the country and for a great Ice Storm from Kent to Exmoor and the Cotswolds, and from Sussex to Cambridgeshire and the north Midlands at the end of the month. Reports indicated: Icy Storm hits Britain; London has Heavy Snow, Heavy snow paralyses Britain; Transportation is badly affected (NYT, the 29th of January 1940). Cold broke a forty-six-year record. There were three inches of snow in the centre of London (NYT, the 30th of January 1940). In the close vicinity of London, the river Thames had frozen for the first time since 1814 (Neue Zürcher Zeitung, the 29th of January 1940). These conditions show that continental and maritime air fought their own battle for supremacy. In Britain, maritime site gained back control a few days later. February 1940 was without extreme temperatures. Only the melting of the remains from the Ice storm caused widespread flooding.

1 Gunton, H.C. (1939/40); 'Report on the Phenological Observations in British Isles from Dec. 1939, to Nov. 1940', in: Quarterly Journal of Royal Met. Soc. 1941, p.67f).

Notice: The facts stated in the previous two paragraphs give a strong indication that Southern North Sea has been cooled down too much and too early due to enormous naval activities since September 1939, a principal factor for the emergence of arctic winter in Northern Europe and a key subject in the following chapters.

The Netherlands

It was the same with the Netherlands: the coldest winter since 1830 (NYT, the 20th of February 1940). Some further reports say:

The 6th of January 1940: Drift ice in the East Scheldt. Ameland temporarily cut off from the mainland by ice. River Maas is frozen over from Woudrichem to Heusden[2].

The 12th of January 1940; Amsterdam: Floating ice is halting traffic on the rivers Rhine, Maas and Yssel. The ports of Amsterdam and Rotterdam are being kept open with considerable difficulty. The cold increases the losses already caused by war conditions. For instance, the number of ships calling at Rotterdam has dropped from 1,300 per month, before the war, to 380 now. (NYT, the 13th of January 1940)

The 14th of January 1940: At least two ships were crushed in ice packs on the Rhine and Ijsselmeer Rivers and thirty others were damaged severely. (NYT, the 14th of February 1940)

The 21st of January 1940: Heavy ice drift reported on the west Scheldt.

The 13th of February 1940; Amsterdam: Hundreds of persons abandoned their homes in the face of crushing ice packs boiling up from ice-locked canals, rivers and seas. Europe suffered tonight in the paralysing grip of the bitterest cold in more than 100 years. Weather Bureaus in Amsterdam recorded the lowest temperature ever recorded in this country: 11.2 degrees below zero Fahrenheit (-24°C). For the Netherlands, which has a rather mild climate, this is more severe than the lowest temperatures recorded in Minnesota. The average for the whole country was 1.4 Fahrenheit degrees above zero (-17°C).

---

2 Frankcom, C.E.N.; 'Ice conditions in the Baltic and Danube Areas December 1st 1939 to January 23rd 1940', in: The Meteorological Magazine, Vol.75, February 1940, pp. 1-8.

Water transportation in the Netherlands has been completely paralysed. Canals have been covered with thick ice for more than six weeks, while traffic on the Rhine and Waal stopped on the 11th of January. (NYT, the 14th of February 1940)

Notice: The cold came early and was severe. It prolonged for two full months. Every aspect points out to the impact that naval activities had on North and Baltic Sea conditions.

Denmark

"It is Denmark's worst winter since 1860". (NYT, the 15th of February 1940) What else was reported? A few examples:

The 28th of December 1939: Snow storms sweep Denmark (Frankfurter Zeitung, the 29th of December 1939)

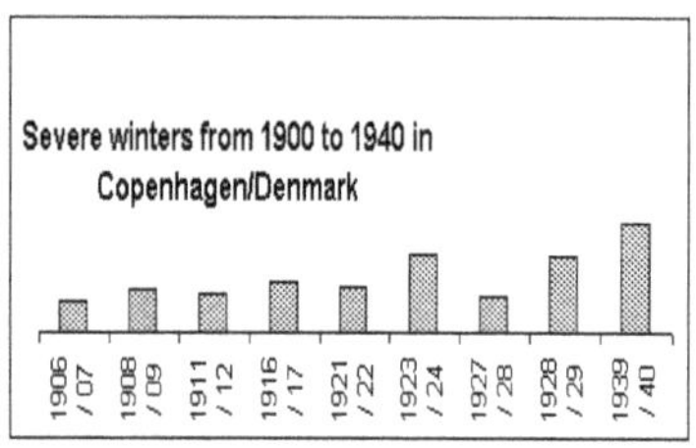

The 3rd of January 1940: Heavy snowstorms reported again from Denmark and traffic at Jutland is affected. (Neue Zürcher Zeitung, the 3rd of January 1940).

The 17th of January 1940: In Copenhagen, 14.8 degrees below zero Fahrenheit (-26°C) was registered early today; there was no sign that the cold wave would abate soon. Heavy snowstorms accompanied the cold, and traffic in many parts of Denmark was impeded or brought to a standstill. (NYT, the 18th of January 1940)

The 13th of February 1940: At Copenhagen temperature dropped to 13 degrees below zero Fahrenheit (-25°C). (NYT, the 14th of February 1940)

Sweden

On the 21st of February 1940, the New York Times (NYT) reported: "In Sweden all cold records were broken in the last twenty-four hours, the coldest since 1805". On the basis of data of four months, i.e. December 1939–March 1940, the winter of 1939/40 ranked the 9th on the list of the coldest winters after 1757, trailing behind the winters of 1880/81 (rank 6), 1837/38 (rank 5) and 1808/09 (rank 2). On the basis of data for three months, the winter is ranked the 10th, outranking the winter of 1892/93 (rank 9)[3].

Finland

High in the North, the winter situation 1939/40 was special due to the war that Russia started against Finland on the 30th of November 1939 and it requires a detailed assessment in one of the subsequent chapters. Below, there are only a few cases of relevant weather information from December 1939:

The 1st of December 1939: "Bombs dropped on Helsinki, civilians were hastily leaving in mist and rain in the northern winter". (NYT, 'The Week in Review', the 3rd of December 1939)

The 2nd of December 1939: "Snow began falling on Helsinki where relief workers sought to extinguish fires and to clear away rubbles before Russian bombers returned again with a rain of death". (NYT, 'The Week in Review', the 3rd of December 1939)

The 10th of December 1939: "Violent fighting in knee-deep snow on Finland's eastern frontiers, at the Arctic Circle was reported today". "Hostilities in the northern sector were said to be proceeding in weather 4 degrees below zero Fahrenheit (-20° C)". "In addition to the Red Army troops killed in battle, many others were reported to be dying of cold and exposure after being isolated from their supply trains and bases in the snow-piled wastes". (NYT, the 11th of December 1939)

The 24th of December 1939 - Report by James Aldridge (extract from NYT, the 25th of December 1939): "The cold numbs the brain in this Arctic hell, snow sweeps over the darkened wastes, the winds howl and the temperature is 30 degrees below zero Fahrenheit (-34.4°C). Here the Russians and Finns are battling in blinding snowstorms for possession of ice-covered forests. ...I reached the spot just after the battle ended. It was the most horrible sight I had ever seen. As if the men had been suddenly turned to wax, there were two or three thousand Russians and a few Finns, all frozen in fighting

3 Liljequist, Gösta H. (Severity); 'The severity of the winters at Stockholm 1757 – 1942', in: Geografiska Annaler 1-2, 1943, p. 81-104; and as an extended paper in: Meddelanden, Serien Uppsatser, Stockholm 1943, pp.1-24.

attitudes. Some were locked together, their bayonets within each other's bodies; some were frozen in half-standing positions; some were crouching with their arms crooked, holding the hand grenades they were throwing; some were lying with their rifles shouldered, their legs apart... Their fear was registered on the frozen faces. Their bodies were like statues of men throwing all their muscles and strength into some work, but their faces recorded something between bewilderment and horror." (NYT, the 25th of December 1939)

The 28th of December 1939: "Russian forces in winter cold, 30 degrees below zero Fahrenheit, and amid blinding storm... (in) the bitterest weather conditions of any war ever fought". (NYT, the 29th of December 1939)

The 29th of December 1939; Petsamo Front: heavy snowstorms are continuing. (Neue Zürcher Zeitung, the 29th of December 1939)

The 30th of December 1939: According to reports from Kirkeness, in North Norway mighty snowstorms blew over North Finland. Horrible cold prevailed in the Finnish north front area. Temperatures have fallen to 40°C below zero, a cold of such magnitude is seldom seen in this area in December. Weather experts consider larger military actions impossible. (Hamburger Anzeiger, the 30th/31th of December 1939)

The 31st of December 1939: According to a review of the first war month, the Russians attack on seven fronts with 700,000 men. Russian losses are estimated at 35,000 killed, 100,000 wounded, 332 tanks destroyed or captured. (NYT, the 31st of December 1939)

Baltic Countries

A full assessment of weather conditions during WWII still needs to be written. Conditions during winter 1939/40 must have been 'killing' as some reports imply:

The 24-27th of December 1939: In the Eastern parts of the Baltic countries (Russian West border) temperatures fell to -17°C from the 24th to 25th, and below 20°C one day later, extending to the Baltic coast, with -14°C in Klaipeda and -17°C in Gdynia (Bight) on 27th of December[4].

4 German daily weather charts of 'Seewarte'.

The 13th of January 1940: Bitterest cold wave for years, which sent temperatures in the Baltic countries down to as low as 40 degrees below zero Fahrenheit, ended abruptly today. The mercury rose rapidly to a few degrees below zero. Parts of the Baltic Sea have frozen over and floating and pack ice are likely to interfere with shipping for some time. (NYT, the 14th of January 1940)

The 13th of February 1940: In Estonia, Latvia and Lithuania, more than 10,000 persons suffered from severe frostbite. At least five persons froze to death in the three Baltic countries, where temperatures reached 54 degrees below zero Fahrenheit (-47.7°C) for the first time in 160 years. Baltic Sea was frozen over. (NYT, the 14th of February 1940)

Central Europe (e.g. Hungary, Rumania)

Weather was erratic, very cold, very snowy, and possibly the coldest for fifty or more years, but not the coldest for a century or record breaking. However, some reports demonstrate the severity of this winter.

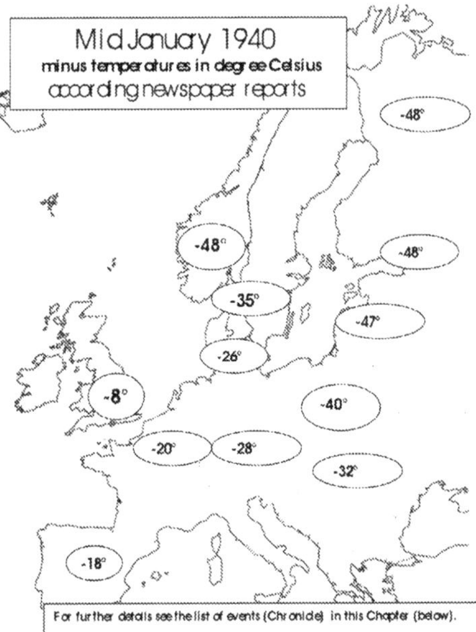

The 22nd of December 1939: A very severe snowstorm brought shipping in the Black Sea and the lower Danube river to a standstill. On the coast, temperatures dropped to 15°C below zero. Snow also fell all over Bulgaria on the 21st-22nd of December, starting a new cold weather episode (down to -16°C): -20°C in Northern Bulgaria.

The 29th of December 1939: Ice closes Danube to German supplies; rail traffic expected to be hampered by snow. "Cold winds have been recently blowing at the west of Russia. Constantly low temperature in the river valley indicates that a general freeze will set in soon". (NYT, the 30th of December 1939)

The 10th of January 1940: Cold weather, worst in Hungary since 1929, is expected to break all previous records. The Danube is a solid sheet of ice. (NYT, the 11th of January 1940)

The 11th of January 1940: In Rumania, temperatures are of 40 degrees below zero Fahrenheit (-40°C); Bulgaria was reported to be suffering under the worst cold in the memory of living persons (NYT, the 12th of January 1940). Riga –41°C; Budapest -26°C, Vienna -25°C, Sofia –22° C (Neue Zürcher Zeitung, the 11st of January 1940).

The 17th of January 1940: Cold Paralyses Northern Europe. The unexpected swiftness with which temperatures fell was featured in almost all weather reports. After a comparatively warm weather during the weekend, the temperatures began suddenly to drop towards the bottom of the thermometers. A typical report from Riga said that the temperature was at freezing point on Monday morning (the 15th of January) and at 22 degrees below zero Fahrenheit yesterday morning. Then it tumbled to 47.2 degrees below zero – a drop of 79.2 degrees in about thirty-six hours (NYT, the 18th of January 1940).

The 22nd of January 1940: Severe snowstorms swept Europe from the Adriatic Sea to Scandinavia (NYT, 23 January 1940).

The 13th of February 1940: Europe suffered tonight... in the cold wave which extended from the Arctic fringes of Norway and Finland... the Baltic countries to the Netherlands and Hungary. (NYT, the 14th of February 1940)

The 15th of February 1940: All cold records in Europe were broken last month and just when it was hoped the worst was over, another cold wave has bound the whole continent. (NYT, the 15th of February 1940)

The 15th of February 1940: Budapest suffered today from the bitterest cold in sixty years, 28 degrees below zero Fahrenheit (-33°C). (NYT, the 16th of February 1940)

War winter 1939/40 in Germany

Most of the naval activities of the initial war months occurred in the proximity of Northern Germany's coast, in the North and Baltic Sea. The location of Germany in Europe is of great importance in tracing the reasons for an extreme winter after only four-month warfare. That is why no other country had to look so far back in its historical weather recordings to find comparable winters, with the same coldness magnitude. Vast parts of Germany experienced the coldest winter in more than 100 years. In the early 1800s, the Little Ice Age had reached its heights and, suddenly, Northern Europe was back in an Epoch of Cold.

The centre of cold stretched from Amsterdam, via Bremen, Hamburg, Berlin, to Königsberg (Kaliningrad). Naval activities were the most intense in the Helgoland Bight and Southern Baltic Sea, starting with a ten days battle from sea to shore in the Gdansk area (in early September) and with the laying of many dozens of mine fields along the German coast. A detailed picture will be provided later.

Hamburg, a port city on the river Elbe and close to North and Baltic Sea, experienced record conditions despite its usually maritime weather conditions, with winter temperature averages just above zero degrees Celsius. Instead, for almost two months, from the 1st of January to about the 20th of February, average temperature was below -12°C. The Elbe was heavily iced. With a big headline newspaper, "Hamburger Anzeiger" had claimed on the 23/24th of December 1939: "The Elbe will never be frozen over, since 1874/75 icebreaker would keep the shipping fairway open". Only a short time later, nature creates extreme problems to the German navy: heavily frozen seas and rivers. Many naval vessels could not be moved for a considerable period of time.

For Berlin and Halle it was the coldest winter in 110 years. The assessment is based on the 'summary of the daily mean data from November 1939 to March 1940'. For Berlin (correspondingly for Halle), the data noted for 1829/30 is the 'cold sum' figure -791°C, for the winter 1939/40 the figure - 736°C[5]. These data are confirmed by other researche as well. The coldest months of January in Berlin since recording has started, in 1719, are: 1823, 1838 and 1940. With regard to the winter of 1928/29, February (-10.4°C) was colder than February 1940 (-7°C), but as January 1929 is not among the 20 coldest winter months, the winter 1939/40 ranks higher on the list of cold winters. For Dresden, about 150 km south of Berlin and close to Halle, the winter of 1939/40 (December-February) was also the coldest in 110 year, surpassed only by the winter of 1829/30.

At the most eastern end of the southern region of the Baltic Sea, former Königsberg (later Kaliningrad), with long-term winter average of –2°C, had to cope with following mean temperatures:

	Medium	Maxi-mal	Minimal	Deviation from means	Lowest
January	-10,7°C	-7,2°C	-14,4°C	-8,0°C	(14.Jan.) - 25,4°C
February	-11,4°C	-7,9°C	-15,8°C	-9,0°C	(24.Feb.) - 25,8°C
March	-2,2°C	0,7°C	-5,4°C	-2,8°C	(13.Mar.) - 15,1°C

Summary

The evidence of extraordinary winter conditions is overwhelming. It is further possible to clearly demonstrate that the whole Northern Europe, from Riga to Budapest and London, fell prey to arctic conditions. Cities like Amsterdam, Hamburg, Berlin and Dresden registered record cold never experienced in more than a century. While the impact and appearance of winter 1939/40 is now presented, the next move is to establish how this could happen. After all, global and regional weather is based on physics. Nothing happens without a cause.

5 Stellmacher, R. and Tiesel R.; ‚Über die Strenge der mitteleuropäischen Winter der letzten 220 Jahre – eine statistische Untersuchung', Z. Meteorol.39 (1989) 1, p.56-59.

Navies churn seas

Laws of physics governing Hot Soup in a Cup

Laws of physics also apply to hot soup in a cup. WWII unleashed tremendous military forces unheard of in history. Millions of soldiers marched up and down the battlefront. Thousands of naval ships ploughed oceans and seas day and night. When war broke out, the most affected seas were the Baltic and North Sea. Both of them would have normally stored heat to their highest capacity by the end of August. Since the last Ice Age, they lay idle in autumn to serve as a substantial heat reservoir during the forthcoming winter season, when days are short and sunrays contribute little to regional weather conditions. Together with the Gulf Current, west of Great Britain and Norway, these seas ensure moderate winters in Northern Europe. These seas decide whether Western Europe, at the north of the Alps, has maritime or continental winter climate. Winter 1939/40 turned out to be extreme continental in Northern Europe.

Allowing navies to participate in a war at sea, in Northern Europe's natural heat reservoir, is like hastily stirring a hot soup to cool it down for quick consumption. Once the soup in a bowl is cooled down, it will not warm up again naturally. Likewise, once the heat storage of Northern and Baltic Sea is diminished, water will warm again only during the next year's summer. Once the navies were out at sea in autumn 1939, the inevitable happened. Arctic cold was to come during winter 1939/40. Naval activities during the first four war months (from September to December 1939) were a force to reckon, as it will be demonstrated in the following section. Although it might appear as if some sort of naval history is presented, this is in no way intended. It is presented only with the purpose to awake the awareness that warring navies in early WWII days were effective enough to stir and churn the seas about like a spoon moving in a cup of soup.

"A spoon in a cup"

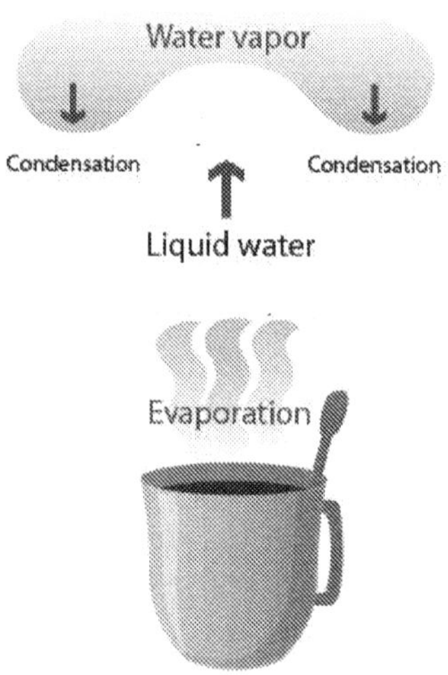

Dimension matters when considering the effect of a spoon stirring the soup in a bowl. In oceanic terms, Northern Europe's enclosed seas are only 0.2% of the global sea surface and a mere drop with respect to the total volume (0.0026%). Nevertheless, they play a vital role as their size is roughly one-fourth of North-Western Europe. With regard to the effect of a 'turning about' of sea areas, the available depths also matter considerably. In North and Baltic Sea, depth is not significant, i.e. a mere average of 50 meters. In comparison, Mediterranean Sea has an average depth of 1,500 metres and sunrays warm the sea even in wintertime. It matters if a ship moves through a moderate water depth or a sea mine explodes only a few meters above the seabed. In those days, battleships had an average size of about 35,000 tons, a draught of 10 metres and a speed of 32 knots (ca 60 km/h). Accompanied by a number of escort destroyers across the seas, battleships turned huge water areas around. Suddenly, there were thousands of naval ships out on the sea, hunting enemies or being hunted from shore, air, surface ships or submarines. Our following task is to describe which mighty forces have been set in motion before the war winter plunged to arctic cold, in mid-January 1940 (for the first time) and in mid-February (for the second time). Our proposition is to demonstrate that the image of a spoon moving in a hot-soup-cup corresponds to the huge naval force which was active in North and Baltic Sea during the initial war months of 1939.

Naval Fleets

By December 1939, the number of main naval ships belonging to Germany, Great Britain, France, Italy, the Soviet Union and

Italy had amounted to more than 1,000 vessels (including submarines, torpedo boats, etc.) with a total tonnage of 2.8 million, plus at least another thousand smaller vessels and boats serving for example as mines sweepers, etc.

- **Great Britain:** 250 big naval vessels (183 destroyers and bigger vessels) and ca. 57 submarines;
- **Germany:** 30 big naval vessels (21 destroyers and bigger vessels) and 57 U-boats.

Merchant Fleet and Convoy System

World merchant fleet comprised 30,000 ships with a total tonnage of about 70 million when war commenced. Presumably not more than two thirds of the fleet were fit for ocean crossing. British fleet was by far the largest, with 20 Million tons, followed by Norway, with 5 Million tons, Germany, with 4.5 Million tons, and France, Holland and Italy, with about 3 Million tons each.

German merchant fleet was swept away from the oceans before the end of the year: taken as war prize, scuttled by its crew or seeking refuge in neutral ports. Vital transportation requirements in the Baltic Sea and ore shipment from North Norway required about 600 ship voyages per month, with additional requirements after the occupation of Norway (1940).

As far as Britain was concerned, shipping was of utmost importance. No effort was spared to maintain it functional. Atlantic supremacy was meant to ensure sufficient supply to Great Britain at any time. Allies introduced the convoy system without delay, a very successful measure during WWI, supported by the First Lord of the Admiralty, Winston Churchill, who considered it "the dominating factor all throughout the war. ...Battles might be won or lost, enterprises might succeed or miscarry, territories might be gained or quitted, but our power to carry on the war, or even to keep ourselves alive, is represented by our mastery of the ocean routes and the free approach and entry to our ports"[6].

Convoying meant that up to 50 ships sailed in four to five columns, frequently altering course by up to 90 degrees

6 Source:www.usafa.af.mil/dfh/harmon_series/docs/Harmon36.doc.

simultaneously (zigzagging), while naval escort vessels formed a shield around them. During WWII, on the 5th of September 1939, the first deep-sea convoy of eleven troop transporters sailed from Clyde for Gibraltar, escorted by the battleship *Ramillies* and eight destroyers. On Wednesday the 6th of September, the first of the East Coast convoys sailed from the Thames up to the Firth Forth. By the end of the war, coastal convoys around the United Kingdom amounted to 7,700, together with 173,000 merchant ships.

The threat of submarines and raiders was felt everywhere. Ships zigzagged the seas on their own. The British cruise liner "Andorra Star" crossed the Atlantic in 10 days (NYT, 13 September 1939), while the US liner "Manhattan" sailed from Bordeaux to the States escorted by two US Navy destroyers in mid-September (NYT, 17 September 1939). Britain announced that it would arm 2,000 merchant ships with guns (NYT, 1 October 1939). Within 12 months, 3,000 vessels were armed with a 4.7-inch gun[7] each. By December 1939, 5,756 ships had sailed in convoys[8]. By the end of the year, only twelve vessels and five stragglers from convoys were torpedoed by U-boats and sunk. The total loss amounted to the tonnage of 421,156[9].

Uboat activities and areas with considerable sinking quotas

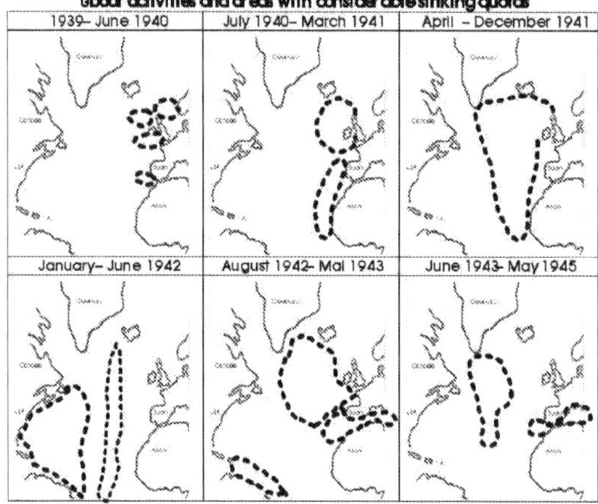

Submarine – U-boats

When war started, German and British Navy had 57 submarines each. Britain eventually employed 270, the Germans about 1,000.

British submarines had the difficult task of intercepting well-protected German shipping around Northern Europe by direct torpedo attacks or by mine laying missions. Although Britain never managed to operate in the Baltic Sea during WWII, Royal Navy submarines

---

7 Slader, John; 'The Fourth Service' -Merchantmen at war 1939-45', Corfe Mullen, Dorset, 1995, p. 56.

8 Winton, John; 'Convoy – The defence of sea trade 1890-1990', London 1983., p. 128

9 Winton, p. 130,

took a heavy toll on German troop transporters, supply ships and escort vessels, quickly forcing the Germans to adopt defensive convoys when operating in the North Sea or, after 1940, in the Norwegian waters. During the Second World War, British submarines were supposed to have sunk 475 merchant ships, 105 warships and 36 submarines and to have damaged many others.

What happened to submarines in North Sea and elsewhere since the 1st of September 1939, for five years day by day, may be illustrated by a news report headlined: "British Submarines' Crew, Bombed All Day At Bottom of Sea, Passes Time by Betting", (NYT, the 6th of October 1939), "the Admiralty today released a story about the crew of a trapped, crippled British submarine who ran a penny sweepstake pool at the bottom of the North Sea while the Germans groped for them with sweep wires and shattered bombs and depth charges for twenty-four hours. During the first hour, six depth charges sounded faintly and, during the second hour, the explosions, louder and nearer, averaged every two minutes". Another report from the same date states: "British destroyer patrolling northeast of the English Channel had trapped two German submarines early this week and forced them into a mine field where they exploded and sank" (NYT, the 6th of October 1939).

However, the submarine warfare during WWII meant both success and failure to German U-boats in North Sea and North Atlantic, which were deputed to cut Great Britain off vital supplies from Canada and USA. About a dozen German U-boats were already in the Atlantic when the war started, in September 1939. Others operated in the European waters. Also in September 1939, groups of three to five naval vessels of the Royal Navy were formed in order to patrol large areas. These groups criss-crossed the seas day and night, searching for U-boats and dropping depth charges when a U-boat was detected or assumed to be around.

On the 14th of September 1939, U-39 operating near the Hebrides shot its torpedo at the 22,000-ton aircraft carrier '*Ark Royal*', but missed. Escorting destroyers *Faulkner*, *Foxhound* and *Firedrake* depth-charged U-39 in a series of attacks, as reported by an eyewitness: "We gained ASDIC Contact with the Sub and each ship in turn went in at full speed and fired a pattern of depth-charges. *Firedrake* attacked last. As we came out of it and heard our depth charges explode, we thought we had missed, until up it came vertical like a huge cigar and then flopped down slowly"[10]. U-39 surfaced briefly, then sank. Attacks of U-29 succeeded a few days later. 22,000-ton British aircraft carrier *'Courageous'* was on an enemy hunt along with four destroyers in the Southwest approaches (Southwest of Ireland), 150 nautical miles WSW of Mizen Head, Ireland, in the early evening of 17th September 1939. The carrier could travel at a speed of 30.5 knots (56 km/h). But HMS *Courageous'* days were numbered. "A German submarine struck a telling blow at the British Navy last night by sinking the 22,000-ton aircraft carrier *Courageous*, with loss of an unknown number of its complement of 1,100 officers and men. It was the first real success scored by the German Navy in this war." (NYT, the 19th of September 1939) From a salvo of three torpedoes, two hit the Courageous on portside. The destruction was devastating as Sub-Lieutenant Charles Lamb describes it: 'There were two explosions, a split second apart, the like of which I had never imagined possible. As if the core of the earth exploded and the universe split from pole to pole, it could sound no worse... In the sudden, deathly silence which followed, I knew the ship had died.' The *Courageous* turned over and sank within fifteen minutes, with a loss of 519 of its crew. Lieutenant Wesmacott 'heard two violent explosions which seemed to lift the ship'. (NYT, the 19th of September 1939)

Depth Charges

This section is about ASW, namely anti-submarine-warfare. A depth charge is a 'drum' containing explosives with a fuse which is detonated at a preset depth and which is based on hydrostatic pressure. Developed in 1916, during WWI, a depth charge could detonate up to 100m depth and carried 150 kg of explosives. There was little development for this weapon between the wars except for a 300kg variant. At the start of WWII, depth charges were essentially the same weapon as it existed at the end of WWI. This situation changed quickly.

In September 1939, The New York Times wrote about the procedures of U-boat hunting: "Once a submarine is located, British naval plans, so far as they were known before the war, call for attack by familiar methods of an enclosing diamond pattern of depth bombs, supplemented, of course, by shell fire and ramming if the submarine could be forced to the surface.

---

10 /www.hmsfiredrake.co.uk/firedrake7.htm

In the diamond-pattern attack, the destroyer goes at full speed to the spot where the submarine, slow and clumsy under water, is thought to be. One depth bomb is charged just before the spot is reached. A few seconds' later two more are lobbed out by a Y-gun so that they land out on either side of the destroyer's wake. In the front part of the diamond pattern, another depth bomb is dropped over the stern, some distance ahead of where the Y-gun fired. This way a large area of the sea is covered by this diamond pattern. The effect is further increased by the fact that the bombs are timed to go off at different levels, so that the area is covered not only horizontally but vertically as well. The bursting area of a modern depth bomb is considerable". (NYT, the 16th of September 1939)

Evaluating the intensity of the destruction caused by the explosion of depth charges from sea surface to sea bottom is not easy. Many naval vessels were not out on sea for combat reasons, but for training, surveillance or testing, etc. For many commanders the situation was new and they took precautions against imminent or assumed threats, as the following report illustrates it: "Russian commanders of the transport ships and torpedo boats were so much afraid of being attacked by a Finnish submarine in the Gulf of Finland that they set off depth charges every 15 minutes or whenever an unconfirmed sighting of a periscope was reported, all that resulting in a total of 400 depth charges having been dropped by the end of the operation that day"[11].

On the 29th of November 1939, at dawn, U-35 was cruising east of the Shetland Islands, in the North Sea. At the sight of the British Destroyer *'Icarus'*, the U-boat crash-dived to 70 m depth and started steering evasive courses. As *'Icarus'* electronic devices for U-boat localisation were out of order, depth charges set for 80m were dropped in order to feign an attack. Two nearby destroyers were alerted. After contact had been established, two more depth-charge attacks followed, jamming U-35 diving plans and placing it at a sharp up angle. Crew was sent to the ship's bow to bring it back on even keel, but all their efforts were in vain. Explosions had also destroyed the fuel and ballast tanks aft. U-35 appeared suddenly at the surface and the crew was ordered to abandon the ship, but they were rescued by their attackers.[12]

---

11 Dyke, van, Carl; ‚The Soviet Invasion of Finland 1939-40', London, 1997, p.54

12 Source: /www.u-35.com/war/

“During the first sixteen months of war, an estimated number of 33 U-boats were destroyed in about 4,000 depth charge attacks.”[13] Each attack could mean the use of a few or, from the contrary, of many dozens of depth charges. The total number of depth charges dropped per month could easily reach several thousands. German naval vessels hunted Royal Navy submarines, too. Up to 10,000 or even more depth charge explosions could have occurred below the sea surface during the first four months of the war.

Since then, development of depth charges focused on increasing the depth at which a submarine might be successfully attacked, due to improvements to their sinking speed. Since 1943, the detonation of depth charges carrying a charge of 100 kg of TNT at a depth of 300 meters became possible.

Arial bombing at sea

Neither the German navy nor the British one had a fully operational aerial arm at the beginning of WWII. The German Navy never got one. British Royal Air Force Coastal Command became operational in 1940. However, airplanes charged with bombing missions were operating frequently (British airplanes in the Helgoland Bight and German airplanes on England’s East coast) or were attacking the enemy in the open sea. On the 3rd of September 1939, Britain was in possession of a fully operational unit of 2,600 aircrafts[14]; the Germans had nothing less.

A few out of many hundred events are listed below in order to offer you an outline of what happened during the first few months of the WWII.

The 4th of September 1939: The First RAF raid of about 30 planes. Organised in separated groups, they targeted a fleet of Nazi naval vessels in the German Bight (Wilhelmshaven and Brunsbüttel). One officer reported (NYT, the 15th of September 1939): “The enemy held his fire until we were almost over our targets. Then suddenly he opened every gun he could bring to

---

13 Hackmann, Willem; ‘Seek and Strike’, Sonar, anti-submarine warfare and the Royal Navy 1914-54 , London 1984, refers who to six months, but the number 33 U-boats was only reached in late 1940), p.303.

14 Sauders, Hilary St. George; ‘Royal Air Force 1939-1945’, Vol. III, London 1954, p. 379

bear on us. (The pilot described) the anti-air-craft fire 'terrific', especially from the larger warships, which seemed to carry seven anti-air-craft guns on either beam". About seven RAF planes were lost in mission.

The 27th of September 1939: "Nazi Planes Raid the British Fleet" (NYT, the 28th of September 1939). "Yesterday afternoon, a squadron of British capital ships together with an aircraft carrier, a cruiser and destroyers were attacked by about twenty German aircrafts in the middle of the North Sea. No British ship was hit and no British casualties were recorded. One German flying boat was shut down and another was reported to be badly damaged" (NYT, ditto). "This attack was made by fourteen German land bombers", it is said (NYT, the 29th of September 1939). "Last Tuesday, about twenty German planes attacked a British Patrol in the North Sea". (NYT, the 8th of October 1939)

The 29th of September 1939: "Six British planes have attacked a German naval squadron near Helgoland today" (NYT, the 30th of September 1939). "Five out of 11 Hampdens (planes) are shot down by German fighters"

The 9th of October 1939: "British cruisers hunting submarines in the North Sea (southern coast of Norway) fought off German bombers, which attacked repeatedly". "The bombers attacked again and again. And anti-aircraft guns blazed from the decks of the warships" (NYT, the 10th of October 1939). "Also a German naval flotilla with more than a dozen ships; while the British employed 12 Wellington bombers, the Germans sent almost 150 planes to the battle scene but without any success".

The 11th of October 1939: "Since the war broke out", Sir Kingsley said, "the coastal command flew a distance of approximately 1 million miles on reconnaissance, anti-submarine and patrol missions, and provided escort for 100 convoys. Submarines were sighted by planes on seventy-two occasions and, on thirty–four times, the planes were able to attack", he said. (NYT, the 11th of October 1939)

The 17th of October 1939: "Nazis bomb naval base in Scotland". "About a dozen German planes yesterday rained bombs on British naval vessels in the Firth of Forth near Rosyth, Scotland" (NYT, the 17th of October 1939). "Three ships are slightly damaged; two bombers are shot down, crashed in flames at sea".

The 21st of October 1939: Fighter planes shot down four German bombers out of nine which were deputed to attack a British convoy off the Humber estuary.

The 5th of November 1939: "Our outlook shouted, 'Planes right ahead, Sir; three planes; they are diving, Sir'. Our foremost guns opened fire with a roar that drowned everything. The muzzles were elevated almost level with the bridge and yellow flames sprang out, obliterating the shapes of the German machines swooping over the convoy. The sea leapt up in columns where their bombs were dropped." (NYT, the 5th of November 1939)

The 7th of November 1939: First sorties of German torpedo-carrying aircrafts were targeted against a British destroyer, but without any success as the torpedo missed the target.

The 14th of November 1939: "Nazi planes bomb Shetland Island". (NYT, the 14th of November 1939)

The 22nd of November 1939: "Three Royal air force planes send a Dornier (bomber) into the sea before it reaches the coast". (NYT, the 22nd of November 1939)

The 14th of December 1939: Twelve RAF bombers attacked German warships in Helgoland Bight, but ended up by losing six "British Bombers and Messerschmitts fight; both sides lose planes in Helgoland battle" (NYT, the 15th of December 1939). "Nazis claim ten planes have been shut down" (NYT, the 16th of December 1939).

The 17th of December 1939: German bomber planes attacked trawlers near the English east coast and sank 10 boats of approx. 3,000 tons.

The 18th of December 1939: "Driven away from the English coast, two German bombers dived out of the clouds above the 487-ton British motor ship *Serenity* today, riddled its decks with machine-gun fire and then dropped 18 bombs until one struck it and sent it to the bottom". (NYT, the 18th of December 1939)

The 19th of December 1939: 'Air Fleets fight off Helgoland'. '34 down say Nazi'. "The biggest air battle of the war occurred yesterday when British bombers encountered German pursuit ships over Helgoland Bight" (NYT, the 19th of December 1939). The loss was 12 planes out of 24 RAF Wellington bombers deployed.

The 21st of December 1939: "German aircrafts attacked thirty-five vessels, including two neutral ships during the last three days", the Admiralty announced tonight. "Of the ships attacked, one coasting steamer and six fishing trawlers sank." (NYT, the 21st of December 1939)

Sea mines

About 600,000 sea mines were laid by the Allies and the Axis countries in the European and Atlantic waters during WWII. Comparing mining activities during the four autumn months of 1939 to those 65 months that followed (1940-1945), one may tend to think that this short period of four months is hardly significant and therefore it can be ignored. This would be wrong for the subsequent reasons.

During the first four months of war, the 'monthly-average' of mines laid was 10 times higher than during the next five years and could have been somewhere between 50,000 and 100,000 or even more, due to the following facts:s

a. The countries could immediately use their accumulated stockpile;
b. Sea mines were regarded as 'cheap' weapons and it was not difficult to produce them in large numbers;
c. Neutral countries also could and did use mines as a 'defensive measure'.

East Coast Barrier

The British successfully mined their East coast from Dover to Orkneys during the first few months of the war. In September 1939 alone, the British minelayers *Adventure* and *Plover* laid 3,000 mines across the Strait of Dover. In the second half of September, the barrage was completed with 3,636 U-boat mines, which soon paid results, Germany losing three U-boats in October. The British set up the East Coast Barrier, a mine barrage between twenty and fifty miles wide, from Scotland to the Thames, leaving a narrow space for navigation between the barrage and the coast. In late 1939, the British Admiralty intended to lay a 500-mile minefield of unprecedented size, a barrage in a strip of thirty to forty miles. That was a "gigantic effort to check the German submarine campaign" (NYT, the 31st of December 1939). In early January 1940, it was reported: "British naval vessels are sowing some of the last mines needed to complete Great Britain's 30,000,000-pounds protective shield for east-coast shipping, which is the most extensive mine field ever laid." (NYT, the 11th of January 1940) If one assumes that the weight of those mines varied between 300 and 1,200 pounds, the number of mines laid in autumn along the east coast alone would be between 25,000 and 100,000 mines.

A mining mission on the 17/18th of October 1939: The German destroyers *'Galster', 'Eckholdt', 'Lüdemann', 'Roeder', 'Künne'* and *'Heidkamp'* took on their cargo of 60 mines each (except *'Heidkamp'*) at Wilhelmshaven and departed at noon, racing northwards first, at 30 knots, as a misleading measure, then, at dusk, turning westwards for the target area: the mouth of the Humber. In the early hours of the 18th of October, the five destroyers began their task, between the Humber Estuary and the Withernsea Light. On completion, the destroyers headed home at full speed. This minefield of 300 mines eventually sank seven ships.

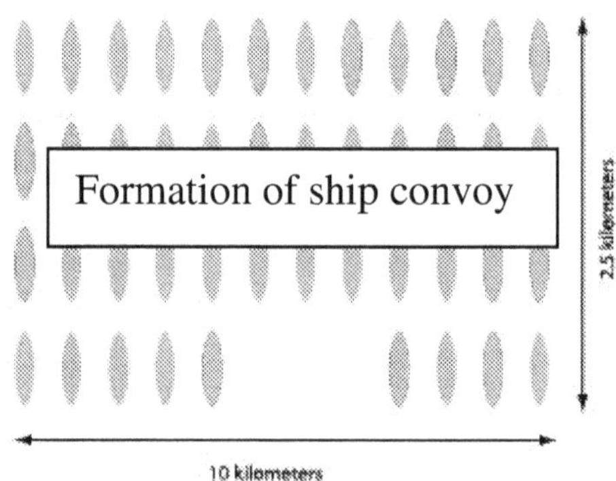

Helgoland Bight (Deutsche Bucht)

German Navy engaged very actively in planting contact mines starting from the Nethelands' coastal waters (near Terschelling island) and going northwards across the Helgoland Bight up to the entrance of the Skagerrak, at a distance between 50 and 100 km off the coast of Schleswig-Holstein and Denmark, called the "Westwall". The most north-westerly point announced by the Germans as 'Dangerous zone' was the position 56°30' North and 4°25' East. That was about half the distance between Skagerrak and Scotland. The first minefield locations were near Terschelling, Esbjerg, Helgoland and two places near Jutland (NYT, the 5th of September 1939). Specific warnings had been given to more than 100 Danish fishing cutters from Esbjerg (NYT, ditto). It was reported that one unidentified cutter had been blown up seventy miles west of Wyl light ship (NYT, ditto). For about three weeks, a flotilla of at least 25 naval vessels was engaged in laying mines along the "Westwall".

It was difficult to verify how many mines the flotilla had planted during the first few weeks as it was not possible to get reliable figures about the stockpile the Germans had on the 1st of September. The number of mines laid during this period could be somewhere between 20,000 and 200,000. But as the distance from Terschelling to 56° 30' North is of about 350 kilometres (170 sea miles) and as the 25 naval vessels deployed for this task were able to cover thousands of mines per day, it seems reasonable to assume that, by the end of September, at least the first 10,000 mines were laid and, by the end of October, 20,000 were in place. The "Westwall" was more or less complete in the following months. According to a NYT report, one minelayer could lay 300 mines per hour (NYT, the 18th of February 1940). During the early days of WWII, one-third of the total of 200,000 sea mines of the German Navy would have been laid in the North Sea.

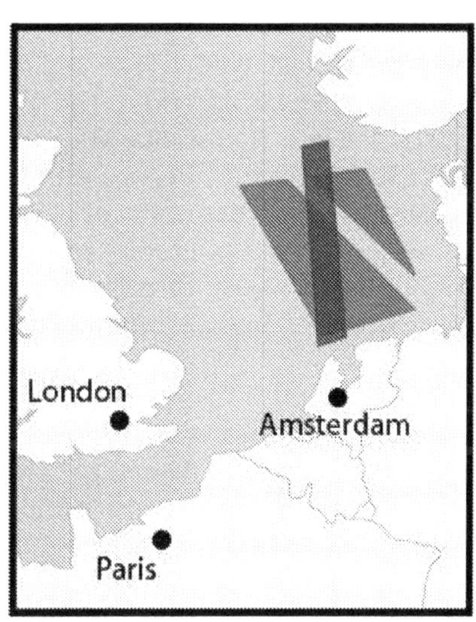

Home Fleet's surface vessels undertook a number of missions as well, with the purpose of laying mines in the German home waters. Such an illustrating example would be the mission undertaken by the British destroyers *Esk* and *Express*, which laid mines where "Westwall" 'exit channels' were assumed to be.

Mining the Baltic Sea, 1939

War had just started when the 1,555-ton, Greek ship Kosti hit a German mine, two miles south of Falsterbo/Sweden, on the 4th of September, and sank after a terrible explosion in the minefield of the Great Belt and west of the Danish island of Zealand. (NYT, the 5th of September 1939) Danish Government made public its plans of planting mines in its own waters. (NYT, ditto) On the 4th of September, the Germans laid about 1,000 mines at the entrance in the Danish waters and continued so during autumn as well. Situation worsened day-by-day for six long years. It is difficult to verify the number of mines the Germans planted in the Southern Baltic Sea. In the Western Baltic Sea, it would have been many thousands before the winter of 1939/40 arrived and, as a result, the German Baltic waters suffered the impact of a compact ice cover since January 1940.

Other riparian countries planted mines as well. With the help of minesweepers *Czajka, Jasolka* and *Rybitwa*, even the Poles managed to drop 60 mines south of Hela (Gdanska Bight), on the 12th of September. The Soviet Navy started laying mines in the Gulf of Finland in late September. A number of mining activities of Germans, Finns and Russians took place in November and December 1939. The total figure of mines laid in various parts of the Baltic Sea in late 1939 could reach several ten thousands.

Finally, more recent information: In 2001, a multinational squadron of minesweepers of the North Atlantic Treaty Organisation and Baltic States was searching for old mines in Latvian waters. According to Baltic experts' estimation[15], over 80,000 mines laid during first and second world wars remained in the territorial waters of Baltic countries.

Chronicle of a few mining events

The number of serious sea mining events during the initial war months presumably goes up to several thousands, out of which only a few will be listed below:

3-9 September 1939: Four U-boats dropped magnetic mines in the estuaries of Orfordness, Flamborough, Hartlepool and the

15 /english.pravda.ru/cis/2001/11/19/21327.html

Downs, sinking four vessels with a total tonnage of 16,000 and damaging one ship of 11,000-tons.

4-20 September 1939: Several minefields laid in Western Baltic Sea to seal off the passage through Danish waters caused the following incident: The US *Mormachawk* sailed with pilot assistance through a German minefield in early September 1939 when five loose mines blew up 500 to 800 yards away. (NYT, the 20th of September 1939)

The 21st of September 1939: Soviet Navy plants mines in the Gulf of Finland to protect Kronstadt and Leningrad. (NYT, the 22nd of Sept.39)

The 17th of October 1939: Mine operation near Humber - German torpedo boats and destroyers sank seven vessels.

The 21st of October 1939: On 21st October and 25th November German mines sank their own German Coast Guard ships, south of the Great Belt. (NYT, the 26th of November 1939)

The 6th of November 1939, off Copenhagen shore: "Gales have loosened several hundred mines in the German mine fiels. Drifting mines exploded breaking windows and frightening citizens with their terrific detonations." (NYT, the 6th of November 1939)

The 23rd of November 1939: Mines sank 22 ships in six days. (NYT, the 23rd of November 1939)

The 1st of December 1939: England claimed to have mined an area of 300 square miles between the Schelde and Thames estuary. The freighter *Sheaf Crest* of 2,730 tons struck a mine and sank. (NYT, the 1st of December 1939)

The 3rd of December 1939: "A British tanker was sunk by mines near the southeast coast of England. *San Calisto* (8,010-tons) struck two mines which went off with such a force that the blast shook buildings on shore". (NYT, the 3rd of December 1939)

The 4th of December 1939: "A third German mine patrol ship was blown up this afternoon, north of the mine fields off Denmark, it sank in less than two minutes; its entire bottom was blown up". (NYT, the 5th of December 1939)

The 5th of December 1939: German cruiser *Nürnberg* lays mines in the area Kristiansand/Skagerrak.

The 6th of December 1939: Sweden mined her waters opposite to Aland Islands. (NYT, the 6th of December 1939)

The 17th of December 1939: Four British destroyers laid 240 mines in the delta of the river Ems.

Minesweeping

Minesweeping was another particularly effective means of churning and turning huge sea areas about day by day since war started. A standard mine was the moored contact mine, a buoyant material filled with explosives of up to 1,000 kg. To nullify their effect, special ships used distant means to cut the mooring chain or wire attached to the mines to keep them afloat. Sometimes they exploded before reaching the surface but if they surfaced they were blown up by rifle shots.

Germans used magnetic mines for the first time in November 1939. The NYT soon reported that: "Some wild stories have appeared here suggesting that the Germans have invented a so-called 'magnetic mine", (NYT, the 22nd of November 1939). Actually, one magnetic mine was discovered on the shore near Southend, UK, on the 22nd of November, and was examined by the Navy's mining school. Only two countermeasures were available against magnetic mines. One was to explode the mine by towing a cable, which passed an electric current through water. From the point of view of the climate, this was the worst possible result. The mine exploded at its location, at a depth of 20, 50, 100 metres or more, producing the highest possible "stirring" effect in the water column above. The other countermeasure was to deactivate the ship's 'magnetism' so that it could pass near the mine without activating it.

Minesweeping proved to be a tremendous round-the-clock operation, travelling millions and millions of miles in the sea for detecting and destroying the 'weapon in waiting'. The efforts made during WWII had been tremendous. German Defence machinery against Allied mining involved 46,000 personnel, 1,276 sweepers, 1,700 boats, and 400 planes, whereas the British Defence against Axis mining involved 53,000 men and

698 sweepers[16]. When, on the 19th of November 1939, five ships were destroyed by mines, the urgent need of a huge mine sweeping operation became obvious (NYT, the 20th of November 1939). The discovery of a 'sample mine', on the 22nd of November, confirmed significantly the effectiveness of these countermeasures. The British Admiralty put quickly a pre-war plan into action, whereby some 800 commercial trawlers, drifters and whalers were requisitioned, fitted out with wire sweeping gear and their crews trained accordingly.

"Stirred and shaken"

The destructions of war at sea are usually accounted in sunken merchant tonnage or enemy naval ships destroyed. The total loss of merchant ships from all causes was of about 380 with a tonnage of 1 million, whereby British, Allied and Neutral accounted for 320 vessels and about 900,000 tons. These are the figures relating to the sunken ships in UK waters:

- September 1939: 33 ships totalling 85,000 tons;
- October 1939: 24 ships totalling 63,000 tons;
- November 1939: 43 ships totalling 156,000 tons;
- December 1939: 66 ships totalling 152,000 tons.

In addition, the Royal Navy lost: one battle ship; three destroyers; one aircraft carrier; one armed merchant cruiser; ca. 10 trawlers; two U-boats; and a number of smaller units. The German Navy lost 9 U-boats and, from its bigger units, the pocket battleship *Graf Spee* on the La Plata, in December 1939.

However, the sinking of about 500 big objects with several thousands of dead sailors and service men may tell a lot about man and material loss, but little about the violent shaking of climatically sensitive seas. Since war commenced, many hundreds of vessels ploughed the seas day and night in numerous naval activities. A battleship at cruising speed of 30 knots causes a water column of about 12 meters over an area of 72 square km, within a period of 24 hours. Only 300 such ship movements over one month are needed for turning the complete North Sea surface layer about. And naval war in 1939 was lasted four months until the arctic winter 1939/40 arrived.

16 Hackmann, Willem; 'Seek and Strike', Sonar, anti-submarine warfare and the Royal Navy 1914-54, London 1984, p.344.

Until that moment, up to several thousands of explosions caused by bombs, sea mines, depth charges and shells had taken place above and under the sea surface of the Northern European seas. The climatically relevant seawater structure was, in the sense of statistical average, severely affected by anthropogenic actions. A cold winter was inevitable as explained in the next section.

Seas reacted to naval churning

The theme

Although physical laws are the same for hot soup and for the "stirred" seas, things tend to become more complex when naval activities occur in the North and Baltic Seas. This is because location, season and applied forces are diverse in many respects in the latter case. This would not matter so much if science had established a comprehensive and sufficient coverage of temperature measures throughout a seawater body a long time ago. Such a system was not available before WWII and is still not available today. Only a few coastal stations recorded sea surface temperatures since long time ago. This is by far too little as far as climate research is concerned. Only a sufficiently complete picture of the interior of the seas and oceans would help detect the course of the climate. Such a hope was out of the sight of the meteorologists in the early 20th century.

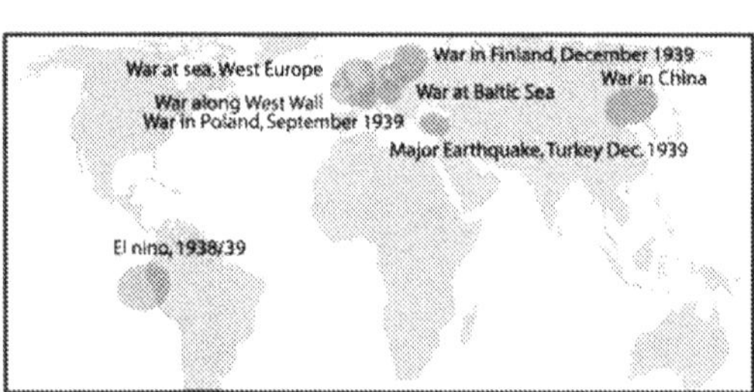

But when the seas determine the pace of the weather and climate one can turn 'the table around' by using meteorological data and citing deviations from usual atmospheric wintertime conditions caused by the turning about of waters of North and Baltic Sea. However, behind each and every reasoning, there stands the overriding fact that, in the autumn of 1939, some mechanism must have invited an arctic winter to prevail in Northern Europe for four months after WWII had started. It is a fact that an uncommon arctic winter could not have occurred without a cause.

Before proceeding further to the conditions concerning the winter 1939/40, a reference may be made to the three cold and snow-rich war winters of 1939/40, 1940/41 and 1941/42, by outlining the interesting observation made by a scientist from Kew Observatory at Richmond/UK in 1943[17]: "The present century has been marked by such a widespread tendency towards mild winters that the "old–fashioned winters", of which one has heard so much, seemed to have disappeared for ever. The sudden arrival at the end of 1939 of what was considered to be the beginning of a series of cold winters was therefore all the more surprising.

Since the winters of 1878-79, 1879-80 and 1880-81, there have never been such severe winters, three in succession, as those of 1939/40, to 1941/42." He further points to another significant aspect with regard to snow conditions in SE England: "Since comparable records began in 1871, the only other three successive winters as snowy as the recent ones (1939-1942)[18] were those during the last war, namely 1915/16, 1916/17 and 1917/18, when snow fell on 23%, 48% and 23% of the days, respectively". Should this statement not raise excitement and confirm outright that 'great' wars leave behind indelible fingerprints? The 'surprise' of three successive cold winters will be come up again at a later stage. At this point it is to note the starting line: the polar winter of 1939/40 came unexpectedly, as confirmed by contemporary WWII witnesses.

Based on the features of Europe's northern seas, the following three topics will be discussed:

- Lost west wind drift due to making the seas steaming.
- Cooling the seas too early.
- Sea ice conditions during winter 1939/40.

Europe's northern waters

North Sea

17 Drummond, A.J.; ‚Cold winters at Kew Observatory, 1783-1942'; Quarterly Journal of Royal Met. Soc., No. 69, 1943, pp 17-32, and: Drummond, A.J.; Discussion of the paper: ‚Cold winters at Kew Observatory, 1783-1942'; Quarterly Journal of Royal Met. Soc., 1943, p. 147ff.

18 Instead usual 10% days of snowfall at Kew Observatory during January and February , there were 1940 (28%), 1941 (32%), and 1942 (44%)

North Sea is one of the principal factors in Europe's climatology. On the one hand, North Sea is a part of the North Atlantic Ocean and is like a big bight. On the other hand, it curves into the landmasses of the European continent. Climatic conditions are therefore transitory. Its climate is neither maritime nor continental. Nevertheless, due to its geographical location, prevailing westerly winds travelling through the hemisphere within a zone of 2,000 kilometres breadth usually ensure a temperate humid climate.

	North Sea diagonals (England – Continent)		
Water depth	Southern section West/East	Middle section West/East	Northern section West/East
	Temperature °C		
Surface	10/12.5 °C	8/15 °C	6/10 °C
7.5 m	11/13 °C	8/15 °C	5.5/10 °C
20 m	11/13 °C	7/13 °C	5.5/8.5 °C
30 m	11 °C	6.5/12 °C	5/7.5 °C
40 m	-	6/11 °C	4.5/6 °C
60 m	-	4,4 °C	4.5/3.5 °C
80 m	-	3,5	4.5/1.5
100 m	-	-	4/1.5

Britain, the most western Atlantic outpost, has its weather influenced by Atlantic depression and presumably would outline a general picture as it follows: between predominant occurrences of depressions, there are often small mobile anticyclones that bring a period of fair weather. Sometimes large, stationary anticyclones effectively act as a 'block' to the regular passage of depressions. These larger anticyclones can often last for over a month and completely change the character of wet, windy and cloudy weather of Britain. If one of these anticyclones established over Scandinavia and easterly winds on their southern side, they can drive very cold air from the continent of Europe. In any of these cases, North Sea plays a vital role in deciding Europe's climate.

The principal factors affecting the climate of any ocean and sea body interior are temperature and salinity. The latter varies in the North Sea more than in any other sea but is less related to the season. Seawater temperatures vary according to depth and to seasons.

It is of great importance to demonstrate developments in autumn 1939 according to statistics and observed air temperature data, *as* seawater and atmospheric temperatures are closely interconnected.

Water depth in the North Sea can be roughly divided into two sections. The southern section comprises a plateau south of a line running from mid-England (Hull) to North Denmark that is mostly less than 40m deep. The northern section is a triangle between North Denmark -Hull - Shetland Islands with a water depth generally ranging between 60 and 120m (the deepest place is 263 m), and the submarine valley along the Norwegian coast with depths ranging between 240 and 350 metres, and 500-700m depths in Skagerrak. The inflow of warm water from the Atlantic Gulf current enters the sea from the north and influences the current system from the surface to the bottom in the northern part only. The 40m deep southern plateau is hardly affected by the northern water, but receives some Atlantic water via the Strait of Dover and some freshwater from the rivers. Thus the North Sea is rich in different water masses, which vary seasonally and fluctuate annually. As all coastlines are subject to marked tidal forces, considerable water masses actually vary on a daily basis.

The annual approximate temperature variation data in three West-East diagonals across the North Sea[19] is as it follows:

Southern section

Due to the shallowness and tidal forces of the water body, its temperature structure can be described as a homogeneous one (from surface to the bottom), with small variations as the average temperatures indicate: December (8.5°C), January (6.5-7°C), February (5.5°C), March (5°C), April (6.5°C), suggesting that water very close to the coasts has lower temperatures during the winter season.
Between May and August, temperatures increase from 8.5°C to 14.5°/17°C and decrease as it follows:

---

19 Tomezaqk,G. und Goedecke,E.; Die thermische Schichtung der Nordsee, Publisher: Deutsches Hydrographisches Insitut, Hamburg 1964

Depth	August	September	October	November
Surface, West-East	14.5-17 °C	14-16 °C	12-13.5 °C	09°-10° (*)
20 m, West-East	14-16 °C	15-16.5 °C	13.5-14 °C	9.5-11 °C

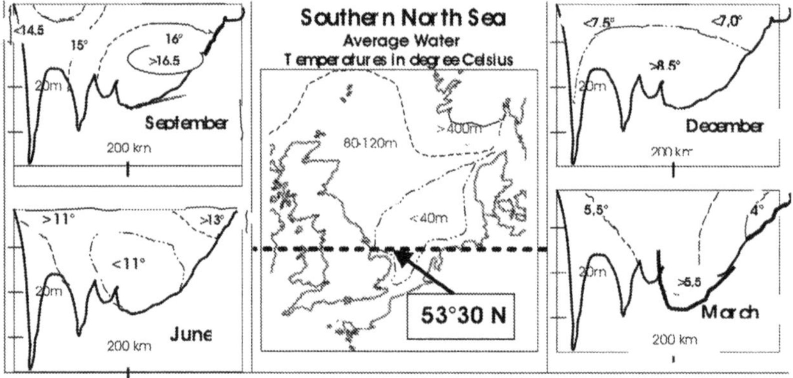

(*) in mid North Sea, the figure is with 11.5° higher than in West & East.

Fairly homogeneous figures of the water body temperature, with 15°/16°C at peak time and the lowest temperature in March (5°C), indicate that the water body experiences an average change of about 1.5°C per month.

Northern section

In March, the lowest annual average temperatures at the surface of the water ranged between 7°C in the northwest (Atlantic water) and 4.5°C in the southeast (Dutch coast). At the end of August, the highest average temperatures at the surface of the water ranged correspondingly (NW and SE) between 13°C and 17.5°C in the Helgoland Bight.

From May to August, a horizontal thermocline builds up but declines during the autumn months. It is worth noting that while temperature level increases at lower water levels (e.g. 20m, 40m) in autumn, it decreases at the bottom (60m). It is therefore possible for the whole water body to be warmer in September than in August. While calculation of 'monthly averages' is an approximate figure, it nevertheless gives an indication that the monthly decrease in temperature (or energy release) takes place in small quantities only from 11°C in August to 4.5°C in March, i.e. on an average it could be as little as just one degree per month.

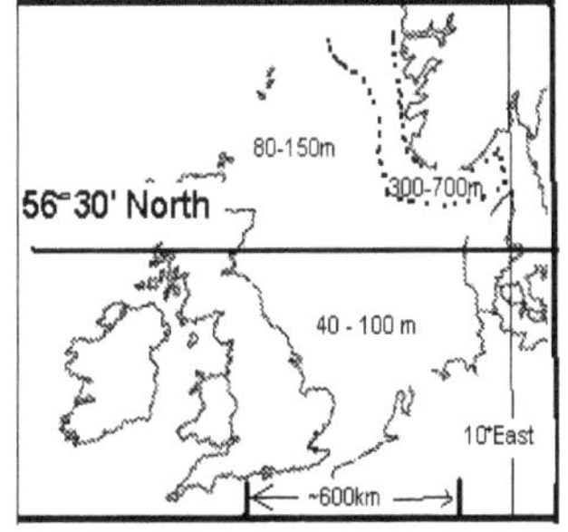

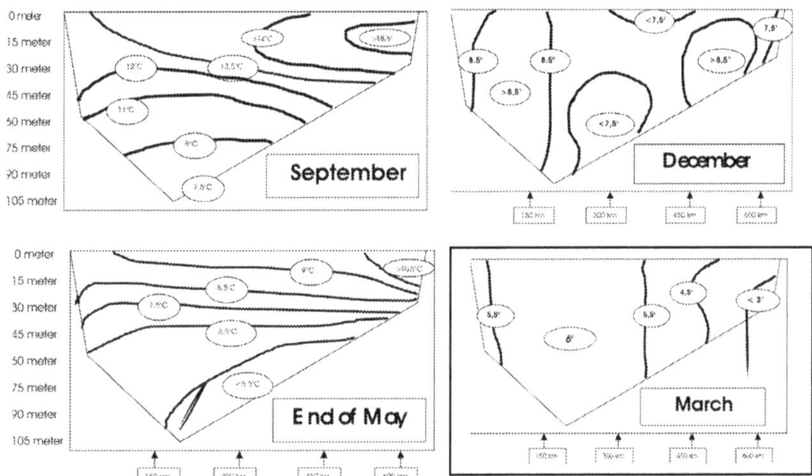

Baltic Sea

In terms of size, the Baltic Sea is a mere 'drop' of water in the world's oceans, but thanks to its strategic location and specific features it represents a 'significant' force and influences the weather in the countries surrounding it. It is an excellent location for the climatology study.

The total area of the Baltic Sea is of 400,000 square kilometres, with an average depth of 55m, including the Gulf of Bothnia (55-294m) and the Gulf of Finland (30m). Except for the eastern part (Gdynia Bight with a maximum of 114m),

Southern Baltic is less than 50m deep. Climatically speaking, an important feature of this sea is a 2,500m high mountain ridge from the north to the south of Norway, drawing a sharp line between maritime and continental belonging. Behind this barrier continental and polar air have much easier access than in areas where Atlantic air travels east at a low elevation level. This frequently guarantees warm summers to Baltic countries by significantly delaying the arrival of continental winter conditions. There is hardly any other sea in the northern hemisphere which can convincingly demonstrate the importance of heat storage and release process throughout all seasons as the Baltic Sea does it.
Actually, very cold conditions cannot prevail on sea and in nearby coastal areas over a longer period as long as the sea is open and not iced. Icing is a very critical point in regional climatology. Every sea area covered with ice loses ten times less energy to the atmosphere than an open sea area[6]. The importance of heat flux can be clearly demonstrated with temperature data records which show that winter average temperatures at the seaside are considerably higher than farther inland whereby temperature sometimes decreases in great leaps, i.e. by 1°C per 50 km or more, depending on the distance from the coast.

From mid-September to the end of February, when air is colder than seawater, water temperature decreases between 13°C and 15°C, which is significantly more than that of the North Sea (9.5-11.5°C). This actually means that the surface temperatures, with an average ranging between 0°C (north) and 3°C (south) in January, quickly come close to zero. Deeper waters (80 metres and below) have just 4-5°C, while water column above varies according to the seasons[20]. These temperature changes during various seasons are effective only from surface to about 80m depth. While surface water reaches its peak temperature by the end of August, lower levels may reach its peak later on (e.g. 40m with 10°C in late October). Therefore, all activities that took place at sea in the autumn of 1939 could have had two principal effects:

---

20 Finnish Institute of Marine Research; M.Leppäranta et.al; "Phases of the ice season in the Baltic Sea' No. 254, Suppl.2; Helsinki 1988

1. Churning the upper sea water layer causes a soup cup effect by increasing evaporation;
2. Turning seawater masses about will force considerable warm water masses to greater depths, which is to 'resurface' later thus contributing to milder air (as usual) or delaying icing processes by days or weeks.

Killing of westerly winds

The western European weather is famous for the predominant flow of wind blowing from the North Atlantic above the Euro-Asian landmasses (from west to east). The wind brings warm air from the depression but soaked up with humidity from the ocean. In contrast, anticyclones influence the weather conditions through high air pressure combined with dry and cold air masses.

This is immediately clear when comparing the climates of Amsterdam and Moscow. The latter has similar latitude as the Netherlands, but the Netherlands have cooler summers and milder winters. This is because Moscow is situated away from the warming effects of the Gulf Stream and other warm ocean currents that could keep winter temperatures mild. Moscow has less humidity and less cloudy air.

Also Northern Germany and Southern Scandinavia which have coastlines to North and Baltic Sea have maritime climate caused by the warm westerly winds of the Atlantic. Further inland or further east, the climate is more continental: marked by greater diurnal and seasonal variations in temperature, with warmer summers and colder winters.

These conditions would have also prevailed during the winter of 1939/40 if German Reichskanzler Adolph Hitler had not started the Second World War. From the 1st of September 1939, huge naval war machineries interfered in the common struggle between cyclones and anti-depressions, between Low and High air pressure areas. To them, North and Baltic Sea serve as a blueprint. Whether the seas are warm or cold determines the prevalence of continental or maritime air. The war machinery changed the weather blueprint so quickly and so decisively that the westerly winds were already sealed off from passing through Central Europe after a few weeks.

North and Baltic Sea reaction

North and Baltic Seas play their role according to the physical laws. By the end of August, they had reached the highest seasonal heat capacity. At this time, the upper water column (down to 30 meters depth) is about 10°C warmer than six months later, in March. If the seas are left in peace and not more than usual winter winds and storms make waves and other internal currents exchange the cold water for warm water at sea surface, then seasonal cooling from September to December and March occurs gradually, but close to long term statistical average. That is what climatology tells ever since: "climate is average weather over a long period of time"[21].

However, statistics become useless if a spoon is stirred forcefully in hot soup or if naval means and forces interfere and turn seas up side down. Warm water starts to steam. The more water is turned and twisted, the more steam goes up. When more steam goes up, physical laws require that rising water vapour is replaced by more heavy air. Statistically, Britain is surrounded by warm water which ensures the wet, windy, and cloudy weather character of The Isles during autumn and winter more than during any other season. But sometimes large, stationary anticyclones act effectively as a 'block' of the regular passage of Atlantic depressions. This is exactly what happened in autumn 1939. Seawater around Britain (particularly in the southern North Sea, Helgoland Bight, and Baltic Sea) was forced to evaporation at a rate above any other climate data average. Air above the seas became 'thin' and needed replacement with 'heavy' air. This replacement air needed to come from somewhere. Heavy air was abundantly available in the depths of Northern Russia and in the Arctic region. Consequently, cold air travelled from North to East, in the direction of Western Europe. The NE winds are not suspected for blocking the depressions from crossing Britain and Central Europe, but should be regarded as a strong evidence that naval warfare acted in North and Baltic Sea like a rapidly turned spoon in a cup filled with hot soup. The next three subsections aim at confirming this picture, discussing 'losing the west wind', 'raining cats and dogs along western war

21 Cf. Houghton, J.T. et.al. (ed), Climate Change, The IPCC Scientific Assessment, Cambridge, 1990, p. xxxv.

front' and highlighting exceptional sea icing conditions in North and Baltic Sea.

'Seewarte' awaits Atlantic depression

While considering the faith of the west-wind during the months between September and December 1939, one might receive an answer from Seewarte. "Deutsche Seewarte", the distinguished German meteorological office in Hamburg, was under the supervision of the Minister of Air Travel and Commander-in-Chief of the Air Force Hermann Goering (between 1935-1945, as already mentioned in the Preface). Although all weather information was classified as top secret by all warring nations, the preparation of daily weather charts and weather analysis was done with great efforts and care. Precise and best possible forecasts were of the highest importance for naval, aerial and military planning. The Seewarte did the job like other Met-Offices: presentation of data, preparation of weather charts and analyses. The daily analysts made numerous comments about an unusual weakness of the west wind and passing of depressions. They wondered, predicted and disputed that the west wind was lost or had disappeared and none of the wartime meteorologists in charge ever realised why. In the following section, some extracts from "Seewarte" weather analysis are reproduced which concern the deviation of the west wind or the movement of low air pressure areas.

Between the 16-28th of September 1939: daily weather charts show a high-pressure area between Iceland and Scotland. The most significant comments of the Seewarte analysts are:

The 19th of September 1939: cyclonic activities over the Arctic Ocean (Nordmeergebiet) are intensive. The west-drift in the North will consequently move more and more to the South.

The 23rd of September 1939: with the advance of air into Middle Europe a more forceful cyclone can develop along this channel (Rinne) which could extend its influence in the Middle Europe later.

> Remark: The two previous extracts show high expectation that cyclonic activities in Middle Europe will resume soon. However, this did not occur as indicated in the following extract, one week later.

The 29th of September 1939: general weather situation towards the end of the month clearly reveals changes indicating the end of the Indian summer spell, which leads to a period of increased cyclone frequency in Europe.

> Remark: This also did not happen, as confirmed by the next extract.

The 13th of October 1939: the first effective gust of maritime air has reached Northern Germany. A continuous west-wind-drift (WWD), however, cannot be expected yet.

The 19th of October 1939: a broad, high-pressure bridge has been formed between the Atlantic and the Scandinavian heights. Again this results in a weather situation similar to those which have been witnessed frequently before, during corresponding month, viz. a high-pressure zone moving from the Atlantic via Southern Scandinavia to Russia, with low-pressure disturbances to the North and South of it.

The 23rd of October 1939: usual weather is changing now and the high pressure bridge which links the Azores high with the West Russian high is broken up. A transition to a west wind situation is on the verge of the German seas.

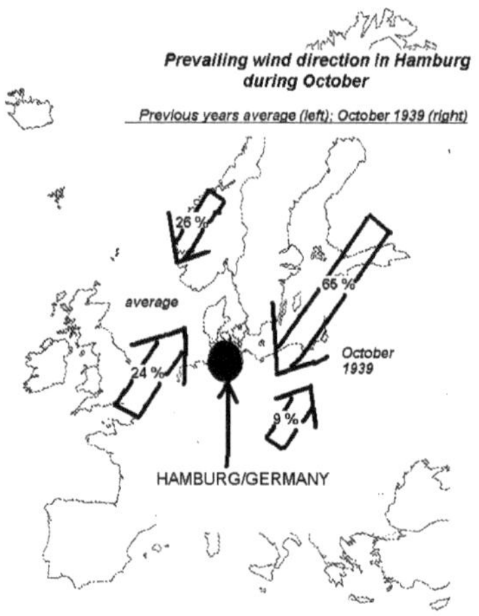

The 28th of October 1939: since a high pressure bridge from Middle Scandinavia to Scotland remains there, a further stream of cold air from the Arctic Ocean (Nordmeerraum) is cut off.

The 2nd of November 1939: an unusual and explicit analysis is given on change in the direction of wind: "Germany lies in the South (Southern part) of the high-pressure area and mostly experiences winds coming from East to North (NE- directions), which is clearly shown by the climatic data from October: Hamburg reported winds from the North-Eastern quadrant on almost two thirds of the dates observed (33% easterly winds out of 65%) while North-Eastern winds accounted only for a quarter (26%) of several previous years' averages. Otherwise, most frequent direction of the wind – South-West (24%) – accounted for 9% of all cases. Thus the observations at this station alone show what the weather charts of an extensive area would obviously indicate."

> Remark: This is a very strong and clear indication that huge air masses moved towards the North Sea (including southern part of Baltic Sea), presumably caused by unusually high evaporation in this sea area. While water of the North Sea was 'stirred and turned', 'steam' rose upwards into the sky causing air to flow in from Easterly direction, which subsequently prevented low-pressure systems to travel along the west-wind-drift channel, via the North Sea and Central Europe, into the eastern hemisphere.

Data for next four weeks are mixed. Four statements made during that month may illustrate the situation as seen by the analysts who thought they were worth mentioning at that time.

The 5th of November 1939: it appears that now – like during many earlier years – a west-wind-drift with lively cyclonic activities will begin to move over Europe at about the middle of the month.

The 14th of November 1939: it seems that a mainly sectional circulation is going to happen in the general weather situation: its pressure field will be characterized by a long, high-pressure zone – Azores–Southern Germany–Southern Russia – and west-wind-drift like turbulence activity in the North of these regions.

The 29th of November 1939: West Siberian high is slowly retreating towards the East thereby allowing the disturbance coming from the West to penetrate still deeper into the regions of European Russia.

Thc 30th of November 1939: a very distinct west-wind weather situation prevails over the North and Middle Europe.

Expectations of 'lively cyclonic activities' did not materialize. At that time, weather men could not imagine seawater changes caused by devastating war machinery.

Westerlies gone

During the first few days of December, we witnessed the attempts of rather weak cyclonic storms to reclaim their common travel path from the Atlantic to the Eastern hemisphere. By the 7th of December 1939, a high pressure field forms near Aachen (West Germany/Belgium), stretching to Norway, the 'last straw' that lead to severe winter conditions. At this time, any Atlantic air power had been lost for Western Europe, as the 'Neue Zürcher Zeitung' brilliantly acknowledged in its issue dated the 14th of January 1940 (extract):

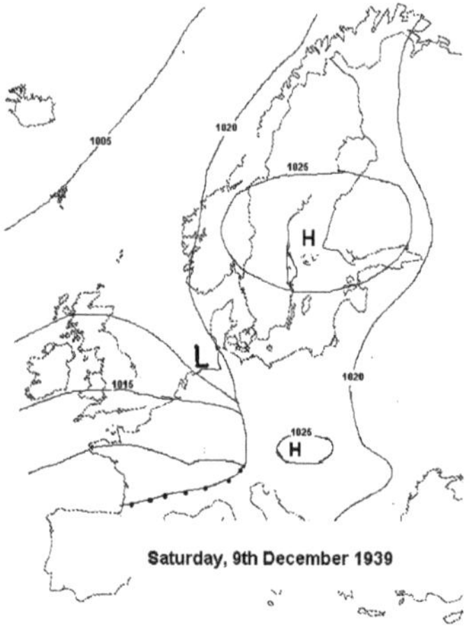

Saturday, 9th December 1939

"Severe cold which invaded the whole Europe in the course of this week was by no means an accidental phenomenon which settled in surprisingly. It rather constitutes the peak of a development which had its beginning in the first week of December. Towards its end, high pressure began to stabilize in North and Middle Europe, keeping away the low Atlantic cyclones from the continent and diverting them mainly through Greenland and Iceland waters, to the Sea.... As soon as occasional Atlantic depressions moved East, through the North and Baltic Sea, they were immediately replaced by the entry of cold air coming from the Greenland area."

So far, this is an impressive analysis. What the weather expert of NZZ had not realised is the fact that the 'blocking' of the westerlies had occurred since September 1939 and that the war at sea could have been responsible for it.

Four further excerpts from the daily Seewarte analysis demonstrate how the 'Seewarte' civil servant on duty judged the developments from December.

The 1st of December 1939: a quite distinct Atlantic frontal zone of the last few days is disintegrating.

The 8th of December 1939: it appears that the influx of warm air from the West is stronger than the retreating stream of cold air, so that the high pressure bridge might stay, although the English frontal zone is currently progressing very slowly towards the East.

The 19th of December 1939: A high-pressure ridge stretches....(etc). These conditions, however, are not likely to exist. The same pressure ridge is attacked from two sides and has gained more than 10mb in the past 24 hours....

The 21st of December 1939: a high pressure area, which installed yesterday over the Northern coast of Scotland, lies today over Central Germany, with a central pressure of 1,034mb. The heavy fall in pressure over the Artic Sea area (Nordmeerraum) has produced a drop there.

After this date, the West Wind Drift was definitely barred from entering Western Europe. The return of the Ice Age conditions became a consequential result.

Changed wind direction

The foregoing investigation emphasized the significance of the changes observed in wind direction, in Hamburg, in October 1939. Wind direction had dramatically changed from prevailing SW winds to dominating NE winds, due to the churning of the sea in Western Europe.

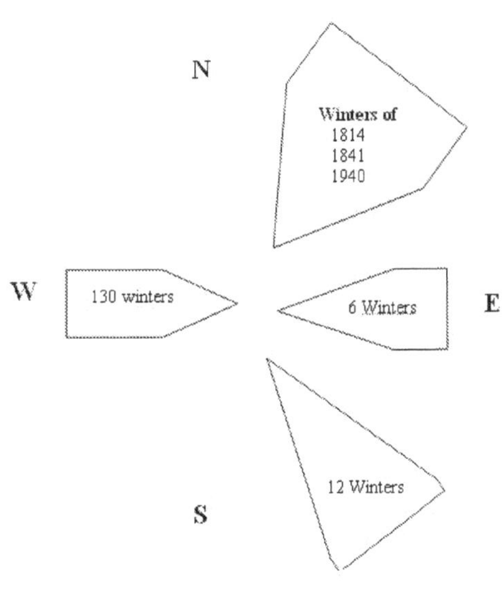

At this stage, it might be worth mentioning that a research conducted by Drummond[22] for Kew Observatory (London), in the early 1940s, mentioned that prevailing wind directions in

22 Drummond, 'Cold winters at Kew Observatory, 1783-1942', 1943, see reference above

South-West England during 155 winters, between 1788 and 1942, had only 21 easterly resultants, whereby the few winters 1814, 1841, and 1940 had resultants from NE to ENE. Another few winters since 1841 (1845, 1870, 1879, 1891, 1895, 1904, 1929) had prevailing SSE to ESE winds. With the exception of the winters of 1801 and 1804, all these 21 winters with predominant easterly winds had temperatures below the average (40.1°F = 4.5°C). While eleven of the above winters had mean temperatures between 34°F and 36°F, only six with westerly resultants had means lower than 37°F, these being: 1820, 1830, 1847, 1855 and 1886.

Observing the way Drummond highlights the exceptionality of the first war winter, one can only wonder why he seemed to have thought that such things happened simply out of the blue. While expressing some surprise, not even the prominent German meteorologist Richard Scherhag made anything out of his conclusion: "the famous winter of 1939/40 was the consequence of a general decrease in general circulation"[23]. And what reduced circulation in the first place? Neither Scherhag nor any of his numerous academic fellows around the world ever asked themselves this question.

Why did it rain cats and dogs?

The picture

First and most important picture: when there is less humidity in the air, it is easier for the cold air to take control. During the winter season, when the Northern Atmosphere is drier, general circulation decrease makes it easier for the polar air to travel to southern latitudes and to determine lower temperatures in many other regions. Some may even wonder about the appearance of such arctic conditions. January 1940 reflected this exact situation. North America, China and Europe froze under extreme low temperatures and there was plenty of snow everywhere. However, the record winter of 1939/40 in North Europe was 'homemade' due to naval warfare in its seas and to the forming of 'dry air' which may have brought its small share[24].

---

23 Scherhag, Richard (1951); 'Die grosse Zirkulationsstoerung im Jahr 1940', in: Annalen der Meteorologie, 4. Jahrgang, Heft 7-9, 1951, p.321-329.

24 In New York about every tenth January was much colder and every fifth winter (January & February).

The next important picture is about the situation in which precipitations actually 'dilute' the atmospheric humidity. If it rains abundantly in one place, precipitations statistically diminish in other places until humidity restores average equilibrium again. This process may take more than a few weeks. If war can cause abundant precipitations during the winter season, nature needs much more time to 'fill' the gap during the summer season. So far this information represents only physical laws and not facts.

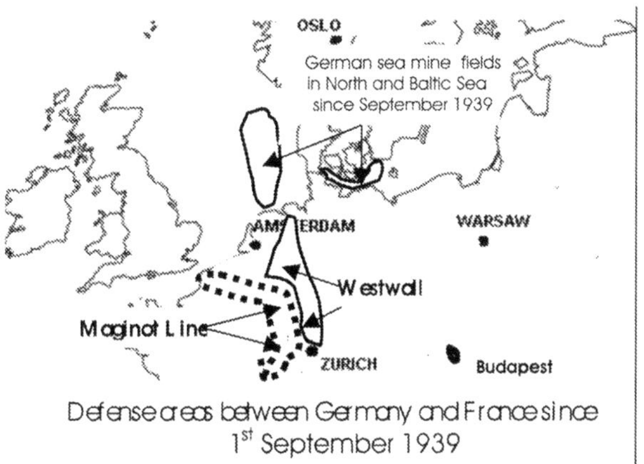

Defense areas between Germany and France since 1st September 1939

World War Two had hardly started when it began to rain excessively in Western Europe, from Berlin and Basel to Paris, Amsterdam and London, for three months, i.e., 200% above average in September, 300% in October, and more than 200% in November. In the Western, Middle and Southern Germany, the quantity of rain recorded at most observation stations was more than double, in some cases even 3.5 times more than usual: Augsburg 366%; Noerdlingen 362%, Kaiserslautern 336 %, Wuerzburg 316 %. Southeast England recorded rainfall of more than three times above average in October 1939. Greenwich saw a higher rainfall only in 1888 and, before that, in 1840. Greenwich total for October (6.16 in.) and November (4.13 in.) together –10.29 inches – was the highest ever since recording had begun at Greenwich. Similar conditions had been observed at Camden Square (London), where hours of rainfall are recorded as it follows: October 77.3 hours, November 96.7 hours. These were 50 hours higher than the average. Some places at the southern end of Maginot/Westwall Line recorded 30 days of rain during October (e.g. Freiburg,); a number of other locations had up to 24 days of rain.

In November 1939, weather conditions were not much better than in October. In general, it was a bit too warm and too wet,

200% more than normal for that season, in Hannover, Aachen, Kassel, Frankfurt a.M., Magdeburg, Ulm, Wuerzburg. This weather conditions actually saved France from being attacked and invaded in 1939. On the 19th of October, the "Yellow" plan for the invasion of France was finalised. On 7th of November, the beginning of the invasion plan was postponed for the first time. A Blitzkrieg was not advisable in such muddy soil conditions. Soldiers and tanks would have been defeated by 'General Mud'. Hitler wanted to go ahead and would have sent the Wehrmacht across the boarders in late 1939, but, due to excessively wet autumn weather conditions, the invasion was postponed until June 1940.

The appearance of excessive rain in West Europe raises a paramount question: where did all water vapors come from?

Where did all the water come from?

Actually one can discuss the matter under two aspects: (1) where did excessive water vapor come from? (2) how was it brought down? The first aspect is more important for this investigation than the second one because it serves as evidence that naval forces increased evaporation rate, which means that the seas lost a considerable part of their seasonal heat budget too early and, this way, their capacity to keep polar air at bay decreased tremendously during pre-winter months.

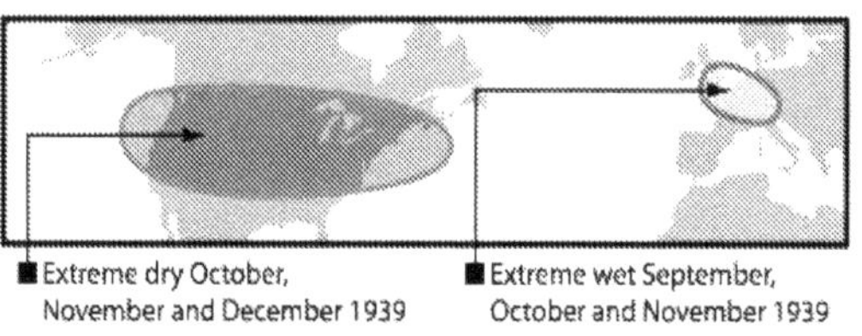

Since the 1st of September 1939, a huge defense area from Basel to Dunkerque (Maginot Line) and from Basel to Emden (Westwall) was activated and manned with one million soldiers on each side. From now on, small and big encounters, shelling, air fights, and aerial bombings occurred frequently. On the 7th of September 1939, The New York Times reported: "First substantial clash saw 700 French tanks and planes moving seven miles over the Saarland border, while 300 airplanes attacked German positions in the Aachen industrial region and munitions area, some 125 miles farther north".

Meanwhile, exploding sea mines and depth charges, shelling among enemy ships or ship versus coastal battery, and thousands of ship movements churned and turned around the waters of North and Baltic Sea. Evaporation rate increased. Soaring water vapour attracted cold air flowing in from north-easterly directions, pushing the excessive water vapour in south-westerly direction towards Westwall and Maginot Line, including South England. A record rain period started there due to three reasons:

1. Naval activities 'produced' a high and constant humidity all over the western war front, including SE of England, North of France, North of Switzerland, Bavaria, and, further north, the Netherlands, the West, Middle and South of Germany (including Berlin and Silesia).
2. Water vapour condenses using the molecules as condensation nucleus. Condensation occurs on a wide variety of aerosol particles e.g. particles of dust, salt, desert sand or smoke. Ambushes and burning down of villages and cities in Poland, in September, and frequent military encounters along the front lines produced abundant condensation nuclei. Clouds could form and 'burst' into rain.
3. Air coming in from north-easterly direction was cold. When high humid air laid over Western Europe and resisted being pushed farther south, arriving air would cool down the high humid air and it would inevitably rain.

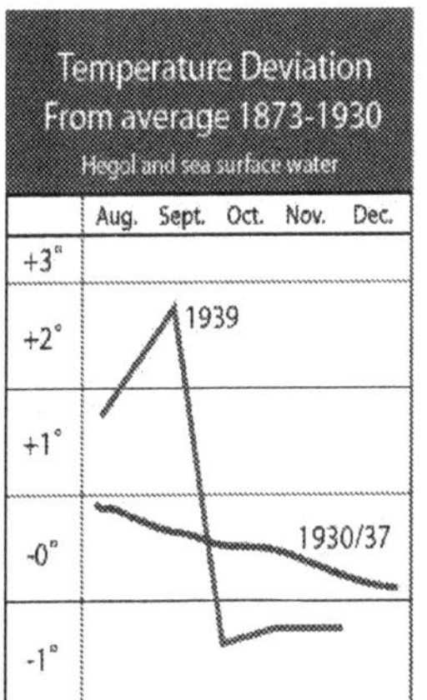

The scenario was perfect. Plenty of water vapour in the atmosphere, abundant condensation nuclei around and a constant arrival of cold air from NE made it rain cats and dogs in Western Europe.

Helgoland Bight water temperature

Reliable seawater temperature data are scarce. 100 years ago, temperatures were measured randomly and at sea surface. That makes data not very convincing. Nevertheless, on the North Sea island of Helgoland, about 50 km off Germany's coast, sea surface temperatures had been taken since 1872. In 1954, Erich Goedecke[25] from Hamburg investigated data series from 1872 until 1950 and observed the following changes:

- A modest temperature rise since 1915 (World War I had just started) lasting until about 1920[26], varying in a narrow band until 1929.
- A strong rise occurred since 1929 until 1939.
- Mean temperature decreased dramatically since 1939 until 1942, then reverted back to the increasing trend of 1929-1939.

One should not rely on this type of data because they can be conditioned by a number of reasons, e.g. too shallow and tidal waters, etc. However, the sudden turnaround in 1939 is interesting as it came simultaneously with the commencement of WWII. Since the 1st of September, huge naval forces and supply ships stayed or navigated close to Helgoland. For a couple of weeks, mine laying flotillas paved huge areas with sea mines. Helgoland roadsteads had become start- and return point for many naval missions. September suddenly showed a 1°C higher deviation than during 60 pervious years, with a record extreme decline during October 1939 and lower than usual average from thereon. If these data tell anything, they confirm that there is a link between naval activities and diminishing heat capacity of North and Baltic Sea, earlier and more lasting than one would usually expect. This means the cooling of seas and attracting arctic air flowing in. Early sea icing and prolonged ice duration are other evidential points which establish a connection between naval war and weather formation.

Sea Icing winter 1939/40

Icing along the Danish, German and Finnish coasts started early and sea ice conditions lasted longer than in dozens of previous years. For example, in December 1938, ice formation started early due to a sudden cold spell, but it lasted only for two to three weeks. The winter of 1938/39 is listed as a quite moderate one, in fact, the warmest for decades. Circumstantial

25 Goedecke, Erich; ‚Das Verhalten der Oberflächentemperatur in der Deutschen Bucht während der Jahre 1872 –1950 und der Zusammenhang mit dem nordwest-europäischen Meere', in: Berichte der Deutschen Wissenschaftlichen Kommission für Meeresforschung, Bd.XIII, November 1952, pp.1-31, & Juli 1954, pp.283-297.

26 Temperature increase from 1915 – 1920 is a strong indication for high naval activities during World War One.

evidences throwing light to the war winter of 1939/40 are manifold and include the following facts concerning sea ice:

- suddenness with which icing started;
- early start and longer persistence of ice;
- severity of icing;
- long duration of the icy period caused by two cold waves, one in January and another one in February 1940.

However, icing had different features in different places. This applies particularly to coastal areas at Germany's North Sea coast on one hand, and Southern Baltic Sea on the other, where the most intensive naval activities took place. This will be outlined in two of the following items. But first we will give a brief description of the Danish and Swedes water circumstances and a final picture will emerge from Northern Baltic Sea where raging Winter War between Russia and Finland left its marks on sea icing.

Denmark - Sweden

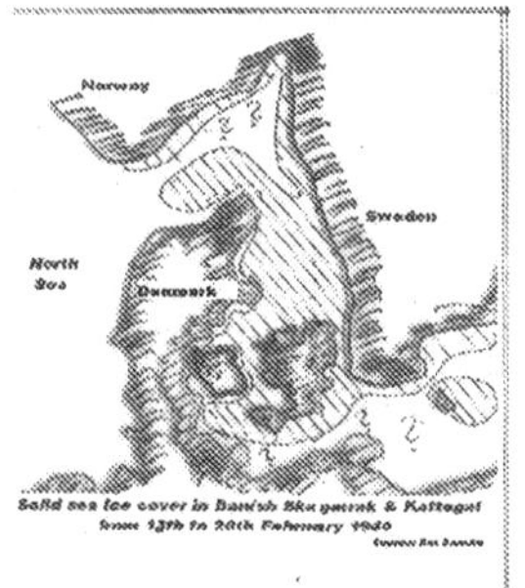

Solid sea ice cover in Danish Skagerrak & Kattegat

First ice was reported around mid December, which increased soon in the inner and closed waters and later on outside this area. The number of ice days had generally been large, a maximum of 115 days. While 34 stations reported more than 100 days, 99 stations reported 75-100 days. Last ice was reported in the Sounds, on the 19th of April 1940. Due to an early start of the winter, there were the severest ice conditions on sea for many decades. The lowest temperatures recorded were in December –22.2°C, in January –24.3°C, in February –27.4°C, and in March –22.0°C. Ships were to be convoyed and accompanied by icebreakers through the Kattegat East-channel if the supplies were to reach Copenhagen. These proceedings were not accomplished without damages to ships convoyed, as well as to accompanying icebreakers.[27] The coldest month in Copenhagen, viz. February, usually has a mean temperature of 0°C.

27 Det Danske Meteorologicial Institute; 'Is- og Besejlingsforholdene i de danske Farvande in Vinteren 1939-40', Kobenhavn.

North Sea - Helgoland Bight

Icing and ice floats emerged on river Elbe on the 16th of December 1939. In Hamburg, about 100 kilometres of river upstream from Helgoland Bight, at a mere 80 km distance from the Baltic Sea, there had been constant temperatures of sub-zero degrees Celsius since the 8th of December. Icing intensified massively since the 26th of December and extreme ice conditions maintained for 90 days, until mid-March 1940.

First ice at Helgoland Bight occurred on the 17th of December, in Tönningen, at a distance of about 80 km from Helgoland, and was immediately followed by all other German North Sea stations south of Tönningen, until the 21st of December. Only at the most northern station of the island of Sylt[28], icing started about 2 weeks later, a clear indication that deeper waters in more northern parts of North Sea had more heat reserves than shallow southern sea areas, which also saw much more naval activities. In the latter case, ice stayed for 60 to 70 days (until the end of February), in the Elbe river delta for 70 to 102 days, at Tönningen for 100 days, and at north of Tönningen for 60 days, from early January until early March.

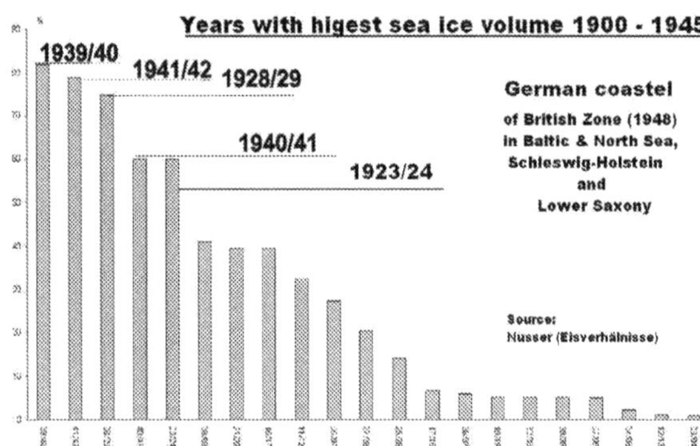

Southern Baltic Sea

Conditions for building up the ice differed in three ways from the average of previous years.

1) Even though ice started to form in the very North of Scandinavia very early, solid sea ice developed at usual time.
2) Ice formation started at first in the southern Baltic Sea as early as mid-December 1939, and

28 Only ca. 80 km north of Tönningen (near Husum), respectively 120 km north of Helgoland island

3) full icing in the Gulf of Finland started only with the cold wave of the 14 –24th of January 1940.

These events should not have come so much as a surprise if naval activities since the 1st of September 1939 are considered:

A) German Navy ambushed Polish coastal positions with intensive shelling in eastern Baltic during September 1939.
B) Germans laid a number of mine fields particularly at the south of Danish waters, with several thousands of sea mines. Denmark also laid sea mines.
C) German Navy patrolled Western Baltic Sea intensively day and night. Danish and Swedish Navies were more active in coastal waters than during peacetime.
D) German Navy trained all their crews, developed weapons and tested them in this water.
E) Since defeat and occupation of Poland in the end of September 1939, navigation and transportation increased many times.

In the South, at Greifswald Bodden (an open bight SE of the island of Rügen), icing started on the 18th of December 1939. Solid ice remained in place without interruption until the 4th of April 1940. Last ice disappeared on the 11th of April 1940.

Western Baltic, presumably including Bornholm, was temporarily ice-covered. We cannot provide a complete picture of southern coast from Lübeck to Königsberg (Kaliningrad) as it is claimed that German surveillance data have been lost. Here are some individual data instead:

The 19th of December 1939: ice reported in Kiel Channel (from Elbe to Kiel), Lübeck and Travemünde, remained there for three months.

The 20th of December 1939: first ice from Stralsund to Palmerort. Since the 1st of January 1940, solid ice continued until early April.

The 21st of December 1939: ice reported in Schlei (north of Kiel) was to stay until the 31st of March 1940.

The 28th of December 1939: ice which was reported in Flensburg (at Danish border) lasted till the 28th of March 1940.

Sweden

Swedish ice expert C.J. Östman[29] summarized his detailed report on Baltic Sea ice conditions in 1940 as it follows (excerpts):

> *"A survey was conducted on ice covering the Swedish coast during the particularly cold winter of 1939/40. As regards the thickness of ice, it was generally greater than usual. Thus the values vary between 75-95 centimetres in the harbours of the Gulf and Sea of Bothnia while the normal is of about 70-75 cm. In the harbours of the Baltic, with the exception of the most southerly ones, the thickness was of 30-60 cm compared to the normal of 25-35 cm. The value of 40-60 cm at the Swedish west coast is about two times the normal value."*

Northern Baltic Sea[30]

The waters around Finland had not seen as much ice as in the war winter of 1939/40 since 1883. And from the 30th of November the region was especially affected by the most devastating winter war ever carried out under the Arctic Circle, where the sun never shines for many weeks. On land, the Russian Red Army attacked with more than 300,000 men on a front of one thousand kilometres. At sea, the Russian Baltic Fleet attacked Finnish shore batteries on islands and coastal points with big shells. Submarines operated in the Gulf of Finland and the Gulf of Bothnia, and laid many thousands of sea mines. Finish Navy was small but still operational. Due to high naval activities, the picture of icing seems to be unclear, which is not the case. It actually confirms that naval activities influenced substantially sea-icing processes.

Just to remind, sea ice formation started first in the southern Baltic. In Hanko/Finland (at the western entrance in the Gulf of Finland), icing started on the 27th of December 1939; solid ice formed on the 4th of January 1940; end of ice came on the 7th of May 1940, at almost the same time as in Helsinki.

29 Östman, C.J.; 'Den svara isvintern 1939/40', Statens Met-Hydro. Anst., Meddelanden Ser. Uppsatzer, No.33, Stockholm 1940, pp. 1-25

30 For data details in section consult item 2_17 on: www.seaclimate.com

However, on the 15th of January 1940, the Gulf of Finland was still open as far as Pellinki. The Gulf of Bothnia was also open in most of its parts. Ice then formed rapidly although the Gulf of Bothnia is far in the North and has a depth of over 200 metres – in the Baltic Sea area the deepest water - holding considerable heat for a long period even during cold winters. An 'ice-bridge' between Turku and the island of Åland (maximum depth of 30 m) formed on the 6-7th of January 1940, about 2 ½ weeks earlier than usual.

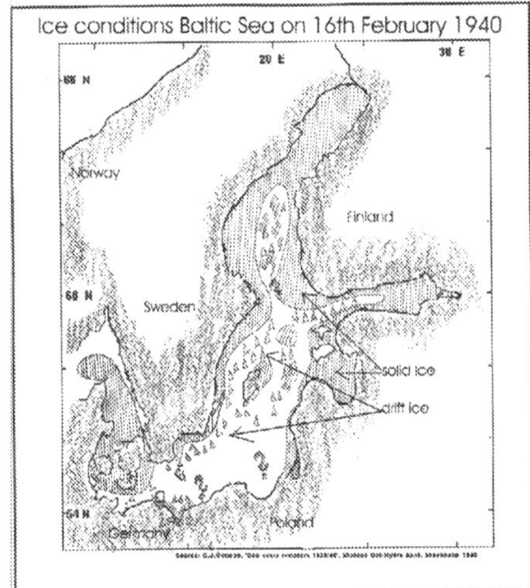

There is no other valid explanation for any deviation in ice formation from earlier averages than the war activities at sea. Most of the factors relevant to the Baltic Sea phenomena are the long open sea areas in the Gulf of Finland, a clear indication that, due to military activities, a high mixing of water took place and delayed ice formation. On the other hand, early formation of the 'Turku-Åland ice bridge' showed that the water of that area had already cooled down enough to freeze; in this case, more than two weeks earlier than in a place like Hanko, less than 100 km away.

Some further ice forming data, chronologically:

Mid-October 1939: some lakes and rivers froze in Northern and middle of Norrland/Sweden, as well as in the NW of Svealand (Middle Sweden), which usually happens only towards the end of the month.

The 8th of December 1939: navigation was closed at Kalix, a Northern port in the Gulf of Bothnia.

The 11th of December 1939: navigation was closed at Oulu. Last vessel sailed on the 7th of December.

The 19th of December 1939: navigation was closed in several ports in the Gulf of Bothnia, except for those which had icebreaker assistance until the end of December or middle of January.

The 9th of January 1940: heavy ice in Riga – navigation possible for powerful steamers only.

The 13th of January 1940: Gulf of Bothnia. A minesweeper and two patrol boats dropped depth bombs in an attempt to cripple a Russian submarine, which had trailed a small Finnish steamer, *Bore*, through the international waters of the Gulf of Bothnia. (NYT, the 14th of January 1940)

The 15th of January 1940: the Finnish ice expert Erkki Palosuo made the following meteorological assessment[31]: “By the 15th of January, the atmospheric pressure in Greenland had reached a remarkably high level, 1,065mb. As a low pressure of 995mb simultaneously prevailed in Central Russia, very cold air began to flow westward at high speed from the northern side of this low pressure and a very severe frosty period began in the region of the Baltic. The outbreak of cold air resulted in an independent ‘cold air plug’ (Kaltluftpfropfen) in Germany, which persisted in the area for nearly a week. On the 24th of January, the cold air plug in the German area began to move towards the Baltic region from where, reinforced, it pushed back to German territory on the 7th of February. On the 12th of February, its centre was in the region of Hamburg from where, moving slowly, it arrived in East Germany around the 20th of February.” This assessment is a convincing explanation for the severely ‘under cooled’ North and Baltic Sea, particularly Helgoland Bight and Southern Baltic Sea. On the 12th and 13th of February, temperatures in Hamburg were down to – 29°C. Hamburg thus became an arctic cold centre.

Chapter summary

While the previous chapter described the severity of war winter 1939/40 on one hand, and the naval activities during four pre-war months on the other, this chapter attempted to link anthropogenic causes with corresponding reactions in regional

---

31 Palosuo, Erkki; ‚A Treatise on severe ice conditions in the central Baltic’, Fennia 77 No.1, Helsinki 1953, p.92.

environment. As navies churned huge sea areas about, the evaporation of the seas increased and eventually changed the prevailing winds, declined the movement of the Atlantic depression on common routes and caused record deviations of the sea water temperatures. At least in one case, the build-up of sea ice conditions in the North and Baltic Seas demonstrates several aspects of the naval war and of its implication in environmental issues.

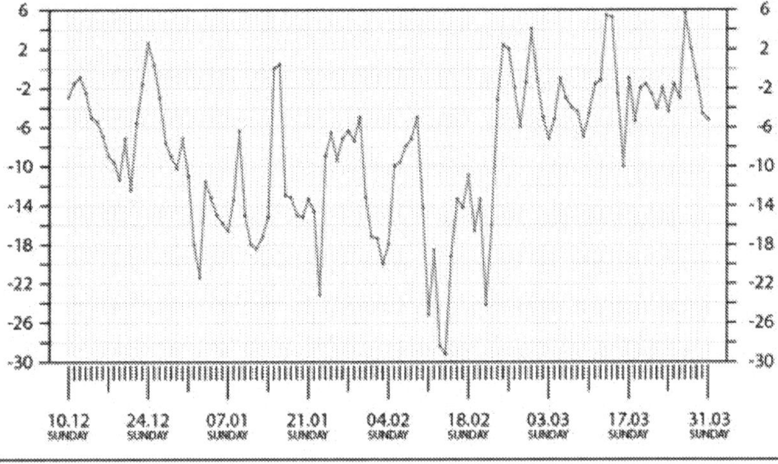

HAMBURG / GERMANY - Winter 1939 / 40

The events presented above are not mere incidents. Why were North and Central Europe affected and why Hamburg became a 'cold air plug'? This city is closely placed between two seas that were most heavily churned during the pre-winter months. Why Southern Europe, Switzerland and the Mediterranean region were not dragged into cold sphere? Why excessive rain occurred along a busy war front between France and Germany while the regions with heavy naval activities only four hundred kilometres further north, from Helgoland to Königsberg, saw less rain than usual? Why sea-icing started more powerfully in the coastal waters of Germany than in an area 1,000 km farther north in Finish waters? All questions could be convincingly explained as being the result of sudden naval activities at sea.

What did or didn't contribute?

Scope of this section

In our previous sections, naval Warfare was established as the cause of the arctic winter 1939/40 in Europe. Further significant events during the final months of 1939 will be presented in this section to support the argument mentioned above. This short period is of utmost importance as climate statistics were unaffected of non-natural influence when war started. In other words, during the initial war months, climate statistics and man-made causation faced each other directly.

It has to be strongly emphasized that the initial four war months should have a very prominent place in climate research. Although military destruction by land, air and sea was modest if compared to later war situations during WWII, military size, material and destructive capabilities were tremendous from the very beginning. From war day zero, the common appearance of an industrialized world changed dramatically. A sudden 'stress' on the environment is imminent, when many million soldiers start to march with thousands of tanks, air bombers and naval vessels. In physics, dynamical processes tend sustaining. Ocean and atmospheric affairs go similarly. Once war commences, the environment remains in its 'natural status' only for a very short period. Very soon, nature adapts and reaches new equilibriums. From that moment on, climate statistics need to be analysed with particular care and reserve.

In addition, the first four war months in 1939 should find foremost place of interest in climate research due to the fact that the influence of the sunrays on climate receded in North Europe since war commenced. During a normal winter season, only nearby seas and oceans are able to sustain common mild winter conditions. They function like a central heating. One should search for an explanation if they fail. The failure of the regional seas "winter heating" has been investigated in the previous three chapters in which we have showed that the arctic winter conditions and the churning of nearby seas reached extraordinary dimensions and that it is possible and necessary to link them together. This makes the main task easily achievable.

Nevertheless, over a short period of time, from the summer of 1939 to January 1940, Europe was not the only place on earth where something happened. Based on the view mentioned earlier that initial months of war are particularly interesting in climatic studies, other climate relevant aspects shall be listed briefly to provide the best possible overview. Only a fairly comprehensive picture may enable the interested reader to draw his own conclusion.

For this purpose a chronological listing of significant events is given, followed by an analysis of possible impact or contribution of these events to the arctic winter 1939/40, in Northern Europe.

Chronology of events

Pre-war months – June to August 1939

(1) El Niño

El Niño occurs once in every three to seven years. There was such an occurrence in 1938/39. The phenomenon begins with an eastward drive of equatorial warm water, which displaces cold surface water off continental American coast, e.g. Peru. Warm sea evaporates there more than usual, resulting in torrential rain along the coast. In Peru, July and August 1939 had been the wettest for past two decades. Indeed, an El Niño event occurred at about that time.

(2) Flood in China

A major flood occurred in China in July 1939. Vast areas in North China's Plains were submerged and the water in the streets in Tianjin (120 km south-east of Beijing) was two meters high so that boats were the only means of transport for more than two months. The flood inundated 3.3 million ha. of farmland and affected 8 million people. Death toll was estimated at 20,000, though it could have been much more.

(3) Russian-Japanese war in China

War was raging on China's soil between China and Japan since 1936, when Russian and Japanese forces of about 80,000 men on each side went into direct clash, on the 20th of August 1939, at Nomonham, a place on the boarder between Outer Mongolia and Manchuku. Battles raged for four weeks. Soviets had transported more than 400 tanks, 200 heavy guns, 400 armoured cars, 500-700 planes and several thousand tons of ammunition, shells, bombs, etc. via Dessert Gobi to the Far East. Presumably not less military equipment had been available with the Japanese Kwantung Army which eventually was the loser in this event, with 20,000 dead men, when the truce was signed, on the 16th of September. The Japan-China war continued with daily bombings, shelling, military encounters and battles.

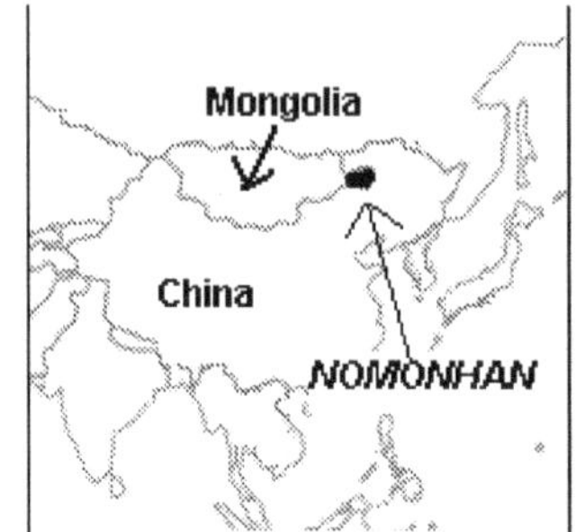

War months - September 1939 to January 1940

(4) Rain and tropical storm in California

In September 1939, California experienced record rains with precipitation up to 370% of normal and an eight days' heat wave since the 16th of September, which was followed by a severe tropical storm[32] (NYT, the 25th of September 1939). It was the heaviest September rain in Los Angeles' weather history and it broke the worst heat wave record in Weather Bureau records, measured in intensity and duration (eight days) (NYT, the 26th of September 1939). It was a month with four storms, including the only storm on record hitting California as a tropical storm until 2003[33], actually crossing the shore at Long Beach.

(5) September anti-cyclone over North Atlantic?

During the early war period, daily weather charts showed a high-pressure area between Iceland and Scotland, between the 16th and the 28th of September. It was a sea area 'crowded' by several dozens of big Royal Navy ships chasing German merchant and naval vessels and German U-boats, 14 of which operated west of Scotland since the end of August. French navy operated near Brest. Convoys sailed. Ships were shelled, torpedoed, scuttled and eventually a number of them were sunk.

32 A tropical cyclone in which the maximum surface wind speed ranges from 39 mph to 73 mph. Hurricane: when winds in a tropical cyclone equal or exceed 74 mph.

33 Jack Williams, 'Background: California's tropical Storms', www: USATODAY, Weather, 12/29/2003.

(6) Sinking of Rawalpindi and Atlantic cyclone

First sea engagement of naval surface vessels in the North Atlantic occurred east of Iceland, on the 23rd of November 1939. New and big German battleships *Gneisenau* and *Scharnhorst* sailed in a flotilla of six naval vessels, when they saw HM Armed Merchant Cruiser *Rawalpindi* of 16,697 tons at some distance. *Scharnhorst* fired salvos over a distance of 10,000 yards (NYT, the 28th of November 1939). One hit the *Rawalpindi's* forward magazine and soon a big explosion sank the ship. The Royal Navy ordered all available Home Fleet ships (ca. 20 big naval vessels) to sail to the scene of action to hunt the German flotilla. This naval encounter was immediately followed by a rapid decrease of air pressure with more than 50mb in 48 hours. On the 26th of November, air pressure was down to 945mb.

(7) USA dried out

This event has only a remote connection with Europe's arctic winter of 1939/40. As mentioned in a previous section, WWII had hardly started when it began to rain excessively in Western Europe, from Berlin and Basel to Paris, Amsterdam and London, for three months. The amount was more than three times the previous averages. What makes this event even more interesting is what happened on the other side of the globe.

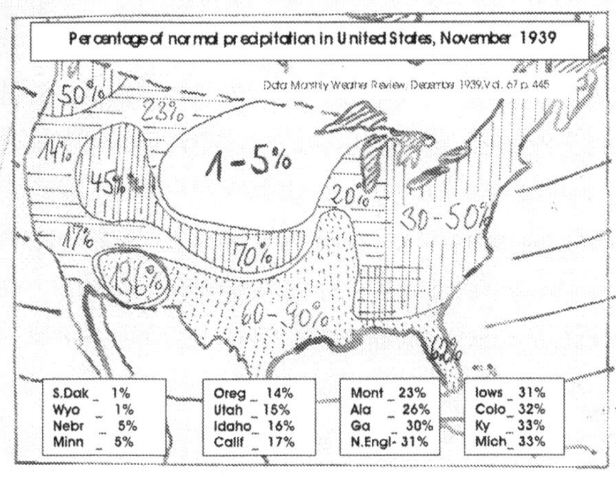

In the late autumn of 1939, the U.S.A. 'fell dry', receiving only a small percentage of the normal precipitations: October 78%, November 44% and December 71%. On the 7th of January 1940, The New York Times reported that November was unusual because of its dry air. According to US Weather

Bureau[34] "the fall season was extremely dry over large areas. From the Rocky Mountains eastward, it was the driest fall on record considering the area as a whole." Therefore, a frame for the arrival of an early winter and a bitter cold and snowy January for the USA was predicted.

(8) Russian – Finish War

Without having declared war, Josef Stalin sent his Red Army and Baltic Fleet to attack Finland, on the 30th of November 1939. At that time, "military observers believed that the total Russian forces in the Leningrad district and the Lake Ladoga region were of at least 5,000,000 men. The number of tanks was estimated at 1,000 and the number of fighting planes at 500." (NYT, the 7th of December 1939) "All in all, the Leningrad Military District command (Red Army) enjoyed a material superiority over the Finnish army by 3:1 in respect of manpower, 80:1 in respect of tanks, 5:1 in respect of artillery of all types and 5.5:1 in respect of aircraft"[35]. The battle took unimaginably destructive dimensions during the full winter period and ended with a treatise only on the 12th of March 1940.

It can hardly be overruled that major military activities went 'hand in hand' with drastic weather changes and deadly low temperatures, for example:

- Invasion of Finland had started - and 'blinding snowstorms' waged along the 750 miles of the battle line. (NYT, the 4-5th of December 1939)
- Russians started a major offensive on the 20th/21st of December - and blizzards occurred and the temperature fell to below -30°C. (NYT, the 21st of December 1939)
- Joseph Stalin had amassed 300,000 of his best troops to attack Finland from the north and the east (NYT, the 27th of December), sometimes shelling Finnish positions up to 48 hours continuously - and snowstorms and unusual low temperatures reached the battlefields. (NYT, the 29th of December 1939; Hamburger Anzeiger, the 30th/31st of December 1939)

---

34 R.J. Martin, 'The Weather of 1939 in the United States', Monthly Weather Review, Vol.67, 1939, pp.444f

35 Van Dyke, p.39-40, reference above

- Russia deployed 2,000 large guns (NYT, the 18th of January), which spat hundreds of shells every minute (NYT, the 1st of February) - but 'a pitiless deathly cold laid a glacial cover on Russia's war machinery tonight with phenomenal 54 degrees-below-zero temperatures'. (NYT, 18 January)

These events are too obvious to be a coincidence. A few years later, William Mandel[36] pointed to the fact that much lower temperatures were experienced in the winter campaigns around Leningrad during the Soviet-Finnish fighting in 1939/40, around Moscow and Leningrad in 1941/42 and around Stalingrad in 1942/43.

December 1939 was extremely variable in terms of weather. The first cold wave came around the 24th of December. The New York Times correspondent, James Aldridge, reported as it follows:

> *"The cold numbs the brain in this Arctic hell, snow sweeps over the darkened wastes, the winds howl and the temperature is 30 degrees below zero (minus 34.4°C). Here the Russians and Finns are battling in blinding snowstorms for possession of ice-covered forests. ...I reached the spot just after the battle ended. It was the most horrible sight I had ever seen. As if the men had been suddenly turned to wax, there were two or three thousand Russians and a few Finns, all frozen in fighting attitudes. Some were locked together, their bayonets within each other's bodies; some were frozen in half-standing positions; some were crouching with their arms crooked, holding the hand grenades they were throwing; some were lying with their rifles shouldered, their legs apart.... Their fear was registered on the frozen faces. Their bodies were like statues of men throwing all their muscles and strength into some work, but their faces recorded something between bewilderment and horror." (NYT, the 25th of December 1939)*

---

36 William Mandel, ‚Some notes on the Soviet Arctic during the past decade', in: Journal of Arctic Inst. Of North America, Vol. 3, 1950, p.55ff

(9) Earth Quake in Turkey – the 27th of December 1939

On Wednesday, the 27th of December 1939, a devastating earthquake in the north-easterly highlands of Anatolia shook the whole of Turkey at 1:57:35 a.m. local time[37]. The quake with a force of 8 on Richter scale caused 35,000 fatalities and injured 100,000 besides making homeless other several hundred thousands. 90 villages and 15 cities over an area of 30,000 square kilometres were completely destroyed. The earthquake produced a tsunami wave of 3-4 metres. A one-metre high wave crossed the eastern part of the Black Sea from South to North, as recorded by several Russian stations. Immediately after the quake, bitter cold, storms, heavy rains, floods and snow fall occurred.

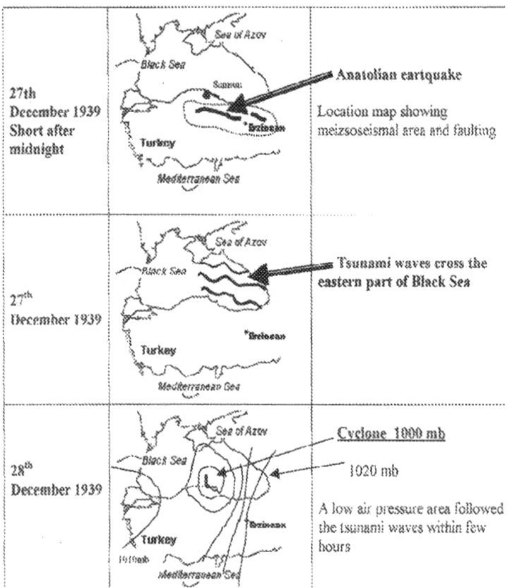

Low pressure from above Ukraine moved into the southern Black Sea, off the city of Sinop/Turkey, halfway between Bulgaria and Georgia, presumably due to quake and related tsunami. A previous high-pressure centre was still in place ca. 600 kilometres away, in Eastern Anatolia. At this short distance, an air pressure difference of at least 35mb generated strong winds that brought hardship to Turkey by way of bitter cold, stormy winds, heavy snow fall and floods. "Temperatures of 22 degrees below zero Fahrenheit (minus 30°C) and strong winds from the Black Sea claimed many lives..." (NYT, the 29th of December 1939) This constellation contributed to sudden cold and snow further west in Yugoslavia and Italy, during the last days of the year.

---

37 Recent seafloor earthquake off Aceh/Indonesia with devastating tsunami in Indian Ocean coastal rim occurred almost exactly 65 years later, on December 26th 2004, at local time 07-57 hours (GMT 00-59 hours).

(10) A bitter cold January in USA and China

January 1940 was very cold all over the Northern Hemisphere, including USA and China. First signs of a 'real' US winter emerged at Christmas time 1939 when, except for the Deep South and California, the United States experienced snow and extreme cold (NYT, the 26th of December 1939). Winter came earnestly with a frigid wave that gripped most of the United States (in early January 1940). Icy north-westerly winds swept New York with force on the 6th of January, causing temperatures to drop to an average of 10 degrees Fahrenheit below normal (NYT, the 7th of January 1940). From the Continental Divide to the Atlantic Coast, there were strange occurrences as compared with normal weather conditions. Frigid waves even touched the northern parts of Florida (NYT, ditto). However, the severity of the winter in the United States was over by the end of January 1940.

A similar cold wave gripped China. According to the newspaper reports, by the end of January 1940, all parts of China reported unusually harsh weather with snow falling in some districts where snow was unknown for twenty years. The cold wave had extended to China's southernmost provinces of Kwangtung and Kwangsi. In Changsha, capital of the Hunan Province, the weather was described as the worst in twenty years. A blinding snowstorm swept Lanchow (Lanzhou), the capital of Kansu, where the cold was said to be the severest in China (NYT, the 23rd of January 1940).

Synthesis of events

Matters to consider

Now that a new stage was reached, we have to think whether the events listed above may have made a significant contribution to arctic winter conditions of 1939/40 in Northern Europe. Previous sections established that naval warfare, due to turning and churning of huge sea areas, must have caused a drop in winter temperatures to such low levels that have not seen in the past 100 years. What role did each of the above-mentioned events play during the second half of 1939?

To begin with, it might be prudent to express clearly that none of the events listed above alone or in combination with any other provided a major contribution for generating the forthcoming winter conditions in Europe. This was decisively caused and sustained by naval war at sea. Yet, it cannot and will not be concluded that contributions on a varying scale from very little to significant levels are possible. Some aspects are logic and easy to present; others are not. This is often in respect of the cause and effect of the weather. The principle applied is: "what was first, the chicken or the egg?"

Actually only two weather conditions out of ten events listed above deserve particular attention. The rest of them are very interesting aspects for understanding the general situation as they may have presumably played a minor role during initial war months, as it will be discussed later in this section.

The most relevant aspects should be discussed first. Out of two subjects, one, which needs a more detailed consideration, relates about rainmaking in Europe, dryness in USA and subsequent cold in January 1940. The second is related to a recent claim that the extraordinary winter of 1939/40 had been caused by the El Niño phenomenon. This shall be reviewed first.

Substantial contributor?

(a) Arctic winter due to El Niño?

An international group of scientists suggested recently that there could be a link between the arctic war winter of 1939/40 and an El Niño event which started in autumn 1939, reached its full strength in January 1940 and lasted, with varying intensity, until spring 1942[38]. According to them, the dominant global feature was the contrast between high tropical and low extra-tropical sea surface temperatures (SSTs) in both hemispheres.

This claim is already weak on facts. As mentioned earlier, an El Niño effect had started in 1938 and reached full strength in South America in July 1939. From then on, the warm water pool causing extra rain, e.g. as in Peru, had been receding. Even if one is willing to accept that a prolonged event occurred, there are not sufficient facts to support the claim. There have been about 25 El Niño events during the past 150 years. It has

38 Broennimann, S.; Luterbacher, J.; StaehelinJ., Svendby, T.M.; Hansen, H. & Svenøe, T.; , Extreme climate of the global troposphere and stratosphere in 1940–42 related to El Niño', in NATURE, Vol. 431, 21 October 2004, pp. 971-974.

already been established that subsequent, long distant effects could have been caused, e.g. increased rain in Florida, flood in Brazil and draught in Australia. During the 25 El Niño periods, there were indeed cold European winters as well as normal ones. For example, during the very cold winter of 1928/29, previous to that of 1939/40, the Pacific saw a La Niña, actually the opposite of a warm water pool under El Niño conditions.

The claim of a prolonged El Niño from 1940–1942 should be treated with suspicion, too. Based on sea surface temperatures (SST), it is not too difficult to dismiss it as too shaky due to various circumstances and war conditions[39]. On the one hand, means and techniques of SST data collection changed considerably during wartime. Talking about a prolonged event over a three-year period fails to give a convincing explanation from the first place. How this could have happened as it does not fit typical El Niño features wherein warm water pools move across equatorial Pacific frequently in multi year intervals?

Regarding the claim that an El Niño would have commenced in autumn 1939, this study attempts to make an altogether different claim. With the commencement of WWII, Europe's seas were turned so much about that they affected weather conditions in distant areas, too, e.g. Northern Pacific. Fresh WWII impacts could have raised the impression that certain statistical deviations have been caused by equatorial Pacific conditions. After all, in late September 1939, California was hit by the only tropical storm ever since such events have been recorded. During this month, severe land wars were fought in Europe and China, causing excessive rain in West Europe. There were thousands of naval vessels out at sea churning the seas so much that they prevented Atlantic depressions to take their common route via Central Europe.

After all this investigation, we will not refute the argument that the El Niño phenomenon from 1938/39 may have had a small

39 Bernaerts, A.; 'Reliability of sea-surface temperature data taken during war time in the Pacific', presented at Symposium on Resource Development, August 8-9, 1997, Hong Kong, in: PACON 97 Proceedings, pp. 240-250; Bernaerts, Arnd; „How useful are Atlantic sea-surface temperature measurements taken during World War II", paper submitted at the Oceanology International 1998 Conference, "The Global Ocean", March 10-13, 1998, Brighton/UK; in: Conference Proceedings Vol.1, pp 121-130; texts are available on: www.oceanclimate.de; and www.seaclimate.de, in section: Previous Essays

share in weather making conditions during the autumn of 1939 and the winter of 1939/40 as far as heavy rain in California, Arizona and Florida, in September 1939, is concerned. They have less, if anything to do with the extremely dry months of October, November and December 1939, in USA. Regarding the excessive rain in West Europe during the first four war months and concerning the closing of the pathway for westerly winds and Atlantic depression through Central Europe, nothing indicates any El Niño contribution. The subsequent arctic war winter in Northern Europe is definitely a 'Europe-made' affair, caused by navies turning the regional seas about.

(b) Rain, dryness and polar air

Rain or no-rain is an interesting issue in the second half of 1939, which definitely had something to do with a snowy and bitter cold in January 1940, in the United States. Physically, the issue has two aspects. Due to thinner humidity in the atmosphere during winter in the Northern Hemisphere, polar air can leave Arctic easily and expand southwards. A further aspect is the wetness of the continental soil. The war in Europe, and with a possible small contribution the war in China, had made the Northern Hemisphere dryer than usual since September 1939. This lasted until snow and frost established different conditions in December. In USA, the Weather Bureau noted that November 1939 was unusual because of its dry air (NYT, the 7th of January 1940). If a strip of land, meadows, fields, forest, and mountains received much less rain than usual over a longer period of time, the evaporation rate will be correspondingly low and, subsequently, humidity will be low, attracting the dominance of dry cold air. This mechanism produced a cold January in the States. With this general picture in mind, the correlation of above mentioned events shall be discussed by first focusing on: 'Wet Californian September', and secondly on: 'Dry US November'.

aa. Wet Californian September 1939

After only a slightly lower precipitation than normal during USA's growing season, from April until August 1939, precipitations were below normal during September, except for

California and four other States[40]. Four storms affected California during this single month, causing almost four times more rain than usual, including the only tropical storm ever moving onshore, with sustained winds of 50mph on the 26th of September 1939. Can these exceptional circumstances be linked to the following four very different and interesting events?

- There was an ongoing El Niño event which reached its peak in July 1939;
- In China a war was going on, including a clash between Japanese and Russian forces, lasting from the 20th of August to the 16th of September 1939;
- A war in Europe started on 1st September saw Poland shelled, bombed and burnt down until Warsaw surrendered on 27th September 1939.
- Since war commenced, weather pattern changed in Europe from usually prevailing maritime to continental conditions, by blocking typical westerlies while, simultaneously, a 1,035mb high-pressure area between Iceland and Scotland dominated the North Atlantic from the 16th of September to the 28th of September.

It is not the intention of this study to prove whether the war influenced weather change over Northern Europe or Northern Atlantic, which can be linked to the only tropical storm ever to enter California. However, war in Europe and at sea in the North Atlantic 'fell' on nature very suddenly. Common atmospheric and oceanic equilibrium

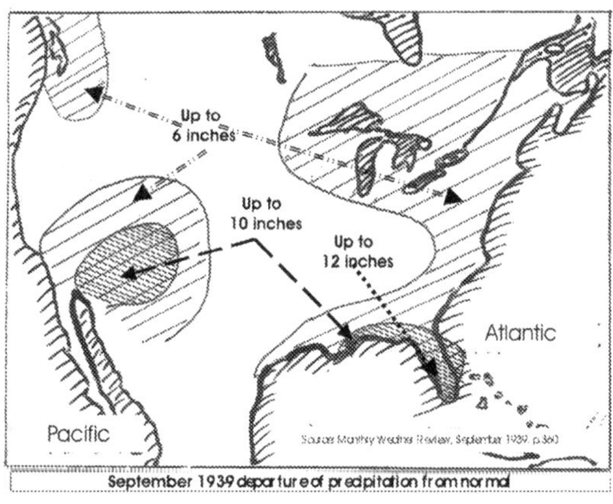

September 1939 departure of precipitation from normal

40 Precipitation in percentage of normal: Calif. 370%, Ariz. 335%, Nev. 327%, N.Mex. 114% and Utha 251%.

was disrupted with extreme suddenness. In so far, it is not impossible that, at quite some distance from Europe, a tropical storm was forced to make a completely unusual move and enter the shore of Southern California.

Concerning the question whether land wars in China and Europe have influenced the intensity of rain in California, this needs to remain unanswered at this juncture. However, a connection to distant events should not be rejected outright. Humid air masses must be available to condense aerosol particles e.g. particles of dust, salt, desert sand or smoke (condensation nucleus). War machineries in Europe and China generated such stuff abundantly. If manned balloons can fly around the world at mid latitude in 10 to 20 days, condensation nuclei can certainly travel from China and Europe to East Pacific region in one or two weeks.

As an interim result, it is possible to establish that neither the interesting Californian tropical storm nor excessive rain influenced weather conditions in Europe. Vice versa, weather conditions due to war may have had generated, on their own or in combination with ongoing El Niño event of 1938/39, unique weather conditions in California during September 1939.

bb. Dry November generates cold January in USA

Wet September 1939 in California is part of a more important aspect when searching for a connection between war conditions in Europe and distant weather anomalies. The issue will demonstrate that not only the cooling of Europe's seas caused by naval war initiated a Little Ice Age winter in Europe but that an unleashed war machinery presumably contributed to winter weather conditions in distant countries, viz. China and USA, as both experienced a bitter cold and snowy January 1940. Physical processes could have been as it follows:

- Military activities support the tendency to excessive rain due to throwing abundant condensation nuclei into the atmosphere.
- Excessive rain in Northern Hemisphere in autumn is particularly critical as it may take more days or weeks

to 'refill' any gap (lower than usual humidity) than during summer season[41].

- With lower water content in the atmosphere, cold heavy air can easily dominate the scene and this air is abundantly available in the Arctic, moving southwards if mid-latitude humid conditions are thin.

The rest of the story of the autumn 1939 is quickly told. Heavy rainfall was recorded in quick succession: in China in July, in California in September and in Western Europe during September, October and November. The result quickly became statistically visible. United States fell dry. In November 1939, USA received only 44% of usual rain, in October and December 1/3 less than the average. After three months with too little rain, soil and ground were too dry for reasonably supplying the atmosphere with humidity through evaporation. The door was open for polar air. From Mountain View, Franklin County[42] minus 20°F (=-29°C) was already reported before mid December (NYT, the 13th of December 1939). Before the year's end, winter came with "a biting northerly wind, driving gray, snow-laden clouds before it. Yesterday, it brought to New York its coldest day of the winter", down to 12°F (=-11°C). (NYT, the 28th of December 1939)

(c) Remaining potential contributor

From 10 events listed above, viz. July 1939 (1 - Flood in China) to January 1940 (10 - Cold USA), only three have not been mentioned and integrated in previous sections, namely: (6) November 1939 cyclone; (8) Russian-Finnish winter war; and (9) Turkey earth quake.

All three events occurred in a different area of Europe, viz. west of Scotland, high in the NE (Finland) and SE (Anatolia). Each of them had a temporary regional effect but certainly did not contribute to forthcoming Little Ice Age winter in Northern Europe. Nevertheless, their context to weather developments is quite interesting:

---

41 Richard Scherhag (see reference above), who analysed disruption in circulation of air in the winter 1939/1940, states with regard to air movements that there must have been a subsequent air-body-transfer (Massentransport) from the Southern Hemisphere towards the Arctic. This remark makes it clear that 'dry air' could have circled the globe for some time before a 'humidity gap' could be refilled. It also confirms that there was a 'humidity gap' in the first place.

42 The New York Times presumably refers to location: Mountain View in New York State, ZIP Code 12969: Franklin County; Latitude 44° 72' N, Longitude 74° 08'.

aa. Sinking of HMS Rawalpindi

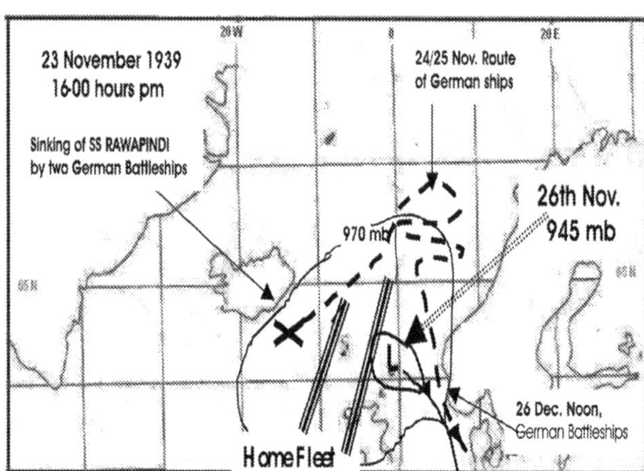

A free fall of air pressure by 50mb in 48 hours, following the first direct naval WWII high sea encounter (SE of Iceland, on the 23rd of November 1939), is interesting to study. It is just about two decades ago that meteorologists began talking about something they called the *Butterfly Effect*. High politics was impressed and nodded agreement. The thesis suggests that, if a butterfly flaps its wings in one part of the world, it can cause a storm in another part. More precisely, the claim says that the flapping of the wings produces a tiny change in the status of the atmosphere which, over time, can result in a much larger effect elsewhere. This effect is often used in connection with "chaos theory", which assumes that the atmosphere is fundamentally chaotic. As such, it is said that it is inherently unpredictable[43]. Is that indeed the case? Is it really only a matter of atmosphere? Can a 15 minutes naval shelling and subsequent aggressive criss-crossing of the sea area by several dozen naval vessels produce sufficient 'butterfly-effect' to turn a modest low air pressure into a violent cyclone? Such situations happened again and again until 1945. The impressive 945mb depression in the aftermath of the *Rawalpindi* event is nevertheless unique as, at that time, in November 1939, the sea area between Iceland and Scotland was still in her natural virgin status. Churning about the warm Northern Atlantic produces a direct atmospheric effect. There is no need for a butterfly around, neither alive nor in theory.

43 Palmer, Tim; 'A weather eye on unpredictability', in: Hall, Nina (ed); 'Chaos – The new scientist Guide to Chaos'; London 1991; pages 69 and 74.

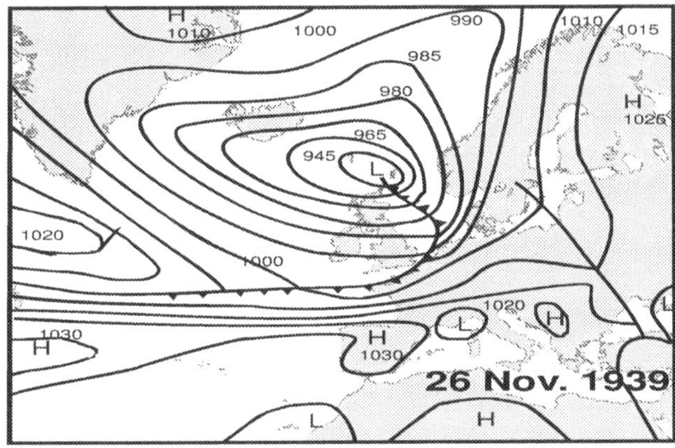

bb. Red Army in Finland for winter war

Several hundred thousands of Red Army soldiers were sent to attack Finland along an 800 miles long boarder, on the 30th of November 1939, when precipitation started with fog, rain and blinding snowstorms. Many dozens Russian naval ships from the Baltic Fleets navigated and fought shelling duels with Finish forces in the Gulf of Finland and the sea area remained ice free much longer than one could have expected. Winter cold had come early.

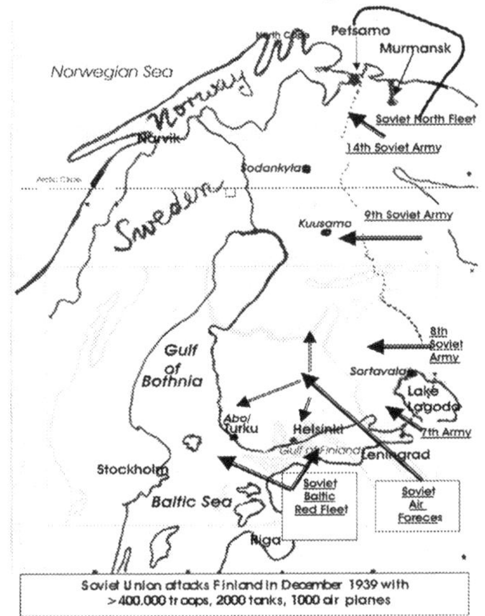

Big military land offensives of tanks, aerial bombing, battery shelling, and ground forces under permanent sunless conditions are highly likely to bring down a lot of water. The mechanism is the same as previously explained with regard to rainmaking process in Western Europe during the autumn of 1939. In winter, there will be snow, out of which much would have reached soil only 100, 200, or more

Kilometers east of Finland, within the Soviet Union territory. Little if any information is available in this respect.

However, Russia was not spared of a bitter cold winter, starting in early January 1940 with the thermometer already at 31 degrees below zero Fahrenheit (-35°C) in Northern and Central Russia, which affected normal activity. (NYT, the 9th of January, 1940) Severe cold continued in Moscow. One week later, the average morning temperature had been of 49 degrees below zero Fahrenheit (-45°C). (NYT, the 18th of January 1940)

Churning of Baltic Sea by naval forces has, for sure, contributed to the severest sea icing since 1883. Nevertheless, the foundation for an arctic winter had been laid earlier and much further southerly. In other words: Northern Europe would have had an arctic winter due to naval war, as explained in previous sections, even if the Winter War in Finland had not taken place. Whether it has finally contributed to overall winter conditions, by 5%, 10% or 15%, is a matter that still needs to be investigated.

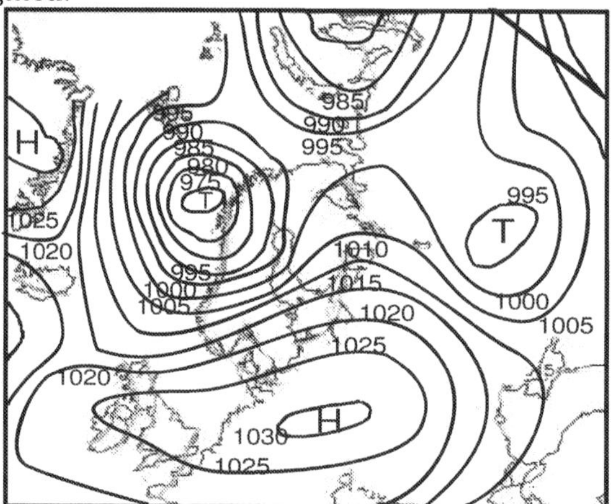

Weather Chart December 21th,1939

cc. Earthquake in Turkey

Anatolia earthquake from the 27th of December 1939 is extremely interesting with regard to temporary weather-making, but has not made any significant contribution to the war winter of 1939/40. What is still not investigated in depth is the chain of events such as quake, Black Sea tsunami, air depression on Turkey northern seacoast (off Sinop City) and a cold wave in Yugoslavia and Italia. A tsunami-generated cyclone ‘shovelled’ cold air from Siberia westwards, as indicated by the following excerpts from newspapers

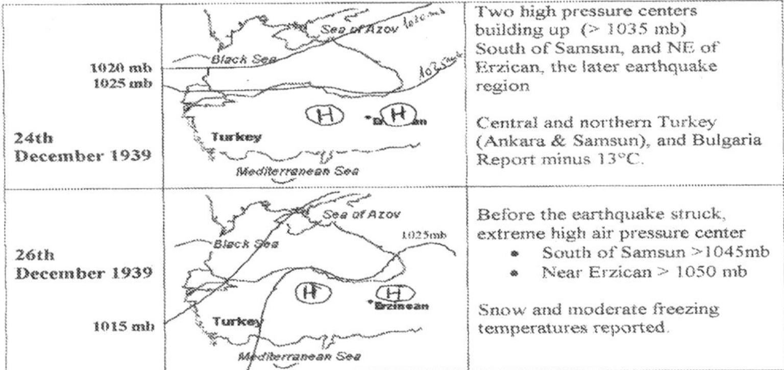

The 28th of December 1939:. “A quake in Turkey was felt around the world”. “Successive aftershocks took heavy toll of life and property in Anatolia region. “Three additional tremors, sub-zero temperature (minus 17°C) and blizzard winds”; “Temperature 22 degrees below zero (minus 30°C) and strong winds from the Black Sea claimed many victims...” (NYT, the 29th of December 1939)

The 29th of December 1939: From Agram, in Yugoslavia, temperature of minus 32°C is reported. (Neue Zürcher Zeitung, the 31st of December 1939)

the 30th of December 1939: “In Naples region, an unprecedented severe snow storm today...”. “Rome’s heaviest snowfall in recorded history - six inches - made the Romans feel as New Yorkers did in the 1888 blizzard. There had been

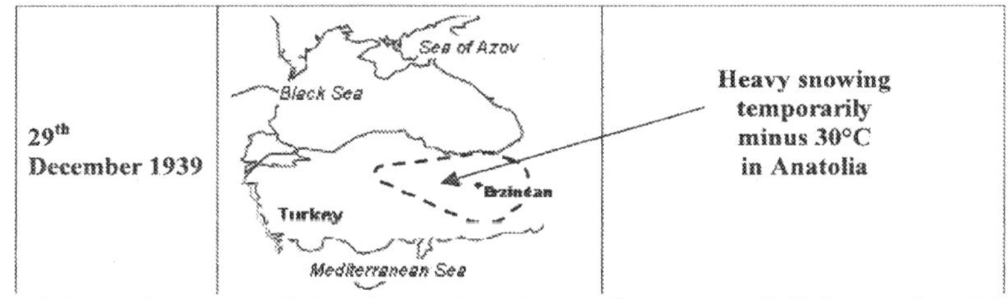

nothing closer to this since the three-day snowfall from the 16-18th of December 1846”. (NYT, the 31st of December 1939)

The 30th of December 1939: a cold wave over the Riviera. Genoa falls of temperature rapidly, extensive snowstorm. Trieste reports heavy winter storms. Malians had –10°C. (Neue Zürcher Zeitung, the 31st of December 1939).

Summary

Which events along with naval war contributed to Europe's arctic winter of 1939/40 is a question which needs to be answered. From 10 events listed above, none was, alone or in combination with other events, decisive enough to throw a continent back into the Little Ice Age.

By far the most interesting element is war-related rainmaking in Europe which subsequently dried-out the North American continent, in November and December 1939, and attracted polar air in USA, in January 1940. This chain of causes is an exciting experiment because, only in the autumn of 1939, atmosphere and seas from Northern Hemisphere were at a virgin state before naval war machinery changed the equilibrium of the marine environments, hundred or thousand times a day, over more than five years.

Which events along with naval war contributed to Europe's arctic winter of 1939/40? Can this question be answered comprehensively? Definitely not! Actually, each of the 10 events listed above would deserve an in-depth research supported by more facts and analysis. The war in China and the July flood; the only tropical storm going onshore in California at Long Beach, in late September, and the low air pressure cyclone in the aftermath of sinking of 16,697 tons HMS *Rawalpindi*, in late November, and, in particular, the winter war under the Arctic Circle during December. Each of the above events has tremendous potential for a better understanding of anthropogenic weather making. It seems high time for meteorology to take up the above-mentioned issues. After all, 65 years have passed since the events have occurred and each event seems to be able to contribute to climate change research. However, the arctic winter of 1939/40 in North Europe cannot be explained by any of the 10 events investigated. The first cold war winter was solely made by naval warfare in Europe's home waters.

- C - Three war years cold package

Suddenly Little Ice Age returned

Imagine that a meteoroid hit earth. Consequently, air temperature would rise with several degrees over a wide region. Most people would insist to be informed and to understand the matter. Assume that winter temperatures fall several degrees below average but that no one talks about it because there is war. That was actually the case during the winter 1939/40 when, in several locations in Northern Europe, average temperatures were 3, 4, 5 or more degrees lower then during all previous decades.

One cold winter may not convince everyone that naval war can be as destructive to climate as a major natural event. Therefore, the initial three war winters will be analysed as a 'package' and each individual winter analysis will demonstrate that there is an ample connection between the arctic war winter and the naval warfare.

Although every of these three winters can clearly stand individually as proof for the anthropogenic influences on weather, their succession is a particular compelling evidence on the naval war impact on regional weather modification. Already in 1942, the Swedish meteorologist Gösta Liljequist[1] stressed that the phenomenon of three successive extreme winters happens very seldom in Northern Europe. The three war winters easily took the leading position among all temperature observation done in the last 250 years.

Lilijequist's remark is logical and easy to explain. Northern Europe is half-continent, half-water. Due to winds, waters release more heat during the winter season. Once cooled down, wind ceases due to the replacement of the cyclone activities by dry, cold air coming with high pressure (anti-cyclones). The less sea surface is disturbed, the less heat is released, until the sea ice appears. In other words, any cold but calm winter situation keeps stored heat at deeper sea level during winter season, which is available for the next winter.

1 Liljequist, Gösta H. (1941/42); 'Isvintern 1941/42'; in: Staten Meteorologisk – Hydrograiska Anstalt, No.4, 1942, pp.2-15.

Naval warfare interferes and destroys this natural process. Whether sea surface water is warm or cold, navigation and warfare still affect it. Seawater is churned and turned with no regard that North and Baltic Sea can sustain maritime winter only when they are able to release heat according to statistical average. That was grossly overturned during the first three war winters. Since 1942, when naval war turned global, Europe's sea areas lost their specific regional 'war-made' winter weather. Extensive naval war in North Atlantic and Pacific easily overruled any special impact of North and Baltic Sea, and thereby ending the three-year artic winter series.

Actually, the statistics for the war winter temperatures between 1939 and 1942 is nothing less than a "Big Bang". In five out of six locations nothing comparable has ever happened since temperature observations have been made and, in only one case, the exception (Wiesbaden) happened 100 years ago. In same places, temperatures were up to 2° degrees lower per month than the next coldest three-year series. This applies for the core winter months January and February as well, when the previous December is included. The distinction between the near-coast location and the inland location deserves our particular attention, too.

Near Seaside Location

Figures show monthly mean temperatures over a three years period [Mean of six (Jan/Feb) respectively nine (Dec, Jan & Feb) months]

De Bilt/The Netherlands, Period 1706 -1993

3 years	Jan& Feb	Dec-Feb.
Long term	+ 4,5°C	+ 5,3°C
1716-18	- 0,7°C	- 0,12°C
1829-31	- 0,86°C	- 0,45°C
1940-42	**-2,46°C**	**- 1,32°C**

Oslo/Norway, Period 1816 -1988

3 years	Jan&Feb	Dec-Feb
Long term	- 3,6°C	- 3,4°C
1845-47	- 6,8°	- 6,9°C
1879-81	- 6,5°C	- 6,5°C
1940-42	**-9,55°C**	**- 7,86°C**

Stockholm/Sweden, Period 1756 –1988

3 years	Jan. & Feb.	Dec.- Feb.
Long-term	- 3°C	- 2,5°C
1766-1768	- 6,23°C	- 5,2°C
1803-1805	- 6,73°C	- 6,3°C
1940-1942	**- 9,11°C**	**- 6,8°C**

It is astonishing that war winter 1940-1942 did not only break all the records but left the next coldest three-year winter package behind. This happened particularly during core winter months January and February. Each of these six winter months was colder with 1,6°C (De Bilt), 2,7°C (Oslo), and 2,4°C (Stockholm) than any previous cold winter, whereby the difference between the 2nd and the 3rd rank was insignificant (less than 0,5°C). The temperature figure for 1940/42 is as unbelievable as a story about a 100-meter sprinter who would have broken the 10 seconds world record in only 8 seconds.

Furthermore, it is revealing that, from this group of three, Oslo (the most Atlantic location, at least from the distance point of view) is taking the lead, presumably due to the very cold sub-surface water which is 700-meter deep at Skagerrak. It is not a coincidence that the coldest January in Oslo series is January 1941. Only half a year earlier, since April 1940, Germany had occupied Norway and had carried on naval activities of huge proportions along the Norwegian coasts. We cannot ignore the fact that the three coldest months of January in all the Oslo series in almost 200 years occurred during the war, more precisely in 1941 (-13°C), 1942 (-12,1°C) and January 1917, with -11,6°C (during World War I, winter which should be carefully analysed)[2].

The three described winters, which are a true record-breaking series, are a strong indication of the role the naval warfare has played. The impact of the naval war is obvious and it is proved by the fact that in the seaside locations the temperature record had been broken at a much higher degree than in inland locations, as the following table proves it:

---

2 It should not be so much of a surprise that the third coldest January occurred during WWI. There were also a lot of naval activities in all North Sea regions. Since late 1916, naval warfare stepped into a new age of destruction, due to newly developed sea mines, submarines and depth charges (see chapter on WWI, below). In so far it might be not too far fetched to assume any link between the biggest naval encounter ever, the Battle of Jutland on the 31st of May 1916 and the record January 1941.

Inland Location

Figures show monthly mean temperatures over a three years period [Mean of six (Jan/Feb) respectively nine (Dec, Jan & Feb) months]

Paris/ France, Period 1757 - 1993		
3 years	Jan&Feb	Dec-Feb
longterm	+3,8°C	+4°C
1829-31	+ 1.5°C	+1,4°C
1879-81	+ 1.8°C	+1,2°C
194042	**+ 0,6°C**	**+1,1°C**

Wiesbaden/Germany, Period 1757 -1961		
3 years	Jan& Feb	Dec-Feb
longterm	+1,5°C	+1,8°C
1829-31	- 3,6°C	- 2,7°C
1840-42	- 1,4°C	-0,7°C
1940-42	**- 3,3°C**	**- 2,0°C**

Basel/Switzerland, Period 1755 - 1970		
3 years	Jan& Feb	Dec-Feb
long-term mean	+ 1,5°C	+ 1.7°C
1766-1768	- 2.2°C	- 2,1°C
1829-1831	- 2,8°C	- 2,2°C
1940-1942	**- 2,9°C**	**- 2,2°C**

Even Paris, which is not so far away from the sea, can blame the war at sea for the temperature modifications. In Wiesbaden (near Frankfurt), winters 1829-1831 kept the lead. Even three stations in Great Britain confirm the January/February record war series 1940-1942, viz. Greenwich[3], Oxford[4] and Edinburgh[5]. From these three, Edinburgh has the smallest negative deviation, with 0,17°C per month, presumably due to the fact that the warm Atlantic current flows into the North Sea in considerable quantities at any time of the year, and the Atlantic is not far away anyhow, while Greenwich and Oxford deviated with 0,7°C per month as compared to the next coldest series (see Footnote).

All the proofs demonstrate that negative temperature records are far away from being a mere coincidence. Sunrays played a minor role during the main winter months, while the North and Baltic Seas can contribute to the winter air temperature only through their available heat reservoir. If that has been reduced

3 Greenwich 1841-1960; Sum January/February, 1940-42 (+ 8,7°C), 1879/81 (+12.8°C), and 1891-93 (+19,5°C).

4 Oxford 1828-1980; Sum January/February, 1940-42 (+ 7,6°C), 1879-81 (+11,8°C), and 1829-31 (+12,2°C).

5 Edinburgh 1764-1960; Sum January/February 1940-42 (+ 7,6°C), 1836-39 (+ 8,6°C), and 1774-76 (+ 10,4°C).

too early, then the regional temperature will drop below statistical averages, and records can fall. 1000 naval vessels crossing sensitive seas in combat missions day and night are as dangerous as a hurricane squeezing heat out of the sea. And if a hurricane goes by after a day or two, naval warfare was a constant presence for months, since the 1st of September 1939.

The following sections will focus, in detail, on each of the three initial war winters: 1939/40, 1940/41, and 1941/42.

The 1st war winter cold centre

Winter 1939/40

War winter 1939/40 has already received considerable attention with its dramatic development and appearance. Over a very short period of just four months of naval war, a lot of heat was exhausted from Northern European seas, to an extent that they could not prevent arctic air from taking reign of the northern part of the continent during January and February 1940. After huge sea areas had been churned and turned about by naval ships and military means again and again, in short succession, most of summer-stored heat has been gone. Riparian countries immediately plunged into icy winter conditions not experienced for many generations. Circumstances give a clear indication about who is to blame.

However, as already indicated in the opening section of this chapter, there is more evidence to prove the link between naval activities and Europe's three cold war winters 1939-1942. Cold, very cold, and extreme cold still leave a lot of uncertainty as long as a baseline is not established for comparison. After having shown two extraordinary exceptions with regard to the unexpected return to Little Ice Age, to the conditions and the exceptionality of three successive cold winters, the third massive piece of evidence is based on record conditions in combination with the intensity of naval activities.

Even a record is not necessarily a record if not clearly defined. Record cold winter can cover many dozen events. Human 100-meter sprint record needs a long precision before being reckoned as an Olympic record. Even identifying the "coldest winter" may raise a number of questions. With respect to the three initial war winters, one can do better by concentration on the cold centre of a record cold region in connection with a major naval activity area. But if naval activities reached their full extent in a wider area (Northern Europe), the cold centre of this wide region during a war winter was exactly where pronounced naval activities had taken place during previous autumn months, and this would prove the connection between the two of them. First war winter (1939/40) is the first excellent example in this respect.

Cold Centre Hamburg (North Germany)

North Germany reported a record cold winter. Hamburg is a focal point between the North and Baltic Sea. North Germany is equally central to both seas. For Hamburg and for Northern Germany, war winter 1939/40 was the coldest of the three initial war winters. Other riparian countries (the Netherlands, Norway, Sweden) experienced their ultimate arctic winter during one of the following war winters.

For Berlin it was the coldest winter in 110 years[6]. The assessment is based on the 'summary of the daily mean data from November to March, with a 'cold sum' figure of -791°C in 1829/30. The corresponding figure for the winter 1939/40 is -736°C[7]. Hamburg was even colder than Berlin, with an extraordinary temperature of –29°C from 14-15 February 1940.

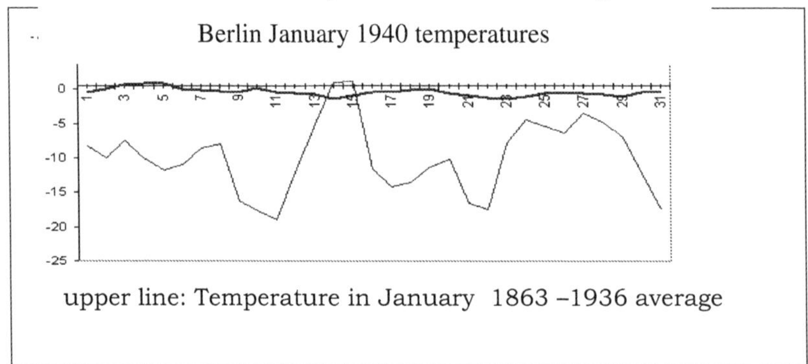

upper line: Temperature in January 1863 –1936 average

6 This applies correspondingly to a number of German cities e.g. Halle and Dresden about 150 km south of Berlin.

7 Stellmacher, R. and Tiesel R.; ‚Über die Strenge der mitteleuropäischen Winter der letzten 220 Jahre – eine statistische Untersuchung', Z. Meteorol.39 (1989) 1, p.56-59.

Since early December 1939, Hamburg's mean temperatures were below zero degrees Celsius, which were an extreme deviation from the long-term average, close to 0°C throughout the whole winter period because of the maritime weather characteristics between the two seas. Why did the situation change so much during the winter of 1939/40?

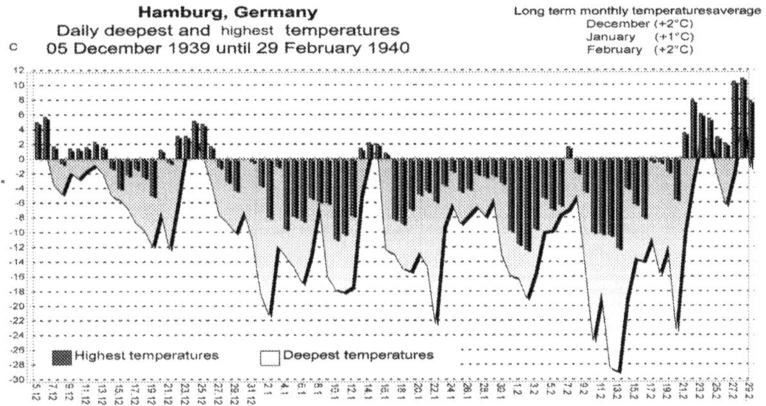

Massive naval activities started on the 1st of September 1939 and, only a few months later, cold air temperatures were close to breaking the record, viz. Southern Baltic Sea from Gdansk to Kiel and Helgoland Bight. Not only had been several ten thousand sea mines already been laid within the few weeks since war commenced, but uncountable ship-coast and ship-ship encounters took place off the Polish coast, in September, while the German Navy trained several ten thousands of navy personnel off its coast and send hundreds of ships in surveillance operations, patrols, mine detecting, mine sweeping, battle missions and so on. Evidence of a connection between the weather change and the naval war emerged soon. Massive naval activities and record cold occurred concomitantly in the same area.

The 2nd war winter – Arctic Skagerrak

2nd War winter – Arctic Skagerrak

Cold centre, Kristiansand, Oslo, Gothenburg

Three known cities in Norway and Sweden mark roughly the sea area called Skagerrak, or Strait of Skagerrak. In geographic terms, it is the water between Denmark, Norway and Sweden, 57°North and 7°East. It is exactly here that record-braking events occurred during the 2nd war winter. It was extremely cold all over Northern Europe, but South Norway, West Sweden and North Denmark took the ultimate cold temperature trophy. In Oslo, January 1941 was, with -13°C mean temperature, by far the coldest month since 1816[8]. A number of stations observed temperatures never measured before[9]. Vyborg station served Danish Meteorological Institute with –30,2°C, the lowest temperature ever measured[10]. Previous record was of –29.6°C and dated from 1893.

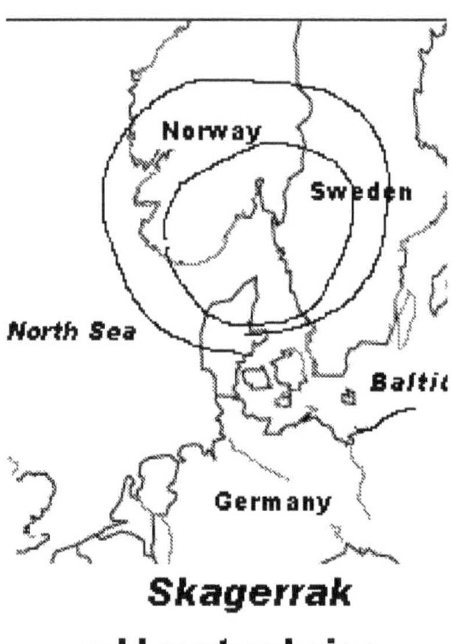

Skagerrak

cold center during winter 1940/41

All the facts mentioned above should not be so much of a surprise if one accounts the circumstances properly. Actually, one should deal with three topics:

First: Applying same conditions and thoughts as raised and explained for the 1st war winter 1939/40. The 2nd war winter was again very cold but the least cold of the three war winters

---

8 The second coldest month was January 1942 (-12,1°C); the third coldest month, January 1917 (-11,6), seven months after the Battle of Jutland, monthly means temperatures at Oslo/Gardermoen (www.wetterzentrale.com/klima/) during time period 1816-1988. The 4th coldest month was January 1867 (-11°C), the 5th coldest month, January 1820 (-10,7°C).

9 Hesselberg & Birkeland, see: References; e.g. Eidsberge (-29°C), Rade (-34,6°C), Freder (-14,5°), Torungen (-19°C), Kristiansand (-21,5°C).

10 Det Danske; Det Danske Metorologiske Institut; 'Is- og besejlingsforholdene i de danske Farvande in Vinteren 1939-40; 1940-41; 1941-42; 1947, Kobenhavn.

1939-1942, due to a simple reason. During autumn and winter 1940/41, the Baltic Sea saw much less naval war activities than during the same time in 1939/40 and 1941/42. In a following section, a brief overview of naval activities and severity of winter 1941/42 throughout North Europe will be given. It will prove, beyond any doubts, that war at sea paved the way for arctic conditions. However, we will focus on the next two topics.

Second: Skagerrak and Norwegian coastal seas over a distance of 2000 km from Oslo to Tromsø became a major naval battleground, from May until June 1940, when Germany attacked and occupied Norway, operation known under the codename “Weserübung”. Norway’s fjords and coastal seas remained under anthropogenic stress after June 1940, until arctic conditions had settled in with record low temperatures in January 1941.

Third: With a depth of down to 700 meters, Skagerrak basin is a unique area in the seawater structure of North and Baltic Sea. With regard to its depth, there are some minor similarities with the Gulf of Bothnia (max. 294m). But Skagerrak is completely different for a number of other reasons, particularly salinity and current system, which includes substantial water inflow from the Atlantic Ocean. Making war in a sea area where water temperatures are permanently below 6°C, at a depth between about 100m deep and the sea bottom, brings up a new dimension in our “hot soup stirring” theory. Logically, if only the surface is hot and the bottom of the soup cup is cold, churning would decrease temperature at surface, reduce evaporation, reduce ‘giving off steam’, and reduce the release of stored heat.
The last two topics are both responsible for causing a record cold winter in the triangle Oslo, Gothenburg and Vyborg area and, therefore, they deserve a more detailed presentation and discussion.

An overview of winter 1940/41

General conditions of war winter 1940/41 in Northern Europe are easy to explain. Even though the winter was very cold, it did not equal that of 1939/40 (Germany, Holland, Britain) or the third war winter 1941/42, particularly in Sweden and the Netherlands. In Germany, the winter 1940/41 ranked the 20th among about 150; in the Netherlands, it ranked the 33rd among about 150 'ice winters' between 1706 and 1946; and in Sweden it ranked the 23rd among the coldest winters since 1757, while the winter of 1939/40 was the 9th or 10th.

All areas close to Skagerrak reached top ranking positions. For Southern Norway, it was established by a number of stations that the lowest temperatures ever measured had been recorded in January 1941. Southern and middle parts of Sweden had been colder than during January 1941 and, in some locations, even colder than in 1860, when most of the meteorological stations in the country had been commissioned. The greatest heat deficit was observed in the inner parts of Götaland and northern Dalarna. Even in Southern Sweden, severe night frost of -20°C and less was observed, which occurs very rarely.

Denmark recorded the coldest January since 1874. It is of particular interest that Northern Jutland of Denmark recorded temperatures varying from –20 to –28°C, while Southern Jutland was about six degrees 'warmer', recording from –16° to –22° Celsius. The cold centre of the winter 1940/41 was around Skagerrak.

Occupation of Norway

WWII had started for just seven months when, in April 1940, Adolf Hitler sent the German Navy on attack missions against Norway. The well-prepared invasion plan "Weserübung" was to take place in one move. A minimum of six locations were targeted, Oslo and Kristiansand (Skagerrak), as well as Stavanger, Bergen, Trontheim, and Narvik, covering a distance of about 2,000 km, with numerous fjords, bights, islands and rocks.

During the campaign which lasted until June 1940, presumably 80 to 120 naval vessels and ca. 1,000 airplanes had been available in the service of the parties at war. Although the Norwegian Navy was small, it was able to lay sea mines with their fleet of a dozen mine layers and to use installed coastal batteries in a great number of locations. One of the first battles occurred in the vicinity of Narvik. On the 10th of April 1940, five Royal Navy destroyers entered the harbour of Narvik, where five destroyers of the Kriegsmarine were seriously damaged, thereof two sunk. Six other German ships were also sunk. British Navy lost two destroyers.

Material and ammunition needed by the German forces were to be transported to various locations by about 50 vessels, with a total capacity of 250,000 tons. Loss of ships and tonnage during this campaign amounted to about 20% of the total ships/tonnage available, including two tank ships of 6,000 tons. The Campaign ended on the 10th of June. During the struggle which lasted four months, a total of 34 naval vessels of about 500,000 tons, including 9 submarines, 19 destroyers or bigger ships, were sunk or damaged. The loss of naval vessels was equal on both sides.

The struggle between the Allies and the German naval forces continued along Norway's coast during the remaining months of 1940. British, Dutch and Polish submarines permanently navigated in the area to search and target German convoys and naval vessels.

Stirring Skagerrak

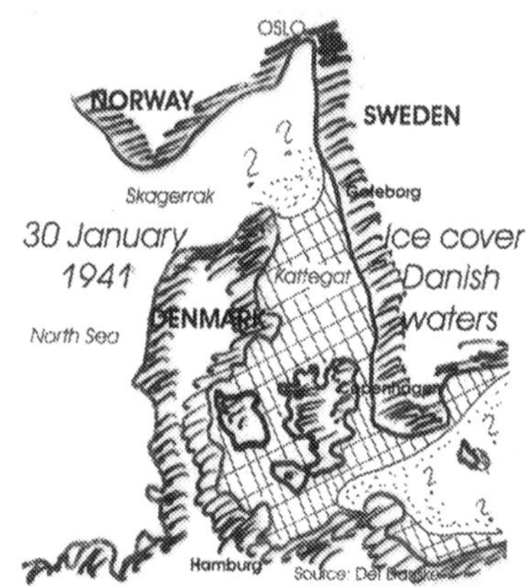

When evaluating any war at sea, we must be aware of the fact that the impact of stirring and churning the seawater body down to a depth of 60-80 meters is nothing compared to the situations which affects lower water masses. Due to a complex current system with quite different water masses coming from different sources, Skagerrak makes it even worst. That is certainly interesting for ocean science but need not interfere with this investigation. Fine-tuned observation may not be needed if experiments are done by brute force. Carrying out war operations in the deep water areas of Skagerrak and along the Norwegian south-western coast is nothing more than a grand climatic adventure. Changed seawater structures will inevitable change winter conditions.

Most of the Skagerrak sea area is below 200 meters deep, the deepest point measuring 700 meters. The average temperature for the whole water body will be of roughly 6°C in March and at peak time, in August, with hardly more than 1-2 degrees warmer. Even if the temperature of the surface layer can exceed 16°C in August, at more than 40 meters deep temperatures never exceed 10°C. As surface vessels have draughts of up to 10 meters, submarines submerged to 100 meters deep and depths charges were made to explode at any place between 5 and 150 meters deep, water structure at Skagerrak was easily stirred. Indeed, temperatures of the surface seawater at Freder and Torungen were lower between August and November 1940 than the long-term averages or the temperatures of the pervious years[11].

One will never know what actually happened with Skagerrak seawater body in the summer and autumn of 1940. Not only that the data series in deep water layer have never been taken, but a complex current system would also limit computer modelling. But the way naval war has immediate impact on deep water layers can be convincingly demonstrated with reference to another location in Vestfjorden, in the vicinity of Narvik. At Skrova, the Norwegian Fishery Directory took deep-water temperatures from 1937 until 1943, except for the occupation months, in the summer 1940. Below 200 meters water body temperatures no longer react to seasonal variations. From 1937 until the Germans' ambush, temperature at the depth of 300m run steadily between 6,6°C and 7,2°C. Suddenly, in July 1940, temperatures were more than 1°C lower and remained on a low and steady level until 1943 (between 5,8-6,3°C). Harbour and sea near Narvik saw a number of naval encounters. Skrova data give evidence of deep-reaching effects. Changing deep-sea water layers by one degree is a very serious climatical matter. Naval war between 1939 and 1945 made its impact many million times. Deep, complex and cold Skagerrak, together with many other deep water areas along the Norwegian coast had to bear many hundred thousands of events which changed the temperature (and salinity) structure of water body in the fjords and coastal seas.

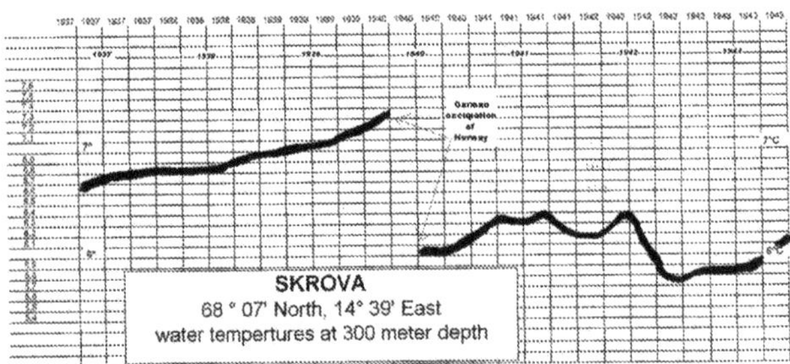

11 Bernaerts, Climate Change & Naval War, Victoria/CA 2005, p. 165

Taking into account that a forceful current system can fairly exchange Skagerrak water[12], the occupation of Norway may be reflected in severe and early sea icing during the winter of 1940/41, which together with the pervious war winter of 1939/40 became heaviest ice winter in the north of Copenhagen in many decades. However, sea icing caused the earlier start of the winter 1940/41 (more than 14 days earlier than usual), while icing of 1939/40 started later than that. It seems obvious that the replacement of Skagerrak surface water took more time than usual, thus allowing an extreme early start of sea icing in Skagerrak and north Kattegat area. As the war was due to naval activities and weather was colder than during peacetime, an arctic winter could break into the region very early and with brutal force.

Summing up Skagerrak Arctic Winter

Climatologically, Norway is a maritime country. Weather is highly influenced by the warm Gulf Currents which extends their reach to the Strait of Skagerrak, and by the Norwegian Current flowing northwards, along the coast. In January, Oslo mean air temperatures ran suddenly amok with 2°C lower than the next lowest means during a January without war since 1816, viz. 1867 that accounted –11°C, while January 1941 recorded –13°C, in a city with a long-term January means of –3,5°C. This month of January beats Little Ice Age conditions in the early 19th century and nobody ever wondered why.

By all means, the answer is presumably the easiest in the world. During the previous nine months, all water areas and many fjords along the Norwegian coast became the battleground for naval warfare. Naval vessels, bombs and depth charges did not only churned and turned seasonally warmed and cooled surface layer of the water (40-60 meter deep), but also operated along a 200-700 meter deep trench, along the coast of Norway, from Sweden (Gothenburg) to the Atlantic (north of Shetland Islands). Deep water and surface water differ by 10 degrees, even more during peak time, in

12 Water entering Skagerrak via the Jutland Current in the southwest, proceeding along Denmark's coast, turning anti clockwise at Sweden's coast to pass near the Oslo Fjord, the Norwegian Coast Current flowing south-westward until leaving Skagerrak and turning northwards and flowing along Norway's coast until reaching Norwegian Sea. In opposite direction a deep counter current injects highly saline Atlantic water into the Skagerrak depths.

August/September. Warfare at sea surface can easily 'restructure' the thermocline of any water layer below. The Skrova case can illustrate this phenomenon (see above). The cold was not only overwhelming, but it also came very early, which is another sign that sea area troubled by war had little heat reserves in store to sustain statistical expectation.

A convincing proof for this causal relation between the war and the cold weather is the fact that all coastal areas around Skagerrak were dragged into exceptional cold conditions with record temperatures never experienced before. This allows only one conclusion: German war machinery (used for Norway's occupation) and naval warfare are responsible for the cold centre winter of 1940/41 which was established at Skagerrak and which influenced Oslo, Gothenburg and Vyborg with record low temperatures.

The 3rd war winter – 1941/42 – Baltic Sea experiment

Frame of Experiment

How can one make an arctic winter and how can one prove it? The first condition for an interesting climate experiment is to exclude the sun. We did it by concentrating research on the winter period during the 1st and the 2nd war winters of WWII. The second condition for improving experimental conditions is to exclude the external influence of the water influx coming from different sources, e.g. the Atlantic Ocean. The Baltic Sea is almost completely disconnected from the oceanic system, salinity is low or inexistent (Gulf of Bothnia) and the current system affected only by local forces (wind, temperature, salinity, and influx of river water). For the completion of an excellent climate change, the third condition is easy to imagine: the forceful stirring and shaking of the water basin. This all happened between June and December 1941 and the following winter proved the effectiveness of the experiment. Northern Europe fell pray to a record icy winter.

'Barbarossa' – Germany attacks Russia

Under the codename 'Barbarossa', Germany planned and ambushed Russia with an Army of 3,000,000 men, 3000 tanks, 7000 artillery pieces, 2500 aircrafts and other war relevant equipment. This happened on the 22nd of June 1941, along a battle line of 2000 km.

It is a well-known fact that, within a few months of invasion, in June 1941, the German Army encountered winter conditions in Western Russia, the severity of which cannot be imagined. It was so much out of tune with the climatic records over many years. And it is not surprising that the German armies had not been prepared to face it. They fell prey to a misjudgement similar to that of the Russian Army in Finland, in December 1939. While military offensive in Finland 'pushed the weather' to very cold temperatures under the Arctic Circle during the winter of 1939/40, the Germans drove the weather conditions 'over the edge' by turning the Baltic Sea 'up-side-down' (see next paragraph). This six-month 'treatment' of the Baltic Sea, in 1941, was several times more intensive than in 1939. A little bit later, snow, freezing and ice conditions became extremely severe along the entire German–Russian front line, from the west of Murmansk, Leningrad, Kalini, Mazhaisk (west of Moscow) to Belowgrad, Rostov, and Sevastopol (Krim). Since mid-November 1941, temperature during daytime was of -3°C, and at night it went down to -7°C. By the end of November, temperature fell to -25 degrees Celsius on the Eastern Front. Along the frontlines close to Leningrad, heavy snowfall blocked almost all German mechanized operations (NYT, the 4th of December 1941). On the 7th of December, the German High Command stated in a communiqué that "despite bitter cold, German and Italian troops have recorded successes in local offensive in the Donets Basin" (NYT, the 8th of December 1941), and that harsh winter forced the abandonment of big operations in the north until spring (NYT, the 9th of December 1941). In December, temperatures went down to -40°C.

Before the severe cold wave hit the Eastern Front, there was a heavy 'mud-period' which lasted from early October until freezing began. It all started with snow on about the 7th of October and went on with rain, bearing quite a number of similarities with the situation discussed in an earlier chapter concerning rain-making on the Western Front, along the river Rhine, in late 1939. Until the end of December 1941, the costs of invasion for the German Army were: 174,000 dead men, 600,000 wounded and 36,000 missing. Germany also lost 758 bomber planes, 568 fighter planes, and 767 other types of airplanes, not to mention the loss of tanks, flaks and vehicles, which was huge. The Russians' loss was considerably higher.

War sideline – Climate battlefield

Immediately, the Baltic Sea became a battleground and its eastern part was churned and turned, from Gdansk to Leningrad. The operation 'Barbarossa' was a fringe war operation area. In climatic terms, it was a major theatre of regional weather modification.

The Germans mobilised about one hundred naval vessels: 10 large mine layers, 28 torpedo boats, and 2-3 dozen minesweepers. Air support was entrusted to the Luftwaffe. Russians had six big war ships, 21 destroyers, 65 submarines, six mine layers, 48 torpedo cutters and 700 airplanes. The considerable number of ships and airplanes became active in six months. The Kriegsmarine lost 35 ships. Russia alone lost 50 naval vessels when evacuating the Reval naval base. The total number of ships which sank in the Baltic Sea during the second half of 1941 is of about 370 (500,000 tons).

Sea mines were a considerable threat. Around 20,000 mines were laid, many thousands being swept and destroyed. Although many of the Russian mines weighted less than 100 kg, the Soviet Baltic Sea Fleet alone laid at least 10,000 mines in the Finnish Gulf and outside the Soviet Ports, in the Baltic Sea (e.g. Riga and Reval). In early August, a dozen of Russian naval vessels laid mines as far away as the west of Bornholm. Probably the last Russian distant operation was a mining operation close to Gdansk (October 20 – November 15).

Many hundreds of daily naval activities caused a great Baltic Sea 'turning and churning' experiment. One devastating experience determined the Russians Baltic Fleet to evacuate their fleet bases at Reval (Tallinn) by the end of August. More than 200 ships had been moved to Kronstadt, near Leningrad. More than 4,000 mines were laid on the way out, some of them placed so close together that the distance between two individual mines was sometimes of only 30 feet. Once the ships were out of the harbour, the convoys were bombed or torpedoed while crossing these minefields. This repositioning operation meant the loss of over 50 ships and some 36 transporters and auxiliaries for the Baltic Fleet, not to mention the total loss of lives (at least 6,000 men were lost).
Another significant event occurred in early December 1941, when the Baltic Fleet desperately tried to evacuate the Finnish island of Hangoe which they had occupied in December 1939.

During its sailing, the 7,500-tons ship *Josif Stalin*, carrying ammunition and military personnel, was hit by four mines that initiated a tremendous detonation, killing four thousand of the troops aboard. 2,000 men survived. Since evacuation from Hangoe started on the 31st of October, the Baltic fleet lost, in half a dozen missions, three destroyers, three fast mine sweepers and other craft and transporters (*Josif Stalin, Andrey Zdanov*), the icebreaker *October* plus a host of smaller vessels.

The 'Barbarossa' operation definitely remodelled Baltic seawater body during the autumn of 1941, to a seasonally water structure never experienced before, particularly the phenomenon of "squeezing" summer-stored heat at such an early date. For the occupation of the vast Russian territory, this may have been hardly more than a small contribution. But for regional weather modification, it was highly effective. This became evident at Malgoviks primary school, in December 1941.

Cold record on the 13th of December 1941

An early date for a cold temperature record should be noted. Swedish Meteorological Service recorded in their annual publication that a new temperature, lower than -50°C, was measured on the 13th of December 1941. At Malgoviks primary school in Norrland (64°37' North, 16° 25' East), this very low temperature was recorded on a plain alcohol thermometer. Actually, on comparison with a common thermometer, this temperature meant -53°C. If such temperature was recorded before mid-December, there may be only two explanations. Either the recording is a gross mistake or deception, or the event had something to do with war at sea. 'Barbarossa' activities in the Baltic Sea could have had a big contribution. But contributions could have also come from other locations. Naval warfare was fiercely conducted in all European waters from Barents to the Mediterranean Sea. German U-boats operated across the North Atlantic. Since August 1941, the Allies supplied Russia with weapons and urgently needed equipment. Convoys sailed from England. Until the 8th of December 1941, seven Arctic Convoys departed from Hvalfiord/Iceland and arrived about 15 days later in Murmansk or Archangel. Only six days before the record temperature at Malgoviks primary school, Japan attacked Pearl Harbour on 7th December 1941.

Stockholm's coldness trophy

Location	January 1942			February 1942		
	average Jan. 1942	Normal 1901-30	Lowest 1942	average Feb. 1942	Normal 1901-30	Lowest 1942
Kiruna	-16,6	-11,9	-35,5	-15,8	-11,8	-33,4
Haparanda	-17,0	-10,3	-31	-14,2	-11,2	-30
Umea	-17,2	-7,4	-30	-13	-7,4	-27,8
Östersund	-16,9	-7,9	-31,4	-11,2	-6,8	-26,4
Karlstad	-12,3	-3,2	-25,2	-10,8	-3,1	-24,6
Stockholm	-10,6	-2,5	-28,2	-10,5	-2,6	-18,8
Karlshamm	-8,4	-0,3	-22,5	-6,6	-0,6	-16
Malmö	-7,5	+0,3	-25	-6,2	-0,2	-20

All figures in minus Celsius degree; source: Statens

More important than a short incident like that from the Malgoviks primary school are record conditions over a longer period and wider perspective. The winter of 1941/42 represents this longer period, while the temperature record over a century offers the wider perspective. Stockholm is a good place to demonstrate this situation, said the Swedish meteorologist Goesta Liljequist, who expressed his amazement about the winter of 1941/42 as it follows: After the two hard winters of 1939/40 and 1940/41 and the difficulties they generated to shipping and fuel supply for the country, one has awaited and expected that the winter of 1941/42 would bring a return of the mild winters, which had recently predominated. Instead this, winter became one of the toughest ever recorded, if not the severest of all winters during the last 200 years[13]. In 1943, Goesta Liljequist made a thorough assessment of the "The severity of the winters at Stockholm 1757–1942". The following data have been gathered from his work[14].

The winter 1941/42 ranks high in the list of very severe winters. In a group of 15 most severe winters since 1757, the winter of 1939/40 ranks about the 10th and the winter 1941/42 is in the top as it follows:

---

13 Liljequist, Gösta H.; see Fn 1

14 Liljequist, Gösta H; 'The severity of the winters at Stockholm 1757 - 1942', Geografiska Annaler 1-2, 1943, p. 81-104; and as an extended paper in: Meddelanden, Serien Uppsatser, Stockholm 1943, pp.1-24.

Rank No	Mean temp. Dec.– March	Mean temperature Three coldest months	Sum of negative monthly means temp.
1	1788/89, - 8.0°C	1941/42, - 9.2° C	1788/89, - 31.9° C
2	1808/09, - 7.6° C	1788/89, - 9.1° C	1808/09, - 30.5° C
3	1941/42, - 7.5° C	1808/09, - 8.7° C	1941/42, - 30.5° C

Liljequist points to the fact that, since temperatures were taken, in 1760, the mean winter temperatures had increased with about 2°C and that this tendency was especially well marked since the middle of the 19th century. Insofar, the deviation from 'normal' became even more evident. A 'true' comparison would actually show that winter 1941/42 was in any calculation –0,5° (right column) to –2,5°C (middle column) colder than winter 1788/89. taking into account the group of the coldest three months (December to February), winter 1941/42 is the coldest since 1757. At that time, mean temperature was of –2,3°C in winter 1756/57. As no data from a previous period are available, Stockholm's winter following 'Barbarossa' could have been the coldest since the last Ice Age, 10,000 years ago.

Swedish January weather turned around

In addition to a very cold period all over Sweden, it is worth noting that the main climate conditions were 'turned around' within the country. Harsh conditions were more severe in middle and southern Sweden than in Northern Sweden. This definitely points to an extremely sub-cold Baltic Sea (including North Sea and beyond). Meteorological circumstances are well documented by official Swedish annual report[15], which says concerning the month of January 1942 (excerpts):

General Overview

During the first few days of the month, moderate westerly airflow dominated. On the 4th of January, a high-pressure zone developed in the NW of Lappland, which brought cold winds in the whole country. On the 7th of January, a small low-pressure area moved over Norrland to the East, where air pressure remained equally distributed but then increased generally. On the 13th day, there was a high pressure zone over the northerly Scandinavia. Wind came from an easterly direction in most of

15 Statens Meteorologisk-Hydrografiska Anstalt, ‚Arsbok', Månadsöversikt över Vänderlek och Vattentillgång , Argang 21-26, 1939 –1945, Stockholm.

the parts of the country until the end of the month. The highest air pressure (1,045mb) was measured in Norrland, on the 21st of January. Together with the easterly winds, snowfall occurred temporarily, particularly on the Baltic coast. On the 24th day, very cold air came from the East and, despite a cloudy sky, the temperatures dropped down from –25°C to –30°C, with a wind speed of more than 10m/sec. On the 26th of January, at the same hour, temperatures recorded were between –35°C and –40°C, with clear sky and calm as far south as Smaland. Especially between the days 25-26 and 29-30, great difference in air pressure was recorded between northerly Sweden and southerly Baltic Sea, with easterly winds (kultje) dominating temporarily in the Baltic Sea.

Air pressure

The average value was higher than the usual all over the country. In the northerly Norrland, deviation was the highest (17-18mb), but decreased gradually towards the south, so that the deviation was still of 4-5mb at Skane. Such high January mean air pressure has never been recorded in Norrland before. Usually, the air pressure in Norrland is lower than in Gotaland. Westerly and south-westerly winds usually dominate. In January 1942, the situation was completely reversed, which caused permanent easterly or north-easterly winds.

Temperatures

The biggest temperature deficit, of about -10°C, was recorded in the inner parts of Gotaland, northern Varmeland, Dalarna and southern Norrland. A number of record temperatures were measured in Gotaland and Svealand. The temperatures were of 6 to 7°C lower than the lowest temperatures known until that moment.

Swedish Summary

The Swedish meteorologist Gösta H. Lijequist[16] wrote immediately after the extraordinary winter 1941/42 (excerpt):

> *The winter 1941/42 was colder than the winters 1939/40 and 1940/41. At Stockholm, it was one of the very coldest winters since 1756, when regular*

16 Liljequist, Gösta H., see Fn 1.

temperature observations were started. If we graduate the severity of a winter according to the value of the mean temperature of the three coldest months of the winter half year, 1941/42 is found to be the coldest winter since 1756.

Baltic Sea Icing

The meteorologist Gösta H. Lijequist assessed also the sea ice along Sweden's coast and Baltic Sea:

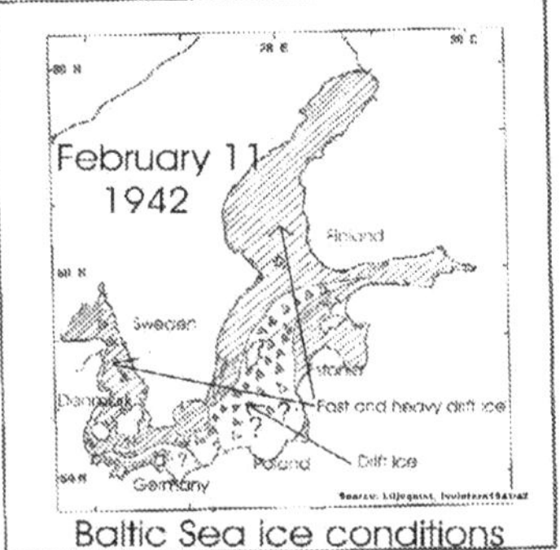

Baltic Sea ice conditions

"The formation and breaking up of the ice took place at a rather normal time in the Gulf and Sea of Bothnia: The formation of ice in the Baltic and on the West-coast started in the first part of January, generally one or two weeks earlier than normally. The ice conditions grew worse after a mighty invasion of cold air on the 24th of January, when temperatures between –25° and –30° C were recorded in the whole country; at the same time, the wind force was 6 Beaufort scale or more.

The thickness of ice was of about 100 cm in the Gulf of Bothnia – the maximum value observed this winter being of 125 cm – and 60 cm in the Sea of Bothnia. In the Baltic, the values varied between 50-60 cm. The ice period was generally longer than in 1939/40 but about the same as in 1940/41, except for the West coast and the Sound, where it lasted longer. On the 6th of June, all Swedish waters were ice-free".

Concluding remark on 'Barbarossa'

Circumstances on churning Baltic waters and meeting devastating arctic conditions on Russian soil demonstrate the interrelation between these two events. Insofar, it is easy to establish that Adolf Hitler shot himself in the feet. At least he should not have touched the Baltic Sea. Not reaching Moscow and fulfilling 'Barbarossa' plan conditions due to early and killingly winter conditions represented the beginning of the end of his ruthless activities. Luckily, at that time science was not aware of such a link and thus could not advice Hitler and his army that they would endanger military goals by simultaneously conducting naval warfare extensively in nearby seas.

When Field Marshal Herman Göring had proclaimed, in February 1940: “Nature is still more powerful than man. I can fight man but I cannot fight nature when I lack the means to carry out such battle. We did not ask for ice, snow and cold – A higher power sent it to us”[17], the winter of 1941/42 proves him wrong. The winter was man-made, more precisely, by Hitler, his Government and his Army. Hitler, Göring and their ruling companions are solely responsible for the coldest winter in Northern Europe since data recording commenced in the middle of the 18th century.

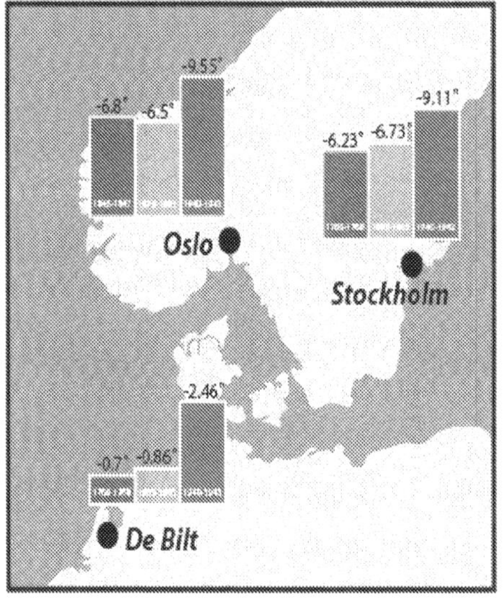

17 See above: Chapter I, Introduction

Three-year winter package

Exceptionality of successive cold winters

Three extreme cold winters in a row are another striking evidence that naval war generated ice age conditions in Northern Europe. A massive demonstration could already be made on the basis of 3-year statistics of winter temperatures recorded in De Bilt, Oslo and Stockholm. Evidence can therefore be based not only on sudden and extreme cold in North Europe in general and at maritime locations in particular but also on the fact that such a situation has never been observed before.

Fortunately, the 'three-year package' theory doesn't rely only on temperatures in order to prove that war at sea was the cause of the cooling phenomenon, but can rely on a number of additional aspects. For example, snow covered the British Isles, sea ice covered the Baltic Sea and the regions which had the most significant naval activities had to deal with record cold temperatures during the next winter.

Mentioned issues offer us a rich investigation field and will be discussed and explained with the help of materials published during WWII or shortly after. That includes early observation and references to the extremely low temperature conditions.

Low Temperatures

Sweden

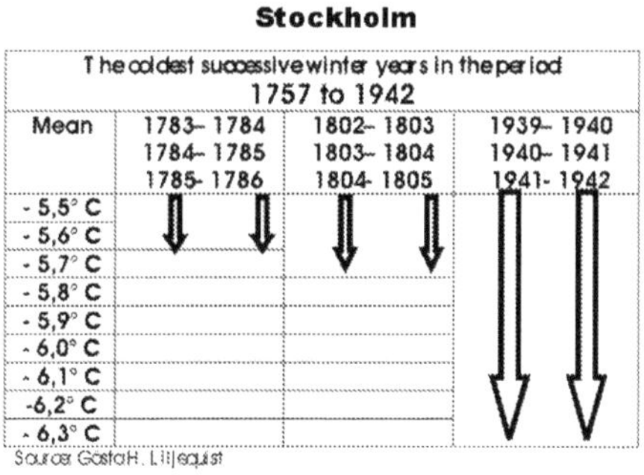

Stockholm

The coldest successive winter years in the period 1757 to 1942			
Mean	1783- 1784 1784- 1785 1785- 1786	1802- 1803 1803- 1804 1804- 1805	1939- 1940 1940- 1941 1941- 1942
- 5,5° C			
- 5,6° C			
- 5,7° C			
- 5,8° C			
- 5,9° C			
- 6,0° C			
- 6,1° C			
-6,2° C			
- 6,3° C			

Source: Gösta H. Liljequist

As already indicated above, G. Liljequist observed: Three ice winters in succession are very rare[18]. During almost 200 years of weather observations at Stockholm, there are only two periods that came close to the most recent one in 1939-42. But none of the previous 'three-winter-periods' (calculated on the

18 Gösta Liljequist, Liljequist, Gösta H. (1941/42); ,Isvintern 1941/42'; in: Staten Meteorologisk – Hydrograiska Anstalt, No.4, 1942, pp.2-15.

basis of mean temperature of three coldest months) had been as cold as the latter, which was 0.6°C colder than the next group of 1802-1805.

Liljequist summarizes his results on Stockholm's cold winters from 1757-1942 as it follows (excerpt): "Since the beginning of temperature observations, around 1760, up to the decade 1931-1940, mean winter temperatures have increased with about 2°C. This tendency is especially marked from the middle of the 19th century. The number of severe winters has decreased during recent years, while mild winters have remained rather constant in number".

Kew Observatory/UK

Even during the „Cold Epoch" (ca. 1810–1850), when 9 winters out of 42 were colder at Kew Observatory/UK than the 1939/40 "winter package", none of these winters was so closely followed by subsequent cold winters as during the winters of 1939/40, 1940/41 and 1941/42[19], which were furthermore commented upon: "The present century has been marked by such a widespread tendency towards mild winters that the 'old-fashioned winters', of which one had heard so much, seemed to have gone for ever. The sudden arrival, at the end of 1939, of what was to be the beginning of a series of cold winters was therefore all the more surprising. Since the winters of 1878/79, 1879/80 and 1880/81, there have never been three winters in a row as severe as those of 1939/40, 1940/41 and 1941/42."[20]

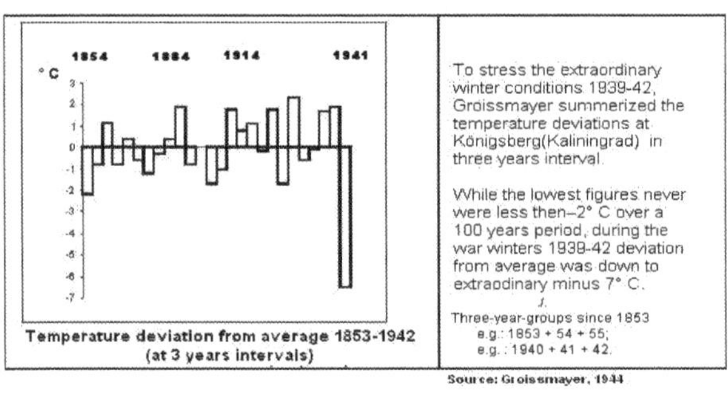

Temperature deviation from average 1853-1942 (at 3 years intervals)

Source: Groissmayer, 1944

Königsberg (Kaliningrad) as early as in war year 1944, F.B.Groissmeyer[21] summarized temperature data according to three year intervals starting in

19 A.J. Drummond.; ‚Cold winters at Kew Observatory, 1783-1942'; Quarterly Journal of Royal Met. Soc., No. 69, 1943, pp 17-32, and: Drummond, A.J.; Discussion of the paper: ‚Cold winters at Kew Observatory, 1783-1942'; Quarterly Journal of Royal Met. Soc., 1943, p. 147ff.

20 A.J. Drummond, ditto, p. 31

21 Groissmayr, F.B (1944); 'Die gewaltigen Temperaturestoerungen auf der Nordshemisphaere 1920-1942', in: Zeitschrift fuer angewandte Meteorologie, Jg. 61, 1944, pp.15-56 (p. 55), (15-24, and 49-56).

1853 until the third war winter 1941/42. The result is shown in the corresponding graph.

Maritime and continental difference

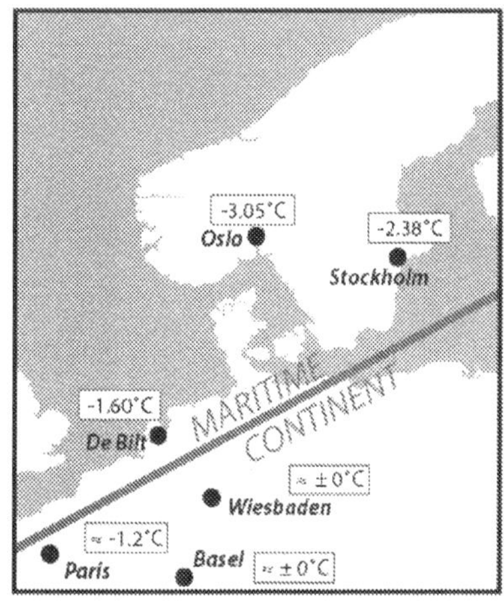

Deviation from three succesive record January & February temperatures during winters 1939/40 - 1941/42

Before moving to the next issue, temperature differences between maritime and inland location, as mentioned in a previous chapter, should be included in a comprehensive 'three year package' list. While record cold winter results were achieved throughout North Europe, the difference between sea and land is remarkable. Land values for January and December were only slightly below previous record (Paris 1,2°C, Basel 0,1°C, and Wiesbaden managed only second place), while close-to-sea locations (De Bilt, Oslo and Stockholm) broke the previous cold records with extraordinary temperature differences from 1,6 to 2,7°C. This is strong evidence that North and Baltic Sea played a big role in generating the three arctic winters. While warm Atlantic water arrives in Europe as usually, colder North Sea water is recorded by the British weather reports.

Snow in Great Britain

A snow-rich winter needs two conditions: abundant supply of aerial humidity, combined with cold air. During the war, Britain flouts like a battleship in a bath tube, filled with warm water and bathing water steaming off. Cold continental air could quickly turn moisture air to fog, rain, ice-rain or snow.

Extreme conditions came quickly. From the 27th of January to the 3rd of February 1940, England did not only face a tremendous snow problem but also experienced the longest-lasting ice-rain event, presumably the severest known. The most effected regions were from Wales, via south-westerly parts of Midlands, to SW and central-southern region. Meanwhile, violent stormy weather brought massive snow to south-eastern England, including snowdrifts reaching heights of 15 feet and more[22]. Surprised? Not really! Over the Atlantic, warm air clashed with cold air, which was actually colder than usually because of the naval warfare in the North and Baltic Seas.

Kew Observatory

In any case, snow in Britain is rare. In the south-east of England, snow can be expected only every 10th day. Any deviation should raise suspicion. During the winter 1939-1942, the rate per month was up to 400% higher. Drummond's table showing percentage of days with snowfall is as it follows:

	December	January	February	Dec.- Feb.
1939 -40	6%	32%	24%	21%
1940-41	6%	36%	29%	23%
1941 -42	3%	42%	46%	30%
Average(1871-1938)	6%	10%	11%	9%

(Source: Drummond, see Fn. 18)

The Isles

Lewis[23] made the following two statements concerning the snow-cover in the British Isles, in the months of January and February of the severe winters of 1940, 1941 and 1942. "The three consecutive winters of 1940, 1941 and 1942 were, however, unusually severe; the snow was considerable and the number of days of snow-laying comparatively large". "Three severe winters in succession like 1940, 1941 and 1942 seem to

22 Cave, C.J.P.; ‚The ice storm of January 27-29, 1940', and Discussion; Quarterly Journal of Royal Met. Soc., Vol. 66, No.285, 1940, pp.143-150.

23 Lewis, Lilian, F.; 'Snow-cover in the British Isles in January and February of the severe winters 1940, 1941 and 1942', in: Quarterly Journal of Royal Met. Soc., 1943, pp. 215-219.

be without precedent in the British Isles for at least 60 years, a similar succession occurring from 1879-1881."

WWI and WWII

At Kew Observatory, A.J. Drummond realised an exceptional situation in 1942[24]: "Since comparable records began in 1871, the only other three successive winters as snowy as the recent ones were those during the last war, namely 1915/16, 1916/17 and 1917/18, when snow fell on 23%, 48% and 23% of the days". The naval warfare caused more humidity in the air and facilitated the inflow of cold continental air over The Isles, thus generating rain, ice-rain and snow in quantities which are above all statistical values.

Change of wind direction

Norway

Hesselberg & Birkeland[25] point to significant climate deviations during the first three war years as reproduced in the following table:

Means deviations for the Period 1940-42

	Winter	Spring	Summer	Autumn
Atmospheric pressure	+6 mb	+3 mbar	+0,5 mbar	+0,5 mbar
Air temp.	-4°C	-1°C	+0,3°C	+0,2°C
precipitation	- 12%	- 8%	+2%	+3%
Wind from north	+24%	+8%	+4%	+7%
Wind from east	-5%	0	0	-2%
Wind from south	-17%	-10%	-6%	-9%
Wind from west	-1%	+2%	+2%	+4%
Approximate figures for Southern Norway (Source: Hesselberg, Fn 24)				

Means deviations during the period 1940-42
from the mean values of the period 1901-30

Hamburg/Germany - October 1939

24 A.J. Drummond, see Fn 18, p. 31

25 Hesselberg, TH., and Birkeland, B.J.; 'The continuation of the secular variations of the climate of Norway 1940-50', in: Geofysike publikasjoner Vol. XV. No.5, Bergen 1944-56; pp. 3-40.

That naval war in North and Baltic Sea reversed long-term climate data became obvious as early as October 1939, when the Deutsche Seewarte meteorologist on duty concluded in his analysis, on the 2nd of November 1939:
"Hamburg reported winds from the North-Eastern quadrant on almost two thirds of the dates observed (33% easterly winds out of 65%) while north-eastern winds accounted only for a quarter (26%) of several previous years' averages. Otherwise, most frequent direction of the wind – south-west (24%) – accounted for 9% of all cases. Thus the observations at this station alone show what the weather charts of an extensive area will obviously indicate as well."

Kew Observatory

Everyone knows that Great Britain's weather comes from the North Atlantic and the wind mostly from westerly directions. From prevailing wind directions in South-West England during 155 winters, from 1788 to 1942, only 21 had easterly resultants, whereby the few winters of 1814, 1841, and 1940 had resultants from NE to ENE. Another small number of winters since 1841 (1845, 1870, 1879, 1891, 1895, 1904, 1929) had prevailing winds from SSE to ESE. Except for the winters of 1801 and 1804, all these 21 winters with predominant easterly winds had temperatures below the average (40,1°F; 4,5°C). While eleven of the above winters had means between 34°F and 36°F, only six with westerly resultants had means lower than 37°F, these being 1820, 1830, 1847, 1855 and 1886[26].

Three ice winters in the Baltic Sea

German coastal sea icing

An accurate indicator of the severity of a winter in Baltic Sea and its bordering countries is the annual feature of icing. Considering the extent and severity of ice during the three war winters of 1939-42, it's possible to provide ample proof that this extraordinary situation could only have been generated by intensive military use of these waters over the time period in question. Main aspects can be summarised as it follows:

---

26 A.J. Drummond, see Fn. 18, p. 31

- First and foremost, there is the suddenness and the severity of each of these ice winters, for which no other cause than the war at sea could be attributed.
- It is possible to establish a direct link between the extent of activities in the Baltic Sea and the degree of icing and of arctic winter conditions:

    - 1939/40: intensive military activities, Gdansk, mining western Baltic and Gulf of Finland, Finnish-Russian war at sea resulted in very heavy ice.
    - 1940/41: there were only general naval activities so the icing was less serious than that of the previous year. Yet, it was a severe ice winter.
    - 1941/42: the Germans invaded Russia and fought with the Russian Baltic Fleet for five months, in the Central and the Northern Baltic Sea, during June-December 1941; this resulted in the most extended and heaviest icing ever observed.

Another proof of great importance is the fact that there has never been such a severe icing. It should be noted that over the observation period the general mean temperatures in Sweden and in the Northern Hemisphere rose roughly with one degree, while the winter temperatures in Stockholm had risen with about 2°C since 1761. This comparison of extreme winter situations from the late 18th or early 19th century to similar events from the mid 20th century will make the latter appear even more severe and extraordinary.

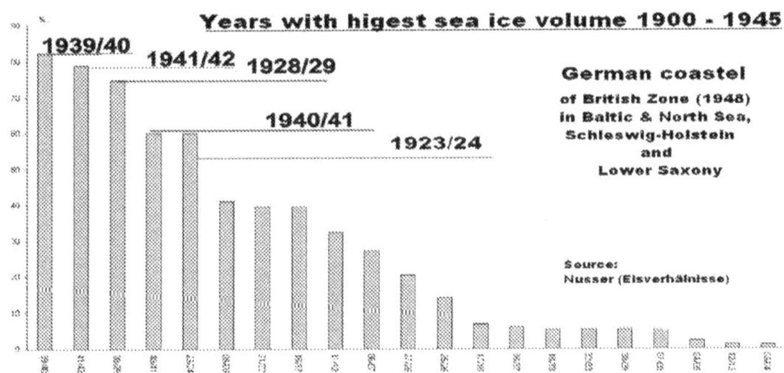

Northern Baltic Sea icing

Another important argument that nothing but the war at sea had turned the Baltic Sea into an ice age sea is the extent of the ice cover during the three years in question. According to a graph made by the Finnish Institute[27], showing the ice cover in the Baltic Sea, 57° North latitude (ca. Visby - Riga latitude), there has never been one group of three successive years with such an important extent of ice cover as the ice phenomenon of the war years of 1939-1942 since 1720 (when such observations were recorded).
As the graph provided by the Finnish Institute actually shows figures only since 1720, the ice cover during the winters of

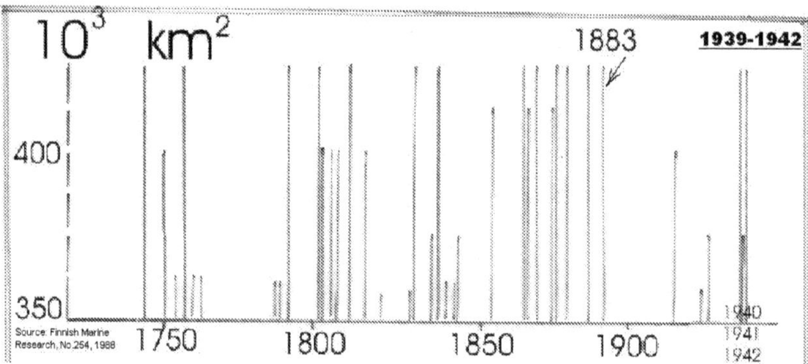

1939-42 could have been the most extensive in many hundred years. From the whole period of more than 200 years, only 15 winters reached the highest possible ice volume, including those of 1939/40 and 1941/42. One of the reasons for this rarity of successive high ice coverage is presumably the fact that, from the moment the Baltic Sea reaches a high ice cover, the water body no longer transfers heat to the atmosphere; the deeper waters retaining, the more heat for the following winter season. But due to the intensive 'stirring and mixing' of the sea by military activities, a record ice coverage had been achieved in the Baltic Sea during the three war years 1939-42, which actually was inevitable. There is virtually no other explanation available.

---

27 Finnish Institute of Marine Research; M. Leppäranta et al.; "Phases of the ice season in the Baltic Sea' No. 254, Suppl.2; Helsinki 1988

Centres of record winters

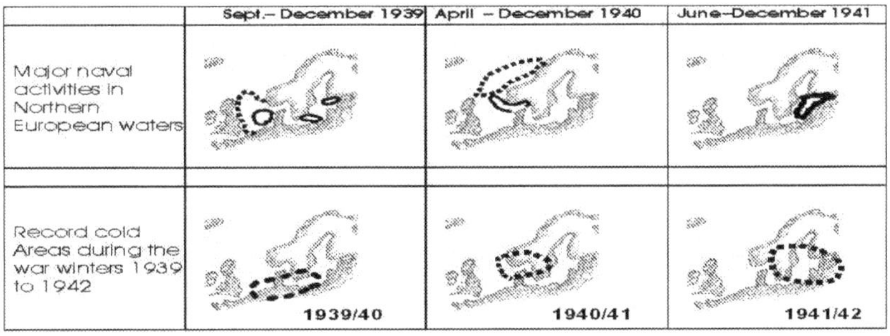

	Sept.– December 1939	April – December 1940	June–December 1941
Major naval activities in Northern European waters			
Record cold Areas during the war winters 1939 to 1942	1939/40	1940/41	1941/42

It is interesting to observe that certain regions reported record climatic events, on one hand, while, on the other hand, they saw intensive military activities 'close by'.

1939/40: Germany reported a record cold winter. In fact, heavy mining, fighting (e.g. Gdansk), military surveillance, transport and exercises took place in the coastal waters of the Baltic Sea, during pre-winter months.

1940/41: Norway claimed to have recorded low temperatures as never measured before at a number of stations in southern Norway immediately after the Germans invaded Norway in the summer, and mine warfare and fighting continued along its coast and heavy ship movements took place between Germany and Norway thereafter.

1941/42: Middle Sweden[28], Denmark[29] and The Netherlands[30] claimed the coldest winter in more than 130 years; after the German invasion of Russia, codenamed 'Barbarossa' brought heavy fighting to the Baltic countries, from June to December. All mentioned locations claimed the third winter of 1941/42 as the coldest, leaving to the first war winter 1939/40 'only' a second place, during a time period of 100 years and more.

28 Gösta Liljequist, see: Fn.17

29 Det Danske Metorologiske Institut; 'Is- og besejlingsforholdene i de danske Farvande in Vinteren 1939-40; 1940-41; 1941-42; 1947, Kobenhavn.

30 At De Bilt (data series 1706-1993) January and February 1942 had been -7,9°C colder than 1941, and -2,4°C colder than 1940. The long-term average is well above zero (about +5°C)

The centre of the cold was 'in the middle of the Baltic and North Sea, somewhere between Hamburg and Skagen/Denmark.

Summary

If we look for the reasons of the sudden arrival of arctic winters in the same time with the naval war in North-European waters, chosen and applied statistic prove convincingly that war at sea prepared the 'ground' for dragging arctic air into Europe, to Atlantic shores.

This investigation observed latter conditions with care because there is no change without a cause. The three arctic war winters 1939-1942 are no exception. At a global level, the law of physics binds people, air and sea. Any hot soup stirred lets steam off and cools down. Any warm lake, sea or ocean, which is churned and stirred during winter season, lets off steam and the summer-warm sea surface layer cools down quickly.

The mechanism is simple and the result, obvious. One can only wonder why science pays no interest to this matter and remains silent on the issue of the WWII winter. Only four months after WWII commenced, North Europe's winter was back to icy conditions last experienced during the 'Cold Epoch', more than 100 years ago. Two extreme winters followed during the naval warfare, which was fought in the North European, waters and in other waters adjacent to them. Nothing is completely explained yet. Conducting a war is devastating but not chaotic to such a huge extent. Three cold winters were the logical consequence of war at sea in sensitive waters. Ending a series of three arctic winters (1939-1942) was only "natural" after Japan had dragged the United States into war, on the 7th of December 1941, and naval warfare went global on an unprecedented scale. A temporary regional cooling impact became a worldwide phenomenon for four decades.

- D - Climatic Impacts of World War I

Introduction

From a climatic point of view, World War I ended with a severe "bang" in late 1918. After four war years, a dramatic shift occurred in the northern part of the Norwegian Sea, at Spitsbergen, and lasted for two decades, until World War II started. Throughout the 20th century there had never been any climatic event as dramatic as this very pronounced one. At Spitsbergen, winter temperatures jumped up by 8°C in a few years. The Northern Hemisphere became suddenly much warmer. The terms "Greening of Greenland" and "Warming of Europe" became common expressions.

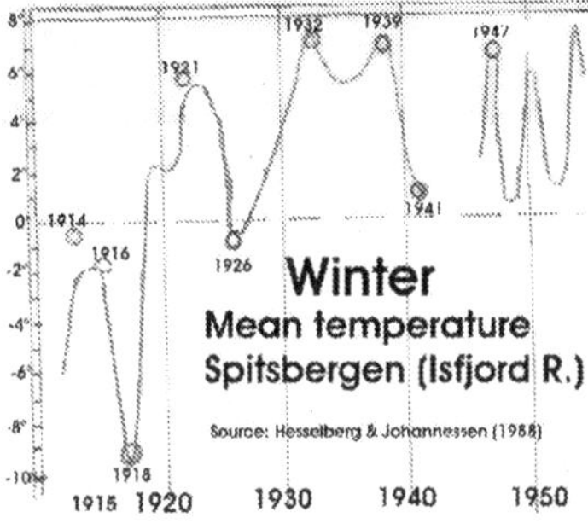

There is nothing clearer than the commencement of a "big warming" that occurred at exactly the same time with the end of WWI, in November 1918. This is not difficult to prove. What is more difficult to show is that naval war caused this event. On the other hand, it is easy to point out the fact that nothing else had happened at that time that could have caused such a dramatic climatic shift. There was no earthquake, no major volcanic eruption, no particularly intense sun spots, no unusual El Niño, and no meteorite fell from the sky. There had been only a devastating naval war, waged for four years at about 2000 kilometres further in the south, around the Isles of Great Britain. As the warming lasted for two decades, until the end of 1939, the warming was sustained and could have remained in place for so long only because of the interiors of the huge and deep Norwegian Sea, which permanently receives plenty of water masses that have passed the British Isles, either on its Atlantic side or coming from the North Sea.

While the chapter focuses on linking the naval war of WWI to the "big warming" since 1918, the following two sections will demonstrate that general weather conditions during WWI already showed similarities to WWII conditions as long as naval war did not went global since 1942.

During WWI, naval war never went global but was fought around Britain, actually starting seriously only in the autumn of 1916 when new naval weaponry became fully available and devastatingly effective, particularly sub-marines (U-boats), depth charges, and sea mines. During the war year 1917, the German U-boats alone sank 6,200,000 tons. The total loss during the war was of 12 million tons, with 5200 ships, plus about 650 naval vessels. Most merchant vessels had been fully loaded with cargoes of all kind, from grain, ore, coal, crude oil, to whatever war parties needed. All that stuff polluted the sea and was taken along with the Gulf Current or the Norwegian Current up to the North, passing Shetland Islands and going either to the Barents Sea or, most of them, to the Arctic Sea, after passing Spitsbergen at the latitude of 79° North.

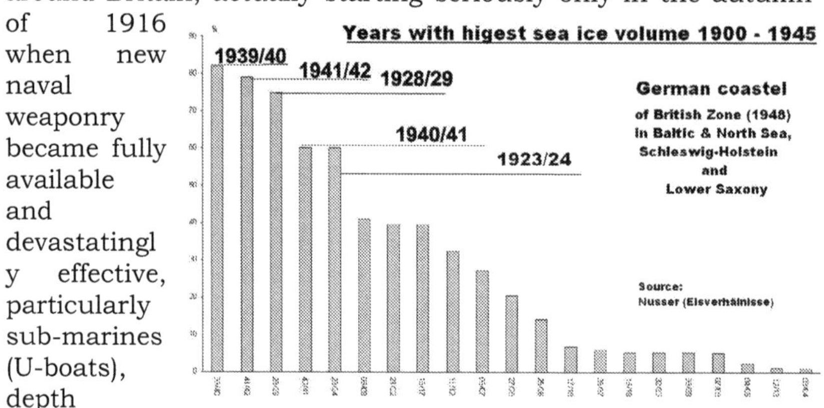

Sinking ships was not all that happened at sea. The sea was churned and turned "up side down" in many ways. For establishing a link between naval war in Europe and the sudden 'big warming' at Spitsbergen more explanations are needed. Before giving more details in this respect, the reader should become aware that both European wars around the United Kingdom, during the last century, had similar weather impacts. After a weather comparison between WWI and WWII, the section will outline the naval forces unlashed during the last two war years, from the autumn of 1916 to 1918, before concentrating on the 'big warming' at Spitsbergen and its WWI causes. It is frankly admitted that this investigation cannot fully prove the latter claim, however there is no better explanation available, yet. Actually, little efforts have been made to investigate the causation of the event anyhow.

Weather Comparison WWI and WWII

Some important factors need to be mentioned first. The land war started immediately in 1914, the naval war commenced fully since the autumn of 1916. On land, there was already the famous icy winter battle in Masuria (north-eastern Poland), in February 1915, between the German Army and the Russian Tenth Army, which determined the German Field Marshall Hindenburg to wonder: "Have earthy beings really done this things or is all but a fable or a phantom?" (citation from NYT, the 7th of January 1942)

If rainmaking along the Maginot Line/Westwall, in autumn 1939, is the comparison element, then the devastating battle of Verdun is much more significant. The German attack on Verdun started on the 21st of February 1916, with one million troops; the battle became the longest of WWI and ended on the 18th of December 1916. French and German Army lost several hundred thousand men each. From a climatic perspective, it is to note that close battle field regions had been wetter than usually, e.g. Baden had 30% more precipitation, in the Black Forest rain level was even 50-80% higher than normal.

The battle of Verdun followed one of the top ranking cold winters during last century. The winter 1916/17 matched closely the record winter 1939/40. To keep in mind! The naval war started its devastating war phase only in the autumn of 1916. Submarines only went into action in 1915, sinking about 100,000 ship tonnages per month, which accelerated to about 300,000 tons per month in the second half of 1916. In addition, in 1916, a flotilla of more than 500 vessels was permanently navigating the seas around the British Isles, sweeping a daily average of 1.000 square miles. Together with the very increased use of sea mines, mine sweeping operations, and depth charges, the result was particularly significant on the weather all over Great Britain. The result can be read from weather records. In Britain, June 1916 was very cold and dull. Rain was persistent in the east and north, e.g. with about 150 hours of rain in Aberdeen and up to 200mm. The next extreme month was October 1916 which was wet and stormy, with record daily rainfall of 200mm. Up to this point, it was the highest daily rainfall ever recorded for the British Isles, and an extremely cold December 1916 followed.

With single events or statistical months, it is difficult to establish evidential circumstances. In addition, more factual data may provide the required proof. Great Britain surrounded by naval war may do it. For this purpose, we refer again to the time witness, A. J. Drummond from Kew Observatory at Richmond (London), who expressed his astonishment in 1943: “The present century has been marked by such a wide-spread tendency towards mild winters that the “old-fashioned winters”, of which one has heard so much, seemed to have disappeared for ever. The sudden arrival at the end of 1939 of what was considered to be the beginning of a series of cold winters was therefore all the more surprising.” He continued: “Since comparable records began in 1871, the only three successive winters as snowy as the recent ones (1939/40 to 1941/42) were those during the last war, namely 1915/16, 1916/17, 1917/18.[1]

Not to miss what naval war may have done on snow conditions in Great Britain, the comparable situation of the war years 1915-1918 shall be explained with the war winters 1939-1942, which were investigated by Lilian F. Lewis[2] who concluded that snow coverage in the British Isles during January and February over the three war winters 1940, 1941, and 1942 were unusual severe; the snow was considerable, and the number of days of snow-laying numerous and without precedent in the British Isles for at least 60 years. According to Drummond, during the first three WWII winters, snow fell on 23%, 48% and 23% of the days which was about 100% to 400% more snowfall than the average. The reasons for such a deviation are easy to explain: snow is likely to fall when humid air cools down. The more naval warfare has decreased sea water temperatures in the sea areas around Britain to below average level, the greater the chance of extensive snowfall due to lower air temperatures.

For the cooling down of the seas around Britain, it is also possible to find hard evidence. In 1935, J. K. Lumby published a seawater temperature series taken in the English Channel

---

1 Drummond, A.J.; ‚Cold winters at Kew Observatory, 1783-1942’; Quarterly Journal of Royal Met. Soc., No. 69, 1943, pp 17-32, and: Drummond, A.J.; Discussion of the paper: ‚Cold winters at Kew Observatory, 1783-1942’; Quarterly Journal of Royal Met. Soc., 1943, p. 147ff.

2 Lewis, Lilian, F.; ‘Snow-cover in the British Isles in January and February of the severe winters 1940, 1941 and 1942’, in: Quarterly Journal of Royal Met. Soc., 1943, pp. 215-219.

from 1903 until 1927[3]. From 1901 until 1914, the temperature varied on a narrow band, from 11.5°C to 12.2°C. During the war years 1914-1917, the temperature dropped to its lowest point of the series, viz. to 10.9° C. By all means that should not come as a surprise when realising what actually happened during World War One for many times:

> "In September 1916, the U-boat flotilla from Zeebrugge alone sank nearly 50,000 tons of shipping in the Channel, without any hindrance from patrol vessels. It was soon clear that the existing methods of combating submarines were simply not working. For example, in one week of September 1916, three U-boats operated in the Channel between Beachy Head and Eddystone Light, an area patrolled by forty-nine destroyers (49), forty-eight torpedo boats (48), seven Q-ships (7), and 468 armed auxiliaries - some 572 anti-submarine vessels in all, not counting the aircraft. Shipping in the Channel was held up or diverted. The U-boats were hunted. They sank thirty ships, and were entirely unscathed themselves." [4]

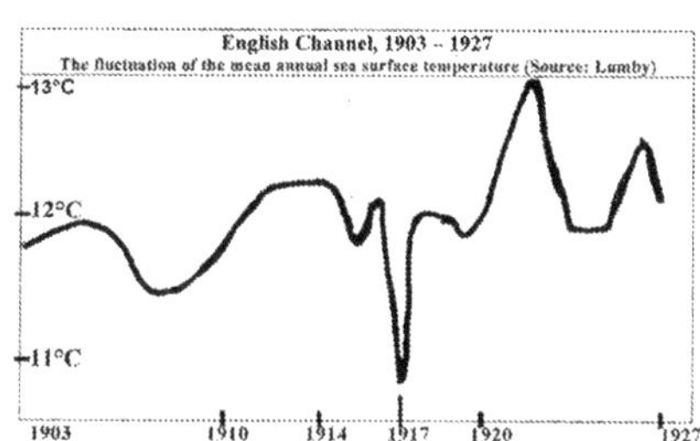

Another investigation of the situation in the Irish Sea over the period 1900 – 1950 made by D.C. Giles in 1949 also shows a deep decline from 1914 to 1919[5]. Sea chilling is inevitable when naval warfare occurs during autumn and wintertime, when thousands of ships movements churn the sea day and

---

3 Lumby, J.K.,; 'Seasonal changes of deep water temperatures'; Quarterly Journal Royal Meteorological Society, Vol.67, July 1941, pp.234-238.

4 Winton, John; 'Convoy – The defense of sea trade 1890-1990', London 1983.

5 Gilles, D.C.; 'The Temperature and Salinity of the Surface Waters of the Irish Sea for the Period 1935-46', in: Monthly Notices of the Royal Astronom. Society, Geophys. Suppl., Vol.5, Nr.9, London 1949, pp. 374-397.

night, when thousands of explosions under and above the sea surface turn sea levels up-side-down. Consequences are obvious: in autumn, the sea cools out quicker and colder air establishes subsequently, followed by more snow which leads to harsher wintertime, and so on. Sometimes, physical conclusions are very simple. The cooling down of Britain and the unusual temperature decline on the Isles, from 1915 until 1918, has its cause in naval warfare and in nothing else.

In conclusion, it can be said that weather anomalies in Britain during WWI and WWII have so many similarities that they can be taken as proof of the impact that war at sea had on weather conditions.

Spitsbergen 1918: warming jump by sea war south of it

The Jump

The most significant climatic event of World War One occurred at Spitsbergen, a remote archipelago between North Cape of Norway and the North Pole. There, winter temperatures suddenly exploded around the winter 1918/19, described by the eminent Norwegian scientist B.J. Birkeland in the year 1930 as being probably the greatest known statistical temperature deviation on earth[6].

The temperature jump which lasted until the war winter of 1939/40 has still not been scientifically explained. A sudden increase with plus 8°C in average winter temperature over a short period of time is an event which could have improved the understanding of the climate almost a century ago. Surprisingly, it might not be so difficult to find clues on causation as it looks in the first place. Timing,

"Big" Warming Spitsbergen

Winter temperature jump in winter 1918/19

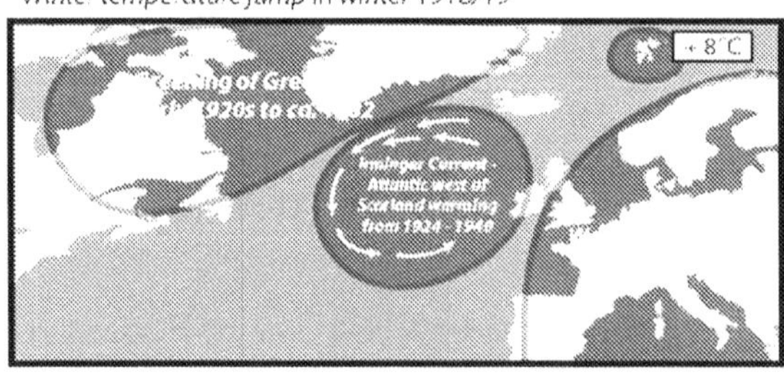

6 Birkeland, B.J.; 'Temperaturvariationen auf Spitzbergen', Meteorologische Zeitschrift, Juni 1930, p.234-236

duration and location may help us exclude or include options and possible causations.

Concerning timing, there was no other force on sight before the winter 1918/19 than a devastating land and naval war in Europe, while nature ran its course without any significant earthquake, volcano eruption, meteorite falling down from the sky, or unusual sunspots.

Concerning duration, it needs to be noted that it was a sustained and lasting event, for two decades in Europe and for one decade in Greenland. From 1920 until about 1930, these events were so pronounced that the terms "Greening of Greenland" and "Warming of Europe" took birth. The sustainability is strong proof that warming was generated in the Northern North Atlantic, north of the Faeroe Island and south of the Arctic Sea.

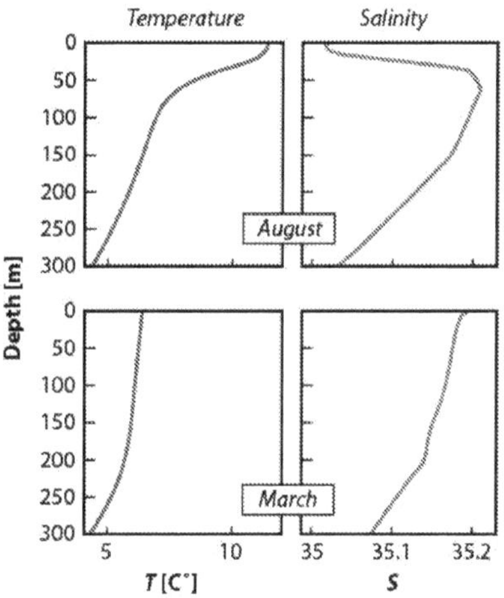

Concerning the location, the sustained warming lasting two decades holds also the clue concerning the direction from which the warmth must have arrived. One can quickly exclude all sea areas around Spitsbergen, except for the Norwegian Sea. The Barents Sea, east of Spitsbergen, contains within its average depth of 300 metres too little water masses to sustain a warming over many years, if not constantly supplied with warm water coming from the Norwegian Sea. The Arctic Sea, north of Spitsbergen, is too cold and widely covered with sea ice to have played any role. The Greenland Sea can be also definitely excluded as a source of warming at Spitsbergen, as the Greenland Sea receives a huge bulk of inflowing water masses from the Norwegian Sea, via the Gulf Current, the Norwegian Atlantic Current and the Spitsbergen Current, and not vice versa.

Actually, the warming can only have been generated in the Norwegian Sea, which means that, during WWI, the southern border of the warming source is immediately connected to the northern border of the naval war area. In addition, on the way to the Norwegian Sea, the most significant warm water supply coming from the North Atlantic Gulf Current was passing Great Britain where a devastating naval war had been waged for four long years. Viewing the distance between Spitsbergen and Scotland of about 2000 kilometres under such a perspective, we observe that sea water which had passed Scotland needed only few months to reach Spitsbergen. The warming in the north and the war at sea in Europe can almost be regarded as neighbours. One can thigh both events even more closely together if one considers certain typical seawater behaviour as well. A brief overview shall be given in the next section.

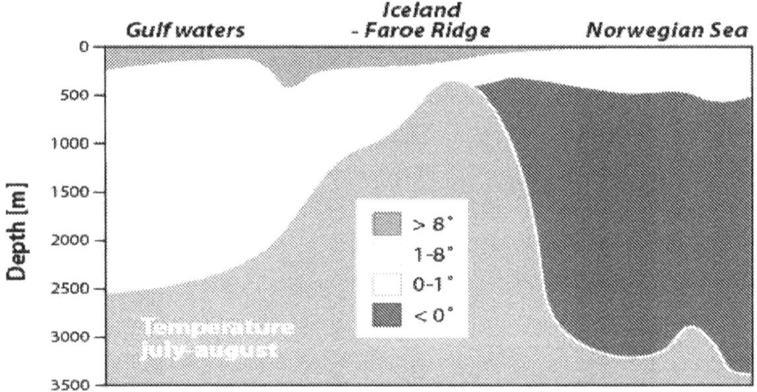

Seawater physics in Norwegian Sea.

In the Norwegian Sea the seawater behaves physically as it behaves everywhere around the globe. Nevertheless, the warm water from the Gulf Current, the high latitude with cold winters, the passing of many forceful low pressure cyclones, and the massive Norwegian mountain ridge with plenty sweet water runoff, as well its size and depth produce a unique wealth and variation of physical appliances.

Fortunately, the basic rules are simple: salty and cold water is heavy and sinks, sweet water and warm water are light and "swim" over more heavy water. Therefore, cold freshwater can form a layer above warm water current. Cold freshwater may stay and flow below of warm saline rich water. And it is much more at stake because water is an excellent isolator. For example, 'swimming' rainwater of several centimetres thick can be as good as a refrigerator shielding stored food from outside temperatures. Without the mixing of rain and melted water near the Norwegian coast, the Norwegian Sea would be frozen over frequently each winter regardless how much warm Gulf water would pass through the Norwegian Sea.

Therefore, there is a long way from registering all principal physical rules to assessing the thousands of possible variations that occur. Usually, the Norwegian Sea surface water, which determines the weather and climate for the whole Northern Hemisphere, is particularly influenced by three natural events: the warm Gulf current, the freshwater from land and rains, and, last but not least, the wind. In addition, after the replacement of sailing ships with machine driven vessels, a lot of surface water mixing took place every day. Particularly during the two World Wars, large sea areas and water masses have been turned upside down.

The significant feature of the Gulf Current water that enters the Norwegian Sea is the high temperature and salinity. As soon as water has been cooled down, it sinks like fruit syrup in a glass with water. Due to high salinity, it is warmer than the water it replaces at lower level. The more water sinks, the more water will follow from the Atlantic, with subsequently more "warming potential" in the area than before. The more water is cooled down by mixing, the more forcefully this water masses will start sinking.

In comparison with salty water, freshwater is very light. Fresh, rain, river, and melt water has the strong tendency to float on brackish and salty water until it gets much colder than the saline water below, or otherwise an external force must occur and determine the mixing phenomenon.

Wind in any form is the most powerful means for sea surface water mixing. Actually, it is practically the only external source nature has at hand to do the mixing. In so far, one cannot emphasise the importance of this mixing means enough. On the other hand, the mixing range the wind reaches is extremely limited and goes hardly further than the 50-meter sea surface layer. All other seawater mixing occur according to internal processes, based on temperature, salinity, and density.

And what does naval war do? Naval war certainly does a lot of water mixing. Particularly during winter time, in any sea area north of the Biscay, it not only forces a rapid mixing between freshwater and more saline water, but also forces cooled down sea surface water to greater depth in exchange of warmer water, until the summer warmed water in shallow enclosed seas is exhausted and arctic air can easily take reign. This has already been explained in great detail in Chapter B. In the next section, we will focus on the sea situation between Britain and Spitsbergen during WWI, whereon the impact on the Norwegian Sea will be discussed to conclude the chapter about the warming of Europe between 1918 and 1939 by severe warming of Spitsbergen due to naval warfare.

Seas under naval stress

Naval warfare 1914-1916

When WWI started, in August 1914, the German Navy had 28 U-boats. Their capacity was limited. By February next year, they had lost 7 U-boats, but had only sunk 10 vessels with a total tonnage of 20,000. This figure accounted for only 10% of all British losses during the first six months of war. Mines sank double as much over the same period, of the about 40 millions ship tonnage available to the Allies. From August 1914 until December 1916, the U-boats sank 2,200,000 tons. This represented the total number of 1,500 Allies' vessels or about three vessels per day. On the other hand, the loss of U-boats also increased, mainly due to a newly developed depth charge with 300 pounds TNT or amatol (in 1915), which became available and fully operable since 1916.

Naval Warfare 1917-1918

The situation became dramatic for Britain in early 1917. U-boats sank more ships than shipyards could deliver. In April 1917, the annual rate of the previous years was reached, with almost 860,000 tons. In 1917, U-boats alone sank 6,200,000 tons. This amounted to more than 3,000 ships.

The total loss of the Allies' shipping was of ca. 12 million tons: about 5,500 merchant ships, 10 battle ships, 18 cruisers, 20 destroyers, and 9 submarines. The total loss in naval units of the Allies and the Axis was of 650 ships (including 205 U-boats) with a tonnage of 1,200,000 tons.

Depth Charges – What it meant to attack a U-boat?

The onslaught by U-boats reached the pinnacle with almost one million tons sunk per month, like in April 1917. Although the British Navy was able to prevent hundreds of attacks, real or suspected, the result was not encouraging. Only a mere 11 U-boats were sunk in four months. New protection measures such as convoying, patrols and a new most promising weapon, depth charges, etc. were regarded as necessary.

While U-boats hunted and torpedoed enemy merchant and naval vessels during the early days of WWI, the scenario changed after 1916. They became the hunted ones and were depth-charged. Thousands of naval vessels steamed the seas around Britain day and night. In May 1918, the experience of the U-boat U-72 may illustrate the situation at sea. In early May, some 75 depth-charges were dropped on the boat by anti-submarine vessels and from an airship. Later, a destroyer arrived and attacked U-72 with another 20 charges. This caused a leak in a fuel tank leaving a trail of oil at the sea surface. 24 hours later, U-72 was again depth-charged, more than 20 times, by two naval vessels. A British submarine sank U-72 a few days later.

Sea Mines

Main minefields in the North Sea were on Britain's East Coast, including the Strait of Dover, Helgoland Bight and the Northern Barrage. A rough figure for each of these areas is of 50,000 mines. The total number of mines in the North Sea was of 190,000 and the total number during the whole WWI was of 235,000 sea mines.

Minesweeping is an activity that stirs and shakes the sea on an unprecedented scale. The 'stir impact' on the seas could possibly be even many times higher than the mine laying and the impact of mines that 'hit a target' together. Between two sweepers in motion 'hung' a sweep wire, with a kite, to cut the mooring rope of the mines. Britain alone had more than 700 minesweepers in permanent operation and Germans also had a considerable number. Possibly 500 ships swept the North Sea day and night.

Operating in a sensible area – Around the Shetlands

Another example: U-boats were a problem for the British. For this reason, between the 15th and 25th June 1917, four flotilla leaders, with about 50 destroyers and seventeen submarines, were sent to an area stretching from NW of Stornoway, round to the north of the Shetlands and eastwards into the North Sea. The idea was to force the U-boats to the surface and to attack them. On sixty-one occasions, U-boats were sighted and attacked twelve times. In practice that must have meant that, in addition to the shelling operation of 75 naval vessels, many hundred depth charges had been dropped. No U-boat was sunk. This episode demonstrates that huge operations may have taken place in the sea, operations which did not go by without any impact on the sea area. However, these were not accounted for in relation to climate change.

Barents Sea and Baltic Sea

The matter is worth a detailed chapter but requires more pages. Although these seas were not the central stage of the operations, they saw immense naval activities and destruction. The intense encounters in the Barents Sea could have played an important role in the strong icing from the high North, in February 1915, and the harsh winter in North-Western Europe, 1916/17. Until early 1915, more than 450,000 tons of coal and 90,000 tons of weaponry had been shipped to the Russian port Archangel. Russian and German navies had laid thousand of sea mines and dozen of minesweepers were permanently in service. U-boats sank 25 ships, in late 1916, and 21 vessels from April until November 1917.

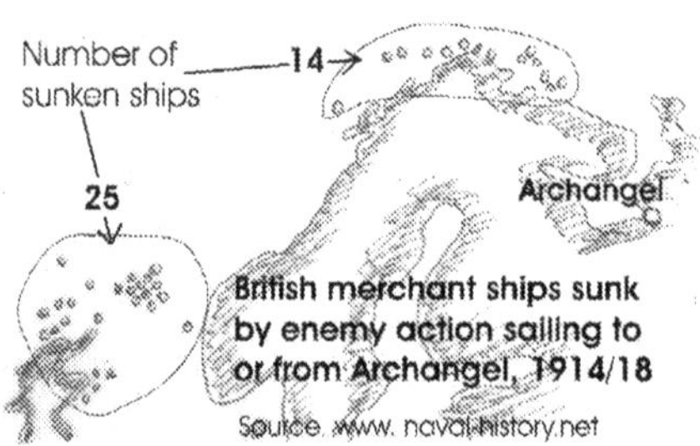

In the Eastern Baltic Sea, many dozen mine fields were laid with some ten thousand mines. Many naval activities took place every day over four years. British and Russian submarines operated successfully. The increasing sea icing during the war years, from 1914 until 1918, can be attributed to naval warfare in Baltic waters.

Northern Mine Barrage

U-boats had been a serious threat to the Allies since 1916. They regarded it paramount to prevent U-boats from leaving the North Sea and enter the Atlantic. To 'close' the northern outlet of the North Sea, a long barrage of about 150 sea miles (ca. 275 km), between the Orkney Islands and Norway, was required. Near the Norwegian coast, the water is 300 metres deep and near the coast of Orkney, of about 100 metres. Sea currents can reach 3-4 nautical miles/hour. That was a challenge and required the development of a new mine, the MK6. The charge consisted of 300 pounds of grade B trinitrotoluol (TNT). The mine itself was supposed to have a destructive radius of 100 feet (ca. 30m) against submarines. Calculations showed that approximately 100,000 mines should effectively prevent U-boats from passing the line. Actually, only about 70,000 mines were laid until October 1918. On the other hand, 20,000 mines were disposed during the laying of the 'Northern Barrage'.

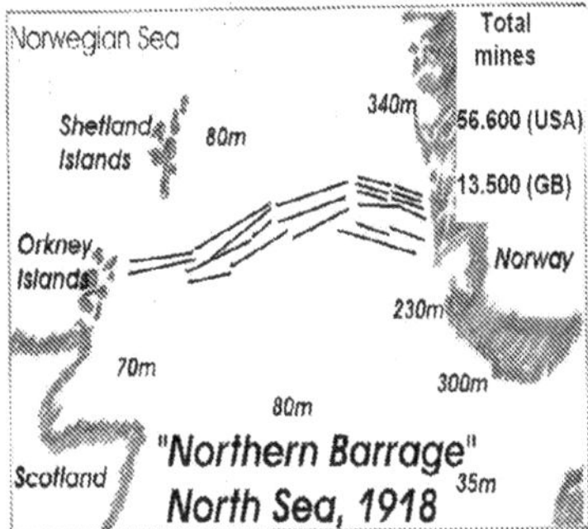

Mines were available by March 1918. Shortly after the mine lay had commenced, mines began to explode. As a report for the USA Government noted, between 3 and 4% of 3,385 laid mines blew up prematurely. In the middle section "A", mines were supposed to be laid as it follows: 10 rows of mines at 80 feet submergence, 4 rows of mines at 160 feet submergence, and 4 rows of mines at 240 feet submergence. The laying of mines ceased when the armistice from November 1918 was in sight.

Mine sweeping started in the spring and ended in the autumn of 1919. From more than 73.000 mines

- about 15% exploded prematurely soon after laying;
- about 15% were disposed;
- from the remaining ca. 50,000 mines
    - more than 30,000 mines were already 'gone' in the spring of 1919, either drifted away or exploded during winter storms;

- 20,000 mines were swept in 1919.

Six months of sweeping operations comprised seven sweeping missions involving more than 70 vessels and 10 supply vessels.

Waiting for an answer to sever warming 1918-1939

Let's face the facts. World War One was the most destructive global event for many years, since the volcanic Krakatoa, three decades ago. Much of the North Atlantic water bound for Arctic regions was part of the naval battleground for four war years before moving northwards towards Spitsbergen. Since 1918, the Arctic warmed twice as fast until 1938 as it had since 1980. From slightly above the Arctic Circle to the pole, the warmest years on record in the Arctic were the years of 1937 and 1938. War winter 1939/40 ended the Warming of Europe. The most convincing conclusion is: WWI must have played a significant role in the warming of the climate since 1918, but how?

We started the chapter on Spitsbergen warming in 1918 by pointing to the fact that two-decades sustained warming could only come from the Norwegian Sea and/or from the northern arm of the Atlantic Gulf current.

The Norwegian Sea basis is a three thousand meter deep hole. The heat reservoir is enormous, enough to keep the Northern Hemisphere ice-free during Nordic winters and to sustain regularly storms and winds. But not only the mass matters, what matters even more is a very delicate balance of water temperatures and salinity at numerous water depth. It may be hundreds or thousands which counts.

In addition, the warm water inflow from the south cannot be ignored. The inflow west of Scotland is the most significant and about 6-7° C warmer than water which travels north, crossing the Iceland-Faroe Ridge. The inflow to Norwegian Sea is roughly eight times the total outflow of all the world rivers or eight million tones per second, while the forwarded energy in terms of heat transport corresponds to an energy output of 100,000 major electricity power plants. In comparison to the 8x106 m3/sec warm water from the Gulf Current, the water transport in the Norwegian Coastal current at the southwest coast is of about 1 million cubic meter per second (1x106 m3/sec), increasing northwards with a speed between 30 and 100 cm/sec or 1 to 4 km per/h. The water needs merely 3 to 8 weeks to reach Spitsbergen. That is all big stuff and a nearby war at sea cannot necessarily compete with such dimensions, might quickly cross one's mind. But nature is not black and white and physics offers thousands of variations. In the same way as a very thin and undisturbed freshwater layer over huge sea areas during winter time would isolate almost completely the sea water body from the atmosphere, hundreds of other activities can change the structure of sea water layers. That must have happened in 1918, and it was a very severe phenomenon, indeed. Two decades of warming do not come from nowhere. Scientists who speak about climatic changes as a matter of expertise have to answer this question.

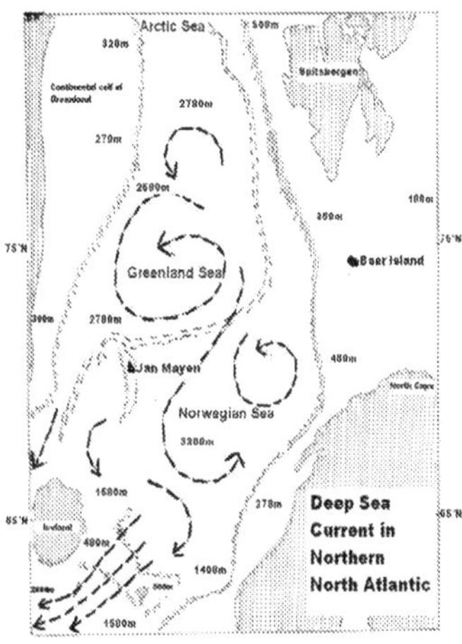

Giving reasonable explanation for the warming of Spitsbergen in 1918 might not be as difficult as it seems at the first glance. One explanation could be based on the fact that naval war around Britain and in the North Sea cooled the water down from September to March, thus affecting about up to 20% of all water that formed the Norwegian Currents, whereby the water from the North Sea had significant lower salinity as compared to the high saline water of the Atlantic. This colder water would go down faster than usually, forcing saltier water (from the inner Norwegian Basin) to the surface. Significant parts of the system were forced into higher motion, and, at the north of Spitsbergen, colder and saltier water flowed quicker into the Artic Basin, which, at its turn, allowed more water to flow into the Norwegian Sea via the Scotland, Faroe, and Iceland ridges. The "experiment" ended with a larger amount of warm water at north of Scotland, after the end of WWI.

There might be other more convincing explanation and we are always interested in any good reasoning. But what we find difficult to accept is that the severe and long-lasting warming of Spitsbergen, which took place almost one hundred years ago, has not been explained yet. After all, almost one century has passed since this sudden and severe warming started, lasting for two decades.

- E - Global cooling since WWII

Introduction

Preamble

These days we talk about warming caused by greenhouse gases released due to human activities. Actually no serious person has any doubt that temperatures are noticeably higher than hundreds of years ago. Thus the matter should not be neglected. We should not neglect either the point on how climate change became a matter of concern 30 years ago. In January 1972, a working conference of top European and American investigators was convened at Brown University to discuss "The Present Interglacial, How and when will it End?"[1] Soon fashionable panic was about global cooling. In 1974, Fortune magazine warned that the temperatures had already

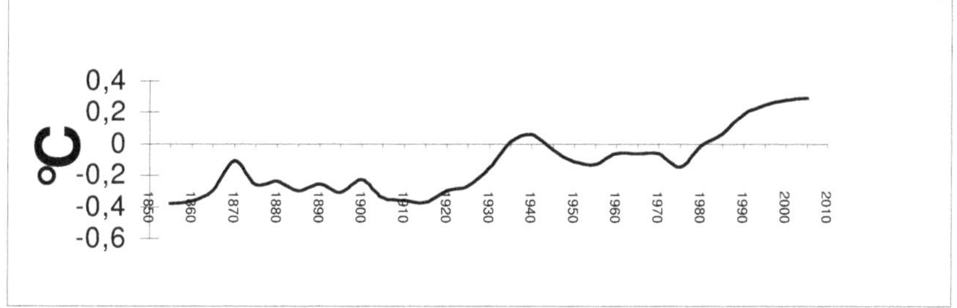

dropped with about 2.7° F (ca. 1,5°C) since the 1940s. Newsweek magazine published the article "The Cooling World"[2] from which the following remarks are taken:

> *"There are ominous signs that the Earth's weather patterns have begun to change dramatically and that these changes may portend a drastic decline in food production – with serious political implications for just about every nation on Earth.*
>
> *A survey completed last year by Dr. Murray Mitchell of the National Oceanic and Atmospheric Administration reveals a drop of half a degree in average ground temperatures in the Northern Hemisphere, between 1945 and 1968.*

1 Robert W. Reeves, Daphne Gemmill, Robert E. Livezey, and James Laver (NOAA), Global Cooling and the Cold War - And a Chilly Beginning for the United States' Climate Analysis Center? Year:?, (as PDF on www)

2 Newsweek magazine, April 28, 1974

Just what causes the onset of major and minor ice ages remains a mystery.

Climatologists are pessimistic that political leaders will take any positive action to compensate for the climatic change, or even to allay its effects. The longer the planners delay, the more difficult will they find it to cope with climatic change once the results become grim reality."

Recent scientific conclusions still remain unclear? Many articles caused panic at that time. The New York Times[3] reported that science saw many signs that Earth may be heading for another ice age, while Science magazine[4] published findings that Northern Hemisphere might face extensive glaciations, and regarded a return of Ice Age as very possible. TIME magazine claimed[5] that climatological cassandras are becoming increasingly scared about their cooling trend findings, which may be the signal of another ice age.

It is interesting that neither then nor since the 1970s, global cooling that started in 1940 was ever linked to naval warfare during World War II. It is even more interesting that neither IPCC nor other groups pressing the global warming issue ever showed interest in analysing the fact of pronounced global cooling during the last century in the first place.

Global cooling during last century

Having gone through three chilling war winters in Europe (1939-1942), world community was ready to go into an even much bigger climate change experiment. With Japan's ambush at Pearl Harbor by dozen of ships and hundreds of bomber air planes, on the 7th of December 1941, a new chapter of anthropogenic climate change started and lasted about four to five years until most of the sea mine fields had been eliminated in 1946/47. Mission was soon accomplished. Climate shifted very pronouncedly into a colder status, for four decades.

By conducting a naval war at a global scale and by turning and churning huge sea areas of Atlantic, Pacific and Indian Ocean, the inevitable happened. Oceans and seas turned a strong warming period since World War I in a modest but nevertheless

3 The New York Times, August 14, 1975

4 Science magazine, March 1, 1975,; and December 10, 1976.

5 Time magazine, June 24, 1974 "

very significant colder period that lasted for almost half a century. Mankind had changed climate after World War I a second time[6]. Actually the experiment had started precisely on the 1st of September 1939. Hitler's war machinery put so much stress on Northern Europe' seas and environment that within four months the area was catapulted back in the Little Ice Age, and experienced the coldest winter for over 100 years. North and Baltic Sea were deprived of their usual winter capacity during three war winters in a row, from 1939–1942. Consequences have been described in detail in previous chapters. However, during the third arctic war winter (1941/42) in Europe, naval war was turned into a global matter.

Any correct answer to the question 'what turned climate in a several decades long cooling phase' would have huge political consequences. Carbon dioxide, which IPCC regards as the major contributor for 'global warming', can definitely be excluded as initiator and sustainers of global cooling from about 1940 until 1980. Who did it then? No one ever observed that, at the end of the third decade (1930s) or at the beginning of the fourth decade, nature did nothing exceptional, for example, earthquake, tsunami, meteorite, exceptional sunspots, etc. Actually, there was nothing of such kind; nature resumed its normal course. Industrial plants and combustion machines released abundantly smoke, soot, sulphate, carbon dioxide and other greenhouse gases into the atmosphere, but instead of getting warmer, the world cooled down. It can be concluded with high confidence that none of the mentioned climatically 'external' forces caused the shift toward colling.

If external matters did not determine the cooling, only internal matters could have done it. If one defines climate as the continuation of the oceans by other means (vapour instead of water), oceans and seas are definitely the only source that could and have made climate changing into a cooling down period of four decades. Once questions are settled in, only two options remain to discuss:

- Oceans and seas run their "business" according to their physical conditions, without being seriously affected or influenced by external or global physical events, or by any impact of a several years long naval war.

6 Climate shift due to naval war during WWI is discussed in previous chapter.

- Naval war changed the structure and composition of seas and oceans in a way that made global climate cool down for several decades.

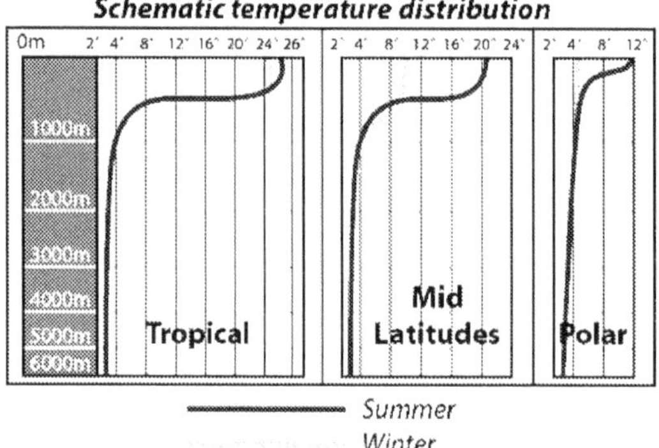

This investigation offers as most likely causation for the significant down turn of temperatures from 1940 until 1980 the war at sea aspect. There are good reasons to point at naval warfare. Previous sections established convincingly that naval warfare in North Sea, Baltic Sea and Eastern North Atlantic generated three extreme war winters in North Europe, establishing evidently a direct connection between war and weather modification. If regional naval warfare can change regional climate, global naval warfare can change global climate. However, demonstrating the latter case is not as easy as it was possible in the former case.

What makes our discussions on global climate changes due to naval warfare even more difficult is the fact that isolating global matters to only the winter season is not an option. The physical features of ocean space and regional seas in question are too different. The same happens in the case of a geographical location, volume of water masses, and any seasonal distinction. What actually did happen to ocean space according time, location, and amount of explosives and naval ship movements is known too few people. How did it change the structure of the sea surface and affected the water body? But no aspect is so dominating as to offer an answer to the question: What forced the oceans to cool down the climate for almost half a century, just 65 years ago?

Approach of section

To establish a link between naval war during WWII and global climate change, the destructive forces unlashed between 1939 and 1945 will be presented in a concise manner. The aim is to demonstrate that, due to the complete lack of any natural event during the relevant time period, only war at sea remains a plausible explanation because it was a sufficient force to play in the league of major natural phenomena. A subsequent section will summarize some principle physical and geographical features of war areas in the Atlantic and Pacific for the better understanding of the highly presumable relation between ocean reactions and naval activities, with the aim of showing that there is no better answer than this one yet. After all, climate research should restrain from scaring anyone with global warming if not able to explain convincingly what made earth atmosphere cooler for four decades since WWII commenced.

In 1988, the eminent scientist Jean M. Grove wrote[7]: "Evidently it will be necessary to understand the climate of the deep oceans before a full understanding of changes in the atmosphere can be achieved". Naval war did many things across all ocean space and ocean depths.

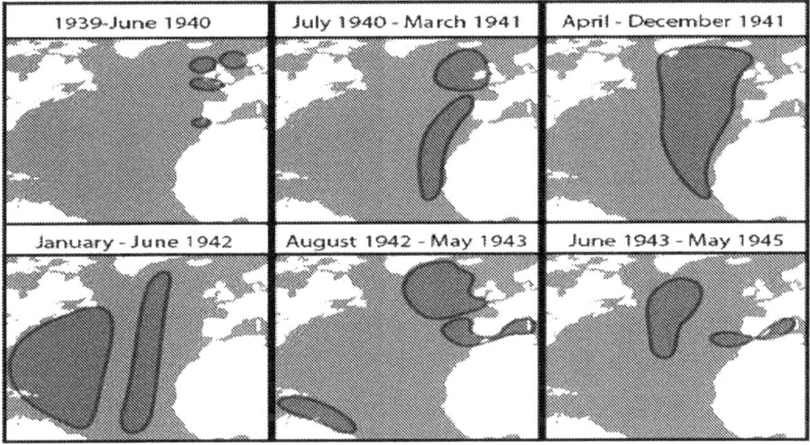

Even the collection of sea surface temperature measurements taken during World War II were severely affected by various reasons and should only be used with outmost reservation[8].

---

7 Jean M. Grove, The Little Ice Age, London/New York 1988, p.363

8 Bernaerts, Arnd; 'Reliability of sea-surface temperature data taken during war time in the Pacific', presented at Symposium on Resource Development, August 8-9, 1997, Hong Kong, in: PACON 97 Proceedings, pp. 240-250; (available on www.oceanclimate.de_ "Pacific SST").

Bernaerts, Arnd (Atlantic); „How useful are Atlantic sea-surface temperature measurements taken during World War II", paper submitted at the Oceanology International 1998 Conference, "The Global Ocean", 10-13 March 1998, Brighton/UK; published in Conference Proceedings Vol.1, pp 121-130. (available on www.oceanclimate.de_"Atlantic SST")..

World Oceans Churned and Turned

Water matters

Summarizing the dimension of a war in the seas will always remain incomplete. It must remain incomplete if not military aspect of enemy destruction is in focus but the temperature and salinity structure of sea water levels. Seas look always the same, before a ship arrives on scene, and after it has left scene, before a sea battle, and after a battle has just ended. Any sign or track left on the water's surface by ship movement, exploding sea mine or sinking ship disappears quickly. Only oil and cargo may disturb the picture of unadulterated nature for a short while. Any scenery of action is back to eternal expression very soon.

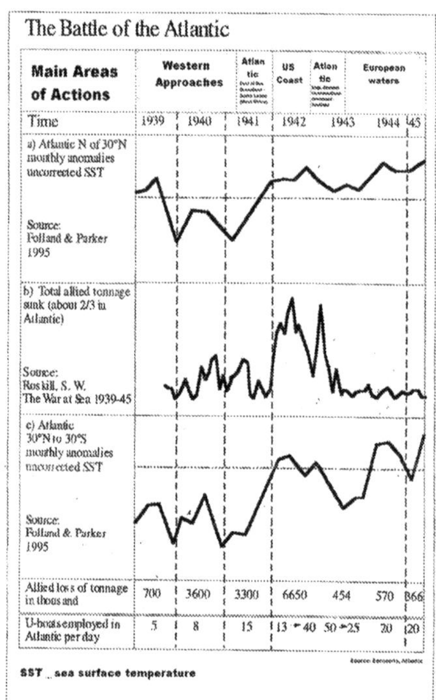

Physical structure of any ocean scene left after anthropogenic action has changed its structure in one way or the other. The physical composition of the sea bodies concerning temperature structure and salinity distribution has inevitably changed. They never turn back to their previous state but strive for a new equilibrium. Some call it a state of chaos, but it is plain physics. This physics, which run the oceans, make climate.

War at sea in the Atlantic, 1939-1941

Naval war and supply across the seas became part of the ocean physics for some time. Allies sailed 300,000 vessels across the North Atlantic. If every ship turned the sea about on a width of 20 meters, the total sums up 6 Million meters, or 6,000 km. This means that, over a corridor wide as from Glasgow to Lisbon, respectively Boston to Miami, the sea surface of North

Atlantic was ploughed through three times. Naval Escort Vessels and freely operating war ships certainly doubled the space of 'turnover'. Many thousands of torpedoes, many hundred thousands of depth charges and bombs, and multi-millions of shells certainly doubled again the already 'doubled space' of turnover the middle North Atlantic. The surface layer was completely 'churned and turned' presumably not less than a dozen times in just over six years. Any 'turning' effect could reach down to a few meters, five to ten meters (vessel draught), 200-300 meters (depth charge), thousands of meters (sinking ships, cargo, ammunition, etc).

As mid-latitude seasonal climatology heavily depends on the upper sea surface layer of about 30-60 meters, global naval war is a force to reckon.

Time period matters

The issue of climatic change during WWII has two distinct periods, viz. the period before Pearl Harbour and the one thereafter. From September 1939 until early 1942, naval warfare was largely confined to European waters. Great climatic relevance of the war at sea in the Northern Europe became dramatically clear during the extremely cold winters of 1939/40, 1940/41, and 1941/42.

Outside Europe's waters, naval activities during 1940 and 1941 were largely confined to Eastern North Atlantic. The most affected areas were the transportation routes from Britain to North America, and the routes from Britain to Gibraltar and Dakar.

U-boats in the Atlantic

A number of German U-boats were already in the Atlantic when the war started, in September 1939. Britain introduced rapidly the convoy system. A convoy consisted of up to sixty, either slow or fast vessels, accompanied by up to ten naval escort ships. The first convoy sailed in September. Also in September 1939, groups of three to five naval vessels were formed to control large areas in the North Atlantic. These groups criss-crossed the seas day and night, searching for U-boats and dropping depth charges when a U-boat was detected or assumed to be around. Also German surface naval vessels, like battleships *Deutschland, Scharnhorst* and *Gneisenau,* sailed in the Atlantic with a number of escort vessels. Until the end of December 1939, the Allies and Neutrals lost 55 vessels with a total tonnage of 300,000 in the Atlantic. Five U-boats were also sunk.

Fighting in the North Atlantic increased during the war years 1940 and 1941. In August 1940, Germans lifted all restrictions on U-boat targets. The number of available U-boats was of 50 (January 1940) and of 230 (December 1941), out of which about 8 were on permanent missions in the Atlantic during 1940, and 15 during 1941. The total loss inflicted on British, Allied and Neutral shipping in the Atlantic by the Axis powers (U-boats, air force, mine, and surface naval vessels) was of 3 million tons in 1940 and of 4 million tons in 1941. These figures relate about 1,500 ships, with cargo, stores and fuel. The Germans lost about 40 U-boats in the Atlantic during these two years.

Atlantic Convoy

To win the war, effective supply was essential. Thousands of accounts have been written about the dramatic events at sea. On the 21st/22nd of September 1940, Convoy HX72 was caught in a twelve-hour battle, in which eleven ships were sunk and two damaged, with a total loss of 100,000 tons of supplies and of 45,000 tons of fuel.

During the early times of the war, convoy escort was small in number and was not always staying with the group for the full travel distance. By 1941, the average size of a convoy was of about forty ships, with six naval vessels as escort. Later, some escorts became quite massive. For example, in 1942, the Convoy ON202 with 38 merchant ships had an escort of 3 destroyers and 3 corvettes; while the escort for the Convoy ONS18 comprised 6 destroyers, 8 corvettes, and one trawler.

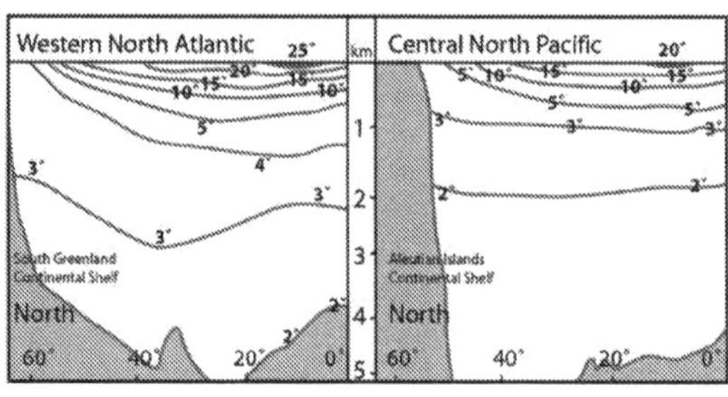

A special aspect concerns the loss of tankers from 1939 until 1941. British fleet lost 1,469 tank-ships and Norwegians, 430 in just 28 months. If one assumes that the average loading capacity of each ship was of 2,000 cargo tons and that half of the sunken vessels were laden, the total oil spill could sum up to two million tons in 2 years, an amount corresponding with the total of all major tank ship oils spills in 1967-2002.

However, U-boats were not acting alone in the North Atlantic. Since the Luftwaffe could operate out of France since the summer of 1940, long-range aircrafts were sent out into the Atlantic to attack supply routes. The total shipping tonnage sunken by Axis airplanes in all sea areas during the first two war years is claimed to be of 1.5 million tons.

War at sea in the Pacific: 1942 -1945

On the 8th of December 1941, The New York Times reported: Yesterday morning, Japan attacked the United States at several points in the Pacific, with a major attack on Pearl Harbour. President Roosevelt ordered United States forces into action and a declaration of war was expected soon. Seven hostile actions from a naval ship off the coasts of San Francisco to Malaysia were reported (NYT, the 8th of December 1941). This was to continue for four years. Allied forces, viz. USA, Britain and Holland, had a total strength of about 220 big naval vessels, including 70 submarines; Japanese had 230 naval vessels and 64 submarines in December 1941. Several aircraft carriers were available on both sides, able to deploy many thousands of airplanes. Recording four years of naval warfare in context with ocean water modification in the upper level of e.g. 1,000 metres depths is not achievable by a small study. It could only attempt to kindle readers' imagination as to what the war could have done to the ocean temperature and salinity structure. Oceanic matters have been discussed in the

Main Naval Activity Area 1942 - 1945

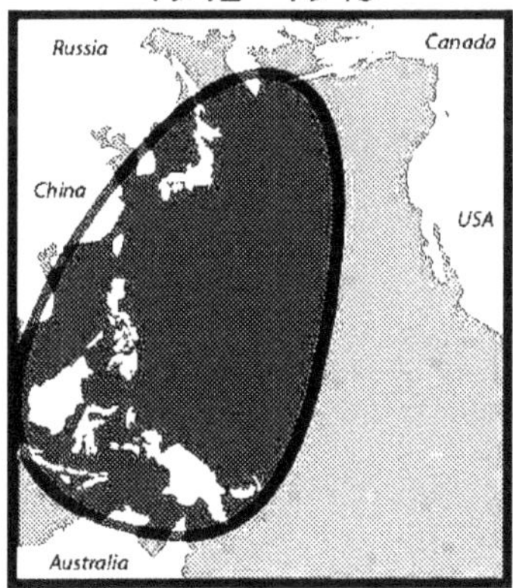

corresponding chapter: 'Ocean system affected', mentioning that the sea surface temperatures were low from 1945 until 1977[9].

The clash of the naval forces in the Pacific had no precedent. The fighting included all means and military options. Heavy battles were fought. In May 1942, the combatants had already met in the Coral Sea each with three-dozen ships and several hundred airplanes. On the 5th of May, in a first attack, the US Navy destroyed one Japanese destroyer, three minesweepers, and 4 smaller vessels, with 22 torpedoes and 76 bombs (each weighing 450 kg). Further attacks followed during the next days. On the 8th, each side lost about 35 aircrafts. A mighty explosion sank the aircraft carrier Lexington. The Battle of Midway saw even more naval vessels, more airplanes, and more destruction and losses, in June 1942. The Japanese alone deployed more than 200 big naval vessels under five separate commands. The USA and Japan lost a huge number of naval vessels (more than 120,000 tons) and 400 airplanes.

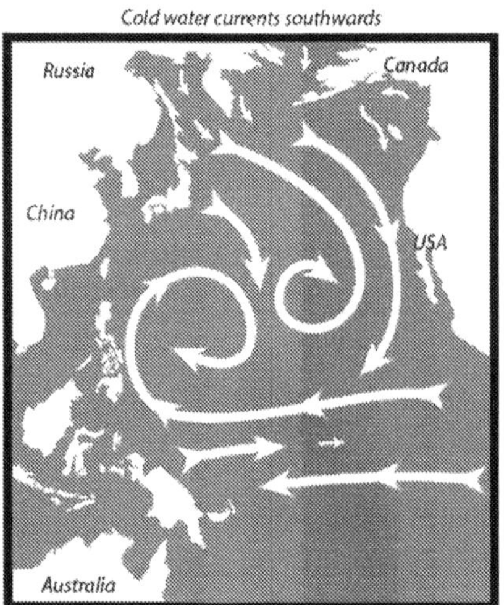

North Pacific surface currents

Aircrafts played a significant role in the Pacific war. Japan's front line strength was its air power consisting of about 4,000 planes; the USA had 4,000 in January 1941 and 22,000 in July 1945. After taking over Okinawa, the US Third fleet had deployed 26 aircrafts carriers, 64 escort carriers and 14,000 combat aircraft for a final attack on Japan. Japanese loss of combat aircraft was of 37,000 (army and navy); the USA lost 8,700 in the battle. Material loss in that battle was gigantic. Japan lost more than 500 warships (including 150 submarines), with a total tonnage of about 2,000,000, the figure in merchant tonnage was about 8,000,000 of which 5 Mio (1,150 ships)

9 Source: www.pmel.noaa.gov/

have been sunk by US-submarines and 1.5 Mio by airplanes. A special chapter could possibly be written on the sinking of tanker tonnage resulting in oil spills. During the war years Japan had some 700,000 tonnage permanently afloat and lost over the war period 1,500,000 tanker tonnage. The US lost 52 submarines. Many of them fell pray to depth charges. Standard Japanese depth charge contained about 230lb of explosives. Anti-submarine bombs carried by aircraft were 131lb and 550lb each, the latter being preferred when available. The Japanese had no means of determining the depth of a submarine to be targeted and so the pattern of attack usually was dropping of depth charges with a variety of settings on the time fuse. The Japanese lost 150 submarines, many of them to depth charges. It is necessary to consult special literatures available in great number and detail even to imagine what happened in the Pacific war theatre. One cannot help getting the impression that WWII left its imprint on Pacific seawater body.

War in the Atlantic: 1942 -1945

Aerial warfare over the Atlantic

The use of planes in the Atlantic war made tremendous headway since the USA entered the war after Pearl Harbour attack, in December 1941. The US production was estimated at 127,000 planes in 1942, exceeding the total number of German aircraft production during the whole war period. It meant that more aircraft with much better quality and capability were available for surveillance, bombing and combat missions in the Atlantic. In August 1942, only eighteen American B-24 aircraft, called 'Liberator', were available for Atlantic convoys. These planes had a range of 2,400 miles, fuel tanks of 2,500 gallons and reached heights of 30,000 feet. From winter 1942/43 onward, long-range aircrafts were assigned for anti-submarine warfare in the Atlantic. They sank 33 submarines between April 1943 and September 1944. 209 long-range bomber aircrafts were available for the US navy in July 1942. The number increased progressively up to 2,200 searching and chasing U-boats, between June 1943 and May 1944.

Vice-versa, U-boats got very little support from the Luftwaffe in 1942 and 1943 but even that little help diminished after D-Day (1944), while the Allies' air force presence in the Atlantic improved impressively. The British Coastal Command flew approximately 238,000 sorties, totalling 1,300,000 flying hours. Fourteen U-boats were confirmed to have been destroyed by Coastal Command and another twelve damaged.

German Luftwaffe had not been well equipped to put up a significant performance in the North Atlantic battle. However, they had in service a few hundred long-range four-engine planes, which flew from bases in France, in 1941. During the month of August 1941, they succeeded in sinking more than 300,000 tons of shipping, i.e. almost one-third more than the U-boats sank in the same month. Axis airplanes shall have sunk a total of about 800 merchant ships in all war theatres. Even if less than half of that number has been sunk in the sensitive waters of the Northern Atlantic and Northern Pacific, it actually meant the use of many thousands of bombs and the felling of hundreds of planes in the oceans as well.

U-boats off Florida and Cape Hatteras - 1942

There was a short period, from January until June 1942, when U-boats operated extremely successfully along America's East coast. Within half a year, they had sunk about 400 vessels. In two weeks, a handful of U-boats could sink 25 ships with a total tonnage of 200,000, of which 70% were tankers. In the summer of 1942, U-boat operation 'Paukenschlag' (Drumbeat) ended. The US Navy had become effective. The Gulf Current flows from Florida to Cape Hatteras, before turning at Cape Hatteras into the Atlantic to go eastwards, to Europe. The warm current on one hand and the colder Atlantic water off Cape Hatteras on the other built a highly sensitive water body which had a significant impact on daily weather, seasons and climatic conditions in the Northern Hemisphere. Waging a war at sea in these waters is presumably effective in producing changes to the seawater sphere.

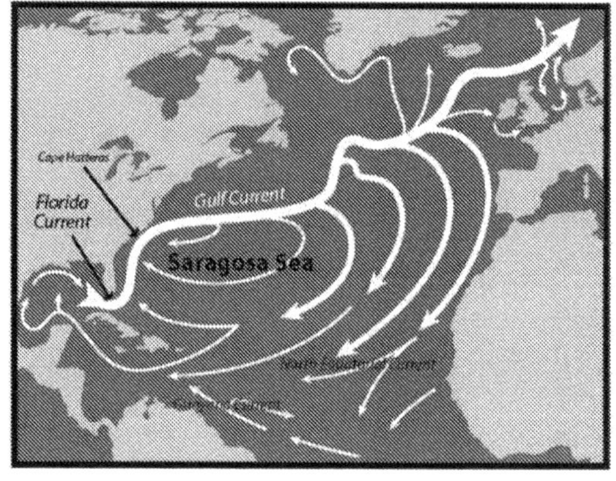

U-BOATS

In August 1942, the U-boat fleet had reached the number of 340, with almost 300 boats more than three years before. During the whole war period, the U-boat force had comprised about 1,100 boats, from which 850 participated in at least one combat mission and 630 were destroyed in enemy attacks.

Loss incurred by German U-boats attacks (all told) is of 2,822 vessels (14,220,000 tons). 152 Italian boats sank 132 vessels (700,000 tons). Axis U-boat fleet (German, Italian, Japan) is credited with the sinking of 25 big naval vessels, 41 destroyers and about 150 other naval vessels. The main field of operation of the U-boats was the Atlantic. They were quite successful only from 1942 until March 1943.

Atlantic Convoys

As already mentioned above, the Allies completed over 300,000 Atlantic voyages during this period of the war. The heroic story of merchantmen has been told and re-told in uncountable essays and books. Here is only one case.

In March 1943, two convoys, viz. SC122 and HX229, encountered forty-four U-boat attacks on their route. During the three-day battle that ensued, twenty-three merchantmen from the two convoys were killed. At the same time, convoy HX229A, which included thirteen tankers, eight refrigerators and four cargo liners (39 ships), was routed northeast, towards Greenland. There they came upon Arctic conditions. Three convoys with a total of 131 ships carried about 1,000,000 tons of cargo – petroleum fuel, frozen meat, food, tobacco, grain, timber, minerals, steel, gunpowder, detonators, bombs, shells, lorries, locomotives, invasion barges, aircraft and tanks.

Tanker

The destiny of many tankers proved extremely disastrous for their crew and presumably for the ocean area, too. The Allied and Neutral countries had about 1,000 tankers in their permanent service since 1942. Between December 1941 and May 1944, the loss of tankers with a size over 1,600 tons was of 4,221 ships.

Report 1 (extract):
October 1941: "Attacking from inside the convoy between the seventh and the eighth column, U-432 torpedoed the Norwegian tanker *Barfonn*. U-558 destroyed British *W.C.Teagle* and Norwegian *Erviken*, both laden with aviation spirit. Tankers could merit the description of 'floating volcanoes'.

Report 2 (extract):
The 15th of November 1942: "Shortly after 3.00 a.m. all hell was let loose. The Avenger was hit by two torpedoes and, being little more than a large floating petrol can, it blew up instantly in a sheet of flame... An enormous bright red glowed on the near horizon where Avenger blew up".

Ammunition ships

Report 3 (extract):
1942: To the southwest of Ireland, the convoy SC107 lost fifteen merchantmen from its forty-two vessels, during the last week of November. The attack came from a pack of sixteen U-boats. After sinking two vessels and the *Empire Linx*, U-132 was on target for being bombed by a Liberator of 120 Squadron. Then, from beneath the water came a tremendous explosion: *Empire Linx*, an ammunition ship, blew up. It is assumed that U-132 was within lethal range and thus became a victim of its own victory.

Report 4 (extract):
1941: Sugar carrier *Silvercedar* had been loaded in New York with high explosives in the holds and bombers on deck. Amidst the wind gale of 8-9 Beaufort, a torpedo struck her in hold No.3 which was loaded with condensed milk. *Silvercedar* blew up with a mighty explosion and sank in less than two minutes.

Depth Charges

One of the most effective means of penetrating deep below the sea surface is the depth charge. Depth charges, which could explode at a depth of 500 feet, were in use since 1942. The 'Hedgehog bomb', a highly powered explosive fired by a multi-barrelled mortar and filled with Torpex, was also in use. Its range was of 250 yards ahead of the escort vessel. Attacking ships, it could fire twenty-six depth charges in pairs, set to explode at 500 feet and 740 feet alternately, at intervals of ten-second, whilst continuing to steam ahead of the U-boat.

Report 5 (extract):
1941: U-94 came upon the convoy and sank two ships, then suffered damage from the depth charge counterattack of *Amazon, Bulldog* and *Rochester.* The battle lasted four hours. Attacker account said eighty-one depth charges were used, but the U-boat commander acknowledged only sixty-seven.

Report 6 (extract):
March 1944: On the 29th of February, frigates *Gore, Garlies, Affleck* and *Gould* attacked U-358 with depth charges and Hedgehogs. They held contact virtually continuously until next day, the 1st of March, but although they made one 'creeping attack' of 104 depth charges, which detonated like 'a marine convulsion', their enemy lay very deep, very low and very stubborn. Hunt was carried on for thirty-eight hours. How many depth charges the three frigates eventually dropped in total is not mentioned. It seems it could go into many hundreds.

It seems difficult to obtain reliable figures concerning the number of depth charges dropped in the Atlantic. The total figure could be as high as 500,000 or even more.

The Gunner

Due to experience in WWI, transport ships were equipped with guns to defend against U-boats and surface raiders. Within 12 months of war, 3,000 vessels were armed with a 4.7-inch gun manned by trained gunners, usually six.

Report 7 (extract):
A Focke-Wulf bomber attacked the *Orient City*, sailing in a convoy, at night. The gunner trained his gun as the aeroplane approached and flew straight into the shell-burst. The aircraft's engine stopped as if switched off suddenly. It fell into the sea like a giant leaf. As it crashed, its bomb-load, intended for the Orient City, exploded.

Arctic Convoy

Russians received about 4,000,000 tons of cargo, including 7,000 aircrafts and 5,000 tanks, via the most difficult and dangerous route from Britain to Murmansk. It was climatically the most sensitive sea route, presumably many times more effective for climate changes then naval activities, one thousand miles further south. Out of the total cargo shipped, 7% was lost at sea. Danger came not only from the arctic climate during most of the year, but from the attacks of the German Navy and Luftwaffe from their bases in North Norway as well. At peak time, the Luftwaffe had 264 aircrafts in the area, while the British Fleet Air Arm and the Royal Air Force flew 17 combat missions to North Norway, form January 1942 until November 1944, involving a total of 600 airplanes.

Convoys started to sail in August 1941; the 35th convoy sailed in May 1945. Convoys guarded a total of 715 ships. The loss of merchant ships was of 100, with 600,000 tons. The German side lost five surface naval ships, including a battle ship, a battle cruiser and 32 submarines. British Navy lost 20 surface vessels and one submarine.

To avoid the confrontation with the German forces, the convoys sometimes travelled far to the North. For example, in July 1942, the ships of convoy PC17 navigated close to Edge Island (Spitsbergen) 77°N, at the edge of the ice border, but were still attacked by aircrafts of the Luftwaffe and by U-boats. Few years later, it was observed that a deep fall in temperatures occurred at Franz Josephs Land (80°N, 53°E), in 1950, with over 5°C in one decade after the mean temperatures varied between -10°C and -11°C from 1936 until 1950.

Report 8 (extract):
An anti-aircraft gunner, on service on the high-octane tanker, the steamer *Bolton Castle* which was sunk by the ill-fated Arctic Convoy PQ17, reported: "We were sunk in the ice fields and the ship sank in thirteen minutes. Sunken by three bombs of a Junker 88, the *Bolton Castle*, which had hundreds of tons of cordite in cargo hold 2, looked 'like a giant Roman candle'."

Out of the 35 cargo ships and three rescue vessels of the convoy PQ17, only 11 vessels and two rescue ships survived.

The convoys were escorted by a considerable number of naval ships. Fighting East and West of the North Cape produced some of the hardest fought battles of WWII. For the Norwegian and Barents Sea, the military presence will not have passed by without any impact on the sea.

Atlantic Sea Mines

The strong barrage of 110,000 mines laid by Britain between Orkney and Iceland, from 1940 until 1943, received little notice. The mines 'Mk XX' were supposed to prevent U-boats from reaching the shipping routs in the Atlantic. Whether the barrage was a serious threat to U-boats or not we do not known, but it seems not. It would have been a tremendous threat to the sea if the mines tended to explode prematurely.

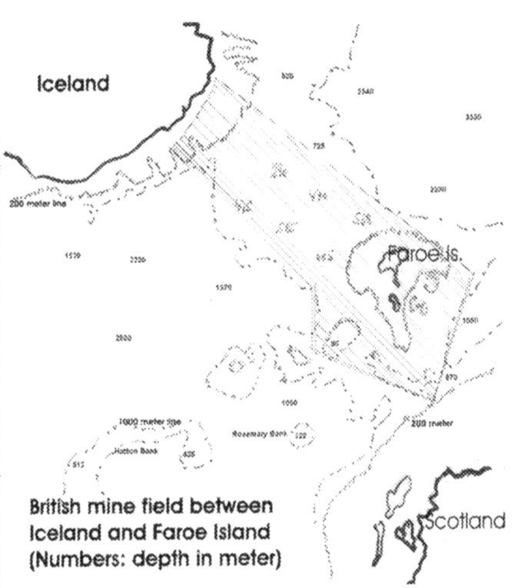

British mine field between Iceland and Faroe Island (Numbers: depth in meter)

It is not clear what happened to the mine barrage after the end of the war. Were the mines 'gone' by 1945? Were remaining mines swept after 1945? The British deployed 300 minesweepers on the assumption that it would take 549 days to clear moored mines and 676 days for ground mines around its coast. The Germans also tackled the issue of deployment with about 400 minesweepers.

Summary

Even though only very little information about the naval warfare between 1942 and 1945 could be conveyed in such a brief presentation, it is hoped to be informative enough to raise the awareness that oceans had been 'stirred and shaken' in a way that could have caused their extra normal cooling for four decades.

F. Time to make the 20th Century Climate Change explained

Summary on how men changed climate twice

The aim of the book is to point the attention to the oceans. In order to explain the real cause of global rising temperatures, scientists started to study the phenomenon in earnest in the 1980's. The aim of the book is to ensure that the mainstream of climate research is not constantly missing the point. Our aim is to establish that anthropogenic climatic changes are really due to two grand field experiments that men undertook during the last century.

The purpose of this book is to show that the activities of war at sea during WWI and WWII correlate perfectly with the only two significant climatic changes from 1900 until 2000: the one that started in 1918 and lasted until 1939 and the second one which started in the winter of 1939-40 and lasted until the early 1980s. The temperature rise during the recent 25 years can be "newly caused", but could also be a résumé of the steep temperature rise between 1918 and 1939, interrupted by WWII.

CO2 gases are the top blamed cause for the so-called global warming. And it seems it is going to remain the same for most of the official world. The aim of the book is to leave no doubt that climate is the continuation of the ocean and that the ocean determines where the climate is heading to. In this scenario, CO2 may have only a remote role to play.

Oceans and seas are very complex. They are only randomly monitored ever since and, even today, not very well understood. But war at sea during two major world wars was a force reckoned immediately even by the ocean. Two climate changes during the last century prove the point. Winter temperatures had risen in Spitsbergen by 8°C, between 1918 and 1939. The whole Europe got warmer year by year. German Chancellor Adolph Hitler started the war in 1939 and Northern Europe was immediately dragged back into Little Ice Age conditions not experienced in 100 years. Two further arctic war winters followed in the region with extreme naval activities until the war at sea went global, in 1942. And what followed without any delay? Can one speak of a surprise that a four decades of global cooling followed? Particularly the Northern Hemisphere felt the cooling, because here naval war was the most devastating and left a pronounced fingerprint in the downturn of global temperatures.

Even though the book section on naval warfare from 1942 until 1945 is short, the link between naval forces and global cooling is overwhelmingly convincing. Actually, it is the first reasonable explanation at all.

Even more reliable proof are the several regional super-large field experiments conducted four times in Northern Europe's waters: 1916/17, 1939/40, 1940/41 and 1941/42, strongly felt throughout the region by extreme winter temperatures. Each time the effect was like a "big shock".

More than 5°C winter temperatures below average are totally out of tune with standard climate that should not allow any rest before not understood. But nothing happened in this respect over more than six decades.

Until now, only one of the most ruthless WWII warmonger, German Vice-Chancellor Hermann Goering, commented the arctic winter of 1939/40 by saying that "a higher power has sent the harsh winter conditions". He was never prosecuted for being together with other Nazi leaders responsible for three polar winters and for four decades of global cooling.

Imagine there is global cooling, and no one cares. Imagine there is global warming and the world is highly concerned. The two assertions do not fit together. The first reflects circumstances more than half a century ago; the latter is the situation now. Insofar, the statements seem to contradict each other. But in a wider sense, they fit well. Someone who claims to be able to explain current global warming must also be able to explain a pronounced global cooling which effected climate only a half century ago. Ignoring the event for over six decades could be more ignorant than relating matters to a 'higher power'.

Remember when unusual powerful hurricane 'Katrina' hit New Orleans, in the summer of 2005. People insisted being informed to understand the matter. Assume winter temperatures suddenly turn to Ice Age conditions not experienced for more than one hundred years, but no one talks about it because there is war. That was actually the case during the winter of 1939/40 when in several locations, in Northern Europe, average temperatures were more degrees lower then during the whole previous century, and WWII war machinery cooled down the earth for four decades.

If this investigation succeeds in proving that two major wars changed the course of climate twice in the last century, it will also prove that shipping, fishing, off-shore drilling and other ocean uses constantly contributed to global warming since the start of the industrialization, more than 150 years ago. A new chapter on the climate change issue could be opened, giving more attention to ocean affairs through forceful use of the potential of the "*1982 United Nations Convention on the Law of the Sea*", which would lead to a better understanding and protection of the stability of our short-term weather and long-term global climate.

340 pages; quality trade paperback (softcover); catalogue #04-2654; ISBN 1-4120-4846-X;
Trafford Publishing, a division of Trafford Holdings Ltd.
http://www.trafford.com
Trafford Publishing , 6E - 2333 Government Street, Victoria, BC, Canada V8T 4P4

About the Book

Climate Change & Navel War

- A Scientific Assessment -

This book has laid emphasis on presentation and assessing details. The book seeks to demonstrate that the industrialized world contributed to at least two significant climatic changes during the 20th century, viz. WWI and WWII. This became particularly obvious when an arctic winter befell Northern Europe only four months after World War II had started, ending a pronounced temperature rise all over the Northern Hemisphere which had started with the end of WWI in 1918.

The book edition presents a wealth of references from newspaper and scientific articles from before the two World Wars and during the wars, which have nowhere been ever presented before. In a conscience step by step approach the thesis is convincingly presented. The work is a big contribution for ocean affairs and certainly will inject 'perestroika' [1] to climate change issue and debate.

Review on AMAZON/UK by: Frank Loebert:

Arnd Bernaerts postulates and substantiates a fascinating theory on the impact of naval warfare on climate in the past century, a theory which appears ever more credible upon studying the scientific material Bernaerts presents. Knowing that everything on the globe is interconnected, Bernaerts work on cause and effect requires serious consideration by scientists, politicians, historians and perhaps also jurists. Bernaerts is to be commended for his bold venture into an area that is novel to many and for making his findings known to the wider public.

[1] NEW THINKING , Perestroika (Russian meaning alter, rebuild and/or reshape).

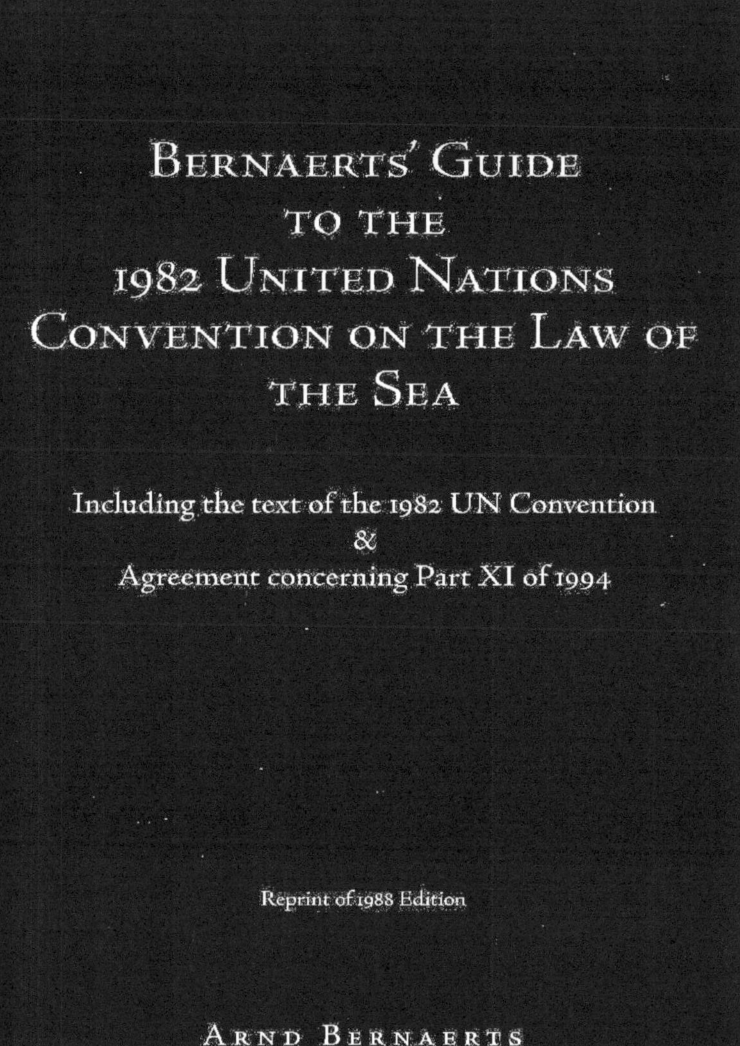

http://www.trafford.com

ISBN 141207665 - X

Preface of the reprint in 2006

More than 15 years ago FAIRPLAY PUBLICATIONS Ltd, Coulsdon, Surrey, England, published the book "Bernaerts' Guide to the Law of the Sea - The 1982 United Nations Convention". The guiding potential of the book to find access to the Law of the Sea Convention is still given. Internet technology and publishing on demand invite to provide the interested reader and researcher with this tool again. Only the Status of the Convention (ratification etc) has been updated and instead of the Final Act, the book edition includes the "Agreement relating to the Implementation of Part XI of the United Nations Convention of the Law of the Sea" of 1994. The corresponding web site neither includes the text of the 1982 Convention, nor the Agreement of 1994. The thorough Index of the 1988 edition is reproduced without changes.

Arnd Bernaerts, October 2005,

ABOUT THE BOOK
Bernaerts' Guide

Comments to Edition 1988

"an invaluable guide to the understanding and implementation of the 1982 United Nations Convention on the Law of the Sea"
Satya N. Nandan, U.N. Undersecretay, in: Book Foreword, 1988

"clearly presented"
R.R. Churchill, in: Maritime Policy & Management 1989, p. 340

"the (book's) concept, which is so wonderful simple, is exactly the factor which makes the book so useful for both the novice as well as the person with extensive experience"
M. Bonefeld, in: Verfassung und Recht, 1989, pp. 83-85

"the work contains much useful background information...."
R.W. Bentham, in: Journal of Energy & Natural Resource Law, 1989, p. 336

"Bernaerts has saved us a struggle"
JG, in: Fairplay Shipping Weekly Magazin, 13th October 1988, p. 33

"this is probably the best edition on the Convention to put into the hands of students"
A.V. Lowe, in: Int'l and Comparative Law Quarterly 1990, p. 16

"it will be an invaluable reference tool and should sit on the book shelves of policy makers and all others who are involved in maritime matters"
Vivian I. Forbes, in: The Indian Ocean Review, May 1990, p.10

FOREWORD of the 1988 edition (extract)

by Satya N. Nandan, Special Representative of the Secretary-General of the United Nations for the Law of the Sea, Office for Ocean Affairs and the Law of the Sea

Revolutionary changes have taken place in the International Law of the Sea since 1945. The process of change was accelerated in the last two decades by the convening in 1973 of the Third United Nations Conference on the Law of the Sea. The protracted negotiations, spanning over a decade, culminated in the adoption of the United Nations Convention on the Law of the Sea in 1982. By 9 December 1984, the closing date for signature, 159 signatures were appended to the Convention, the largest number for any such multilateral instrument in the history of international relations.

The convention and its annexes contain over 400 articles. For many it may be a formidable undertaking to grasp the substance and structure of it without making a considerable investment in time and energy. Mr Bernaerts' guide, therefore, is a welcome addition to the growing body of literature on the convention. It provides a most useful reference tool, which will benefit administrators and policy makers, as well as scholars. It makes the convention accessible to the uninitiated and refreshes, at a glance, the memories of the initiated. With meticulous references and graphic presentations of the provisions of the convention, Mr Bernaerts has given to the international community an invaluable guide to the understanding and implementation of the 1982 United Nations Convention on the Law of the Sea.

www.ingramcontent.com/pod-product-compliance
Ingram Content Group UK Ltd.
Pitfield, Milton Keynes, MK11 3LW, UK
UKHW051130260726
13967UKWH00010B/2960